MAKING IS CONNECTING

For Finn

MAKING IS CONNECTING

The social power of creativity, from craft and knitting to digital everything

Second expanded edition

DAVID GAUNTLETT

polity

First edition published in 2011 by Polity Press
This second edition published in 2018 by Polity Press
Reprinted 2020, 2021

Polity Press
65 Bridge Street
Cambridge CB2 1UR, UK

Polity Press
101 Station Landing
Suite 300
Medford, MA 02155, USA

ISBN-13: 978-1-5095-1347-5
ISBN-13: 978-1-5095-1348-2(pb)

A catalogue record for this book is available from the British Library.

Library of Congress Cataloging-in-Publication Data

Names: Gauntlett, David, author.
Title: Making is connecting : the social power of creativity, from craft and knitting to digital everything / David Gauntlett.
Description: Second edition. | Medford, MA : Polity, 2018. | Revised edition of the author's Making is connecting, 2011. | Includes bibliographical references and index.
Identifiers: LCCN 2017043969 (print) | LCCN 2017052215 (ebook) | ISBN 9781509513512 (Epub) | ISBN 9781509513475 (hardback) | ISBN 9781509513482 (paperback)
Subjects: LCSH: Social networks. | Creative ability--Social aspects. | Web 2.0--Social aspects. | Culture. | BISAC: SOCIAL SCIENCE / Media Studies.
Classification: LCC HM741 (ebook) | LCC HM741 .G38 2018 (print) | DDC 302.30285--dc23
LC record available at https://lccn.loc.gov/2017043969

Typeset in 10.75 on 14 pt Adobe Janson by
Servis Filmsetting Ltd, Stockport, Cheshire
Printed and bound in the United States by LSC Communications

For further information on Polity, visit our website:
www.politybooks.com

CONTENTS

ACKNOWLEDGEMENTS

For the first edition of this book, I acknowledged the help and support of many fine individuals. Here I have ungraciously clumped the key people into this one paragraph and sorted them into alphabetical order. Sorry. But, genuinely, many thanks to: Edith Ackermann, David Brake, Tessy Britton, Nick Couldry, Andrea Drugan, Andrew Dubber, Jenny Gauntlett, Pete Goodwin, David Hendy, Annette Hill, Dougald Hine, David Jennings, Jesper Just Jensen, Anastasia Kavada, Knut Lundby, Anthony McNicholas, Alison Powell, Tim Riley, Amanda Blake Soule, Jeanette Steemers, Paul Sweetman, Anna-Sophie Trolle Terkelsen, Cecilia Weckström, David Whitebread and Thomas Wolbers.

I am also grateful to Tiziano Bonini, who did a very nice translation of the book into Italian (*La Società dei Makers*), and the nameless employees of Samcheolli Publishing in Seoul, who made a neat Korean version with bonus pictures.

For this second edition, I would like to give many thanks to – again in alphabetical order – Fauzia Ahmad, Pete Astor,

Jen Ballie, Mary Kay Culpepper, Susie Farrell, Christian Fuchs, Matt Gooderson, Roland Harwood, Kirsten Hermes, Heidi Herzogenrath-Amelung, Velislava Hillman, Julia Keyte, I-Ching Liao, Simon Lindgren, Sunil Manghani, Winston Mano, Graham Meikle, Kirstin Mey, David Pallash, Mike Press, Mitch Resnick, Isabelle Risner, David Sheppard, Katie Smith, Tina Holm Sorensen, Jonathan Stockdale, Bo Stjerne Thomsen, Clare Twomey and Cecilia Weckström.

Many thanks to Mary Savigar, Ellen MacDonald-Kramer and Elen Griffiths at Polity for being such supportive editors, and I am grateful to Breffni O'Connor, Clare Ansell, Jane Fricker and Leigh Mueller on the production and marketing side.

I should also thank all the sharp, diverse and witty students who helped to refine some of these thoughts by participating in my 'Creativity' module at the University of Westminster in the years since 2010.

In the first edition, I was pleased to acknowledge the UK's Arts and Humanities Research Council (AHRC), and the Research Councils UK Digital Economy programme, for research awards which – as I said then – 'although not specifically supporting this project, did fund related work and gave me time to think about these things'. Those included projects with the reference numbers AH/H038736/1, AH/F009682/1, AH/F006756/1 and EP/H032568/1. For work conducted between the first and second editions, I acknowledge the support of the 'Digital DIY' project, funded by the EU Horizon 2020 Research and Innovation Framework Programme (Grant agreement 644344); 'Digital Folk', funded by the AHRC (AH/L014858/1); 'Advancing Social Media Studies', funded by STINT in Sweden; and 'Community-powered Transformations', funded by the AHRC (AH/J01303X/1).

As ever, huge love to Finn and Edie for supporting and

inspiring me every day. And last but most, all my love and gratitude to Jenny for being such a thoughtful and creative partner in ideas and life and everything.

As always, the responsibility for any weird arguments, spurious sentimentality and unreasonable optimism that you may find here remains my own.

PREAMBLE TO THE SECOND EDITION

Hello, and welcome, or welcome back, to *Making is Connecting*. This tries to be a fundamentally positive book about a fundamentally positive thing – the power of making. Everyday creativity can give us a sense of potency, expressive ways to connect with other people, and a sense of meaningful engagement with the world. This has been true for many thousands of years, but has been boosted and amplified in recent times by the emergence of accessible networked technologies that enable us to connect, exchange things, and inspire each other.

The first edition of this book was written in 2009–10, and came out in 2011. Here I greet you at the start of the second edition, which I revised and wrote in 2016–17, to come out in 2018. 'Making is connecting' is a timeless proposition, and should be a pretty time-proof book, but, you know, things happen, and the *context* changes even when the essence of creativity remains the same. So there are some things we need to deal with here.

NEW GLOOM

Frankly, when we think about the digitally-connected world, things do seem rather less bright and shiny than before. There are three striking and depressing elements, and each is huge. First, governments around the world turned out to be much more committed to *1984*-style mass surveillance – recording *everyone's* online interactions – than ever seemed either possible or likely. It was in 2013 that Edward Snowden bravely exposed the unexpectedly vast level of monitoring and storage of personal communications in the US, and by implication – or explicit extension – everywhere else. A few years on, this fundamental lack of personal privacy seems to be more-or-less accepted as normal.

Second, the corporations running online platforms were revealed as ruthless monopolies that suck vast amounts of money out of the creative ecosystem, while contributing nothing other than services to advertisers. Of course, it was well known that record companies and publishers in the twentieth century were ungenerous to artists, but new modes of distribution – especially for music – have counter-intuitively decimated the opportunities for the majority of artists to make a living. (Jonathan Taplin's 2017 book *Move Fast and Break Things* is especially persuasive on this topic.[1]) Online creativity isn't all about making money. But, in the case of music, say, you would have thought that as we have incredible new technologies that enable people to make and distribute work – and now that so many people have a music-playing phone in their pocket, directly connected to this network – with more than 2 billion smartphone users in the world in 2017[2] – there should be much better opportunities for people to be paid for making music that people want to listen to.

Third, a noisy minority of 'ordinary people' online started

spoiling it for everyone else with vile misogyny, racism, homophobia and other bigotry and threatening behaviour – enabled by the same platforms that in other contexts had seemed so useful for the exchange of creative ideas and practices. There have been 'trolls' and horribleness on the internet since its earliest days, but it seems to have exploded in a few years. In 2014 I remember feeling really sick and depressed when Emma Watson made an excellent speech at the UN about how feminism is for everyone, and was hit with a tidal wave of rape threats and other misogyny. On Twitter, appalled and exasperated, and breaking with my old-fashioned polite tweeting style, I said: 'Hey internet. I spend my professional life saying you people are fundamentally decent. You've really let me down with this Emma Watson shit.'[3]

The repulsive 'Gamergate' controversy,[4] the unbelievable racist and sexist noise from idiots around the 2016 *Ghostbusters* movie,[5] the treatment of female politicians and public figures daily, and many more examples make it *really hard* for hopeful optimists to not just give up in disgust. But you can't leave everything to pessimists, you really can't.

SO IS THE INTERNET ALL BAD NOW?

This book is not all about the internet, but the internet certainly plays a valuable and central role in our story. The three strong reasons for despondency mentioned above offer no positives, except as things to work against and away from. It's hard to discuss anything that happens online these days without being reminded of these dark clouds – and/or being considered stupid for not engaging with them. I guess there are people who look at books like *Making is Connecting*, and think: How can you *still* be optimistic about the power of the internet, when we know all this bad stuff?

And I get it: this is a good question, and not one to be

ducked. But on the whole, the bad things are not much to do with the good things – except that they are enabled by the same technologies. They are *simply different issues*. The positive things can be positive, the negative things are negative, and then we have to work out what to do.

The internet enables people to connect with others, share creative projects, and be inspired by each other, in ways which were not possible before – because it is global and searchable. Previously you could connect and share and be inspired by local people, if you happened to have a way of identifying people in your area interested in the same kinds of stuff. This was difficult, but possible. Doing it quickly and on a potentially global scale was impossible. The fact that the internet enables us to design and make lovely ways to show off our creative abilities, exchange ideas, and build networks of like-minded people who can support and inspire each other, *is still amazing*. It was amazing twenty-five years ago, when the first webpages were being born, and it's just as amazing today. And of course, we have much better infrastructure, hardware and software for doing this stuff, and with more than 3 billion people now online, there's a good chance someone shares some of your creative passions.[6] Is this still amazing, and powerful? Yes it is.

At the same time, we cannot and should not ignore what we now know about the mass surveillance, the aggressive monopoly capitalism of the major online platforms, and the trolling and misogyny. This is all mind-bendingly dreadful. Whole excellent books have been written about each of those issues, but – just so you know – that's not my job here. Those issues are really important, but they are just not what this book is about. We need to arrive at a much better situation in each of those areas. Meanwhile, I still want to talk about the good things we can still do, and the better world that it is important for us to imagine.

INTERNET = WORLD

The thing is: the internet mirrors our world. That doesn't mean that everyone in the world is equally represented on the internet, because the internet mirrors the unfairness and inequalities of our world. The internet also mirrors some nice things in the world, because the world does still have some nice things in it.

The internet enables people to amplify dimensions of the world, making both good and bad things louder and more noticeable. So you can quickly get to inspiring communities, gorgeous designs and wonderful ideas, or just as swiftly you can find offensive, awful and depressing material. It's a complex world, and one person's centre of inspiration might be someone else's epitome of repulsion. And this is not to be taken lightly. There are horrifically awful things on the internet. But they were put there by people. People in the world.

So, dismissing 'the internet' is like dismissing 'the world'. When people say 'How can you still be optimistic about the power or potential of the internet, now that we know all *this* about it?', it *really is* the same as asking how we can still feel optimistic about communities of human beings, considering what we know about various grim aspects of the behaviour of some people. The answer is – the answer has to be – that most people really aren't that bad; and that, even when some of them seem to have turned out really disagreeable, we still have to have hope for, and therefore make plans about, how to make things better.

And, I'm sorry, but it really is stupid to conclude that just because you know X or Y negative things about the internet there's therefore no point being positive about *any* possibilities of online connection, conversation or inspiration. That's just such a binary way of looking at it.

I understand how the brain can get dragged in that way. If you spend time studying the details of some case of neglect or abuse, it's easy and indeed quite normal to feel depressed and think 'Ugh, people are just horrible'. But, they are not. We may all recognize that feeling of revulsion – and the irrational temporary transfer of the feeling about a particular case to a feeling about everything – but it's still irrational. Similarly, people who spend much of their time studying the negative sides of online life will probably, understandably, consider the whole internet to be awful. But it's not. And it's straightforwardly irrational to think that it is. The internet mirrors the world. It's silly to say that everything on the internet, and everything that can be done on it, is wonderful, and it's equally daft to say that it's all bad or should be done away with.

I suppose if you're a proper nihilist, and you're actually signed up to the idea that everything and everyone actually is awful, then we have to allow you to say the same about online life too. But for the rest of us, we have to accept the complicated mix. As a wise person once noted, the typical human existence brings a pile of good things and a pile of bad things. 'The good things don't always soften the bad things, but vice-versa, the bad things don't necessarily spoil the good things, or make them unimportant.'[7]

The piles sit side by side. Focusing all your attention on the pile of good things doesn't make the bad things go away – as people have enjoyed telling me – but equally, emphasizing the negative side-effects (or even planned uses) of technologies doesn't change the positive reality of the good things that have also been done.

There are people who regard themselves as 'critical' theorists, writers or researchers, who think that being critical means pointing out the negative side of everything. But that's not what critical means. I think being critical means having a full understanding of negative threats, and the intended and unintended consequences of things in the world, and balancing this with an awareness of, and engagement with, ways in which we can make life better.

SECOND EDITION: WHAT'S THE SAME AND WHAT'S DIFFERENT

Some parts of this book are unapologetically the same as last time, but other parts have changed much more. In some places I have deleted or shortened things that were in the first edition, to make room for new things – generally parts that seemed longwinded or not so relevant today. In removing those things I have comforted myself with the thought that they are not expunged from the universe forever, because if you really want, you can still get hold of the first edition. Also I am aware that *Making is Connecting* is, to date, my best book, and has a few friends, so some people who already have the first one might get this second one too – and I want those people to be rewarded with a suitably renewed book with whole chunks of new stuff in it.

To make things easy for those of you who have the first edition and want to know what's new – here are the key new things in this edition:

- This 'Preamble' before chapter 1;
- The section 'Draining money from the creative economy' in chapter 7;
- All of chapter 8, 'Making connections and the creative process: From music to everything';
- All of chapter 9, 'Doing it yourself: More lessons from music making and connecting';
- All of chapter 10, 'Platforms for creativity';
- In chapter 11, items 6 and 7 in the previously five-point

conclusion list are new, as is the section on 'Developing and connecting creativity';

- Many other things have been amended, rewritten, added and updated throughout.

1

INTRODUCTION

This is a book about what happens when people make things. I hope it will add to the conversation about the power of the internet and digital technologies – a place where we have seen everyday creativity flourish over the past twenty-five years. But people have been making things – and thinking about the meaning of making things – for a very long time. And the power of making, and connecting through creating, extends well beyond the online world to all kinds of activities in everyday life.

I hope to pull some of these things together, in ways which are hopefully not too obvious as we start. You may reasonably wonder, for instance, how a commentary by Victorian art critic John Ruskin on medieval cathedrals can have affected my understanding of YouTube videos. And you may be surprised when the nineteenth-century socialist and tapestry-weaver William Morris dispenses a blueprint for the making and sharing ethos of social media in general, and Wikipedia in particular, 120 years early. We will note how the former Catholic priest and radical philosopher Ivan Illich outlined the necessary terms of human happiness, forty years ago, see how it lines up with the latest studies by economists and social scientists today, and then connect it with knitting, guerrilla gardening and creative social networks. But not necessarily in that order. We will encounter the 1970s feminist Rozsika Parker, explaining embroidery as a 'weapon of resistance', and several knitters, carpenters, musicians and bloggers, and they will help us to think about how making things for ourselves gives us a sense of wonder, agency, and possibilities in the world.

MAKING IS CONNECTING

This brings us to the title of the book: 'Making is connecting'. It's a perfectly simple phrase, of course. But having spent some time thinking about people making things, and people connecting with others – making *and* connecting – I realized that it was meaningful, and more pleasing, to note that these are one and the same process: making *is* connecting.

I mean this in three principal ways:

- Making is connecting because you have to connect things together (materials, ideas, or both) to make something new;
- Making is connecting because acts of creativity usually involve, at some point, a social dimension and connect us with other people;
- And making is connecting because through making things and sharing them in the world, we increase our engagement and connection with our social and physical environments.

Of course, there will be objections and exceptions to each of these, which we may consider along the way. But that's my basic set of propositions.

THREE REASONS WHY I WANTED TO WRITE THIS BOOK

This book came about because of a number of things I had been thinking about, which I hope are worth listing briefly here.

First, I started out as a sociologist interested in the place of media in people's lives. That was okay for a while, but twenty and even fifteen years ago, the main media that people were usually dealing with were produced by big professional organizations, and it seemed somewhat subservient to be exploring what people were doing with their products. Some of the activity was quite active, thoughtful and imaginative, some of it was mundane, and none of it could score very highly on a scale of creativity because it was all about creative works made by *other people*. Thankfully, the World Wide Web soared in popularity, becoming mainstream in itself, and opened up a world of diversity and imagination where the content itself is created by everyday users (as well as a growing number of professionals). This opportunity to make media and, in particular, share them easily, making connections with others, was unprecedented in both character and scale, and therefore a much more exciting thing to study.

Second, this exciting world of participation was, therefore, an exciting thing to participate in *myself*. I've always liked making things, but they didn't have an audience. With the Web, making writings, photographs, drawings – and indeed websites themselves – available to the world was so easy. It was also rewarding, as people would see your stuff and then send nice comments and links to their own. So I experienced the feeling that making is connecting for myself.

Third, and stemming from the academic interests mentioned in the first point, I was meant to be doing research about what people did, and why, but had always been uncomfortable with the idea of just speaking to them, taking them through an 'interview' for my own purposes, without giving them anything very interesting to *do*. Therefore, over the past twenty years, I have been developing 'creative research methods' where people are asked to *make* something as part of the process. The idea is that going through the thoughtful, physical process of making something – such as a video, a drawing, a decorated box, or a LEGO model – an individual is given the opportunity to reflect, and to make their thoughts, feelings or experiences manifest and tangible. This unusual experience gets the brain firing in different ways, and can generate insights which would most likely not have emerged through directed conversation. I have found that the process is especially revealing and effective when people are asked to express themselves using metaphors. All of this was discussed in my earlier book *Creative Explorations*.[1] In these studies it was clear that thinking and making are aspects of the same process. Typically, people mess around with materials, select things, experimentally put parts together, rearrange, play, throw bits away, and generally manipulate the thing in question until it approaches something that seems to communicate meanings in a satisfying manner. This rarely seems to be a matter of 'making what I thought at the start', but rather a process of discovery and having ideas *through* the process of making. In particular, taking *time* to make something, using the hands, gave people the opportunity to clarify thoughts or feelings, and to see the subject-matter in a new light. And having an image or physical object to present and discuss enabled them to communicate and connect with other people more directly.

Maybe in the end that's more than three, but for all these reasons I wanted to explore the idea that making is connecting.

SOCIAL MEDIA AS AN IDEA AND A METAPHOR

This book does not suppose that creative activities have suddenly appeared in the story of human life because someone invented the internet. However, the internet – in particular through the World Wide Web which emerged in the early 1990s, and the mobile apps which burst into people's lives in the late 2000s – has certainly made a huge difference. The internet made it massively easier for everyday people to share the fruits of their creativity with others, and to collaboratively make interesting, informative and entertaining cultural spaces. This process has been boosted by the emergence of social media. In the first edition of this book, I talked about 'Web 2.0', which was what we called it then, although I had to explain that 'Web 2.0' was not a particular kind of technology, or a business model, and was definitely not a sequel to the Web as previously known.

Nowadays we say 'social media' to mean basically the same thing, and they're all around us, a lot – even if you don't use social media, you hear about them all the time in the news – but it's worth taking a moment to consider the distinctive approach of social media platforms compared to, say, traditional websites.

I used to explain the difference between the older and newer models with a Powerpoint slide showing gardens and an allotment, that I made using LEGO (figure 1). In the first decade or so of the Web's existence (from the 1990s to the early to mid-2000s), websites tended to be like separate gardens. So for example the NASA website was one garden, and my Theory.org.uk website was another garden, and a little-known poet had made her own poetry website, which was another garden. You could visit them, and each of them might be complex plots of creative and beautiful content, but basically they were separate, with a fence between

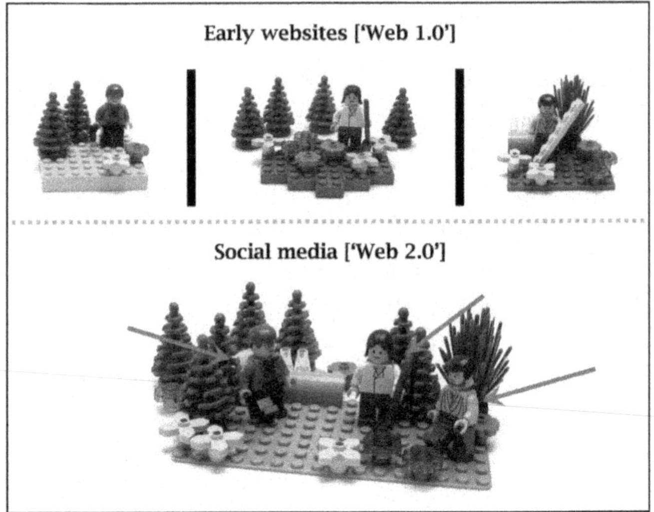

Figure 1: Social media as a communal allotment

each one. There's nothing *wrong* with this model, as such; it works perfectly well as a platform for all kinds of individuals, groups, or organizations, big and small, to make stuff available online. But this model is what we could now call 'Web 1.0'. By contrast, the newer model, whether we call it Web 2.0 or social media, is like a collective allotment. Instead of individuals tending their own gardens, they come together to work collaboratively in a shared space.

This is actually what Tim Berners-Lee had meant his World Wide Web to be like, when he invented it in 1990. He imagined that browsing the Web would be a matter of writing and editing, not just searching and reading. The first years of the Web, then, were an aberration, and it has only more recently blossomed in the way its creator intended.

I clearly remember that when I read about this read/write model in Berners-Lee's book, *Weaving the Web*, when it was published in 1999, it seemed like a nice idea, but naïve, and bonkers. How could it possibly work? I didn't want to spend hours crafting my lovely webpages only for some visitor to come along and mess them up. But of course, my problem – shared with most other people at the time – was that I had not learned to recognize the power of the network. We still thought of everybody 'out there' as basically 'audience'.

At the heart of social media is the idea that online sites and services become more powerful the more that they *embrace* this network of potential collaborators. Rather than just seeing the internet as a broadcast channel, which brings an audience to a website (the '1.0' model), social media invite users in to play. Sites and apps such as YouTube, Twitter and Wikipedia only exist and have value because people use and contribute to them, and they are clearly *better* the more people are using and contributing to them. This is the essence of social media.

So social media are about harnessing the collective abilities of the members of an online network, to make an especially powerful resource or service. But, thinking beyond the internet, it may also be valuable to consider social media as a kind of metaphor, for any collective activity which is enabled by people's passions and becomes something greater than the sum of its parts.

In the books *We Think* by Charles Leadbeater, and both *Here Comes Everybody* and *Cognitive Surplus* by Clay Shirky, the authors discuss the example of Wikipedia, noting the impressive way in which it has brought together enthusiasts and experts, online, to collaboratively produce a vast encyclopaedia which simply would not exist without their millions of contributions.[2] These contributions, of course, are given freely, and without any reward (apart, of course, from the warm glow of participation, and the very minor recognition of having your username listed somewhere in an article's history logs). Both authors then go on to consider whether the Wikipedia model of encyclopaedia-making can be translated across to – well, everything else. In these cases, Wikipedia becomes a metaphor for highly participatory and industrious collaboration. However, most of the time they're not *really* thinking of 'everything else' – it's 'everything else online'. Wikipedia becomes a model of highly participatory and industrious *online* collaboration. But the really powerful metaphorical leap would be to go from digital media to real life – the social world and all its complexities, not just from Wikipedia to other internet services.[3]

So, in this book we will, in part, be taking the message of making, sharing, and collaboration, which has become familiar to the people who enthuse about social media, and seeing if it works in a broader context – in relation to both offline and online activities – and with bigger issues: real social problems rather than virtual online socializing. This connects with the argument – or the hope – that we are seeing a shift away from a 'sit back and be told' culture towards more of a 'making and doing' culture. The 'sit back and be told' position is forcefully introduced in schools, and then gently reinforced by television and the magic of the glossy, shiny and new in consumer culture; the 'making and doing' is what this book is all about.

THE 'SIT BACK AND BE TOLD' CULTURE

Since the historical point at which education became institutionalized in a system of schools, learning has become a process directed by a teacher, whose task it is to transfer nuggets of knowledge into young people's minds. It has not always been this formulaic, of course, and some teachers have always sought to inspire their students to produce their own perspectives on art, poetry, or science. Nevertheless, and in spite of some innovative pedagogical thinking in the 1960s and 1970s, school education since the 1980s has tended to settle around a model where a body of knowledge is input into students, who are tested on their grasp of it at a later point. Over time, the tests have become increasingly formalized, and have been used to assemble league tables of schools, which in turn mean that each school has a vested interest in getting children to do well in the tests. Governments around the world seem to feel obliged to commit to the notion of 'testing and accountability' even though all the evidence suggests that quality learning is destroyed by an over-emphasis on testing.[4]

Meanwhile, the twentieth century was emphatically the era of 'sit back and be told' media: especially in the second half of that century, leisure time became about staying in, not going out, and remaining pretty much in the same spot for long chunks of time, looking at a screen. This remains the case: in 2017, Americans watched on average more than four and a half hours of television per day, much as they had done for several decades, even though this viewing is now joined by the use of other digital devices.[5] In the UK, it's just under four hours per day.[6] This is, of course, a lot, and since it's an average, you know that for everybody watching less than this, there are as many other people watching more. (The good news is that the twentieth-century technology is primarily popular with those rooted in the twentieth century. The steady *average* television viewing figures hide the fact that younger people are watching TV much less – although they are using a much wider range of screen-based services. The Nielsen 2017 data for the US, for instance, shows that the average TV viewing of those aged thirty-seven and under is less than *half* that of those aged over thirty-eight and older.)

Marshall McLuhan's famous statement that 'the medium is the message' can be taken in various ways, but fundamentally it points to the way in which the arrival of a medium, such as television, in our lives, can affect the way we live – not really because of the content of the messages it carries, but from the generally less noticed ways in which it causes us to rearrange our everyday lives. This is a very good insight. Media 'effects', when we are talking about media *content*, are notoriously hard to measure, generally inconsequential, and mixed up with other influences.[7] But the overall 'effect' of the introduction of television – assuming that the broadcasters offer some reasonably enjoyable or informative programmes – was clearly *massive* in terms of how people spent their lives.

Four hours of viewing, as an *average*, and *every day*, was an astonishing transformation in how human beings spent time, compared with the pre-television era. This is not to say that television is full of rubbish or that people are idiots for watching it. It's not impossible to find four hours of informative and entertaining things on telly. But it would be difficult to argue that this was a highly creative or sociable way for people to spend their time, or that this was not an extraordinary change in the way that human beings spent their non-working hours, compared with the preceding few thousand years.

In addition, this relatively passive orientation to time outside work was further reinforced, as mentioned above, by consumer culture. As Theodor Adorno and Max Horkheimer observed in the 1940s, and as many critics have noted since, modern capitalism succeeds not by menacing us, or dramatically crushing our will on the industrial wheel, but by encouraging us to enjoy a flow of convenient, cheerful stuff, purchased from shops, which gives us a feeling of satisfaction, if not happiness.[8] Few of us are immune from the appeal of attractively packaged items, with the sheen and smell of newness, which help us to forget our troubles, at least for a moment.

The notion of the *fetish* might be useful in understanding this. The fetish has sexual connotations, but these are not (necessarily) crucial here. In Freud, a fetish is basically about unconsciously overcoming anxiety through attachment to particular objects.[9] In Marx, the fetish describes the way in which we forget that the value of a commodity is a social value, and come to think of it as independent and real.[10] Somewhere between these two related ideas, we might see the fetish as the common, everyday way in which we find pleasure in the purchase of consumer goods, and acknowledge that it may be silly or irrational, but still a pleasure; and then consistently forget how temporary this diversion is. Between them, television and consumerism can draw people into a dully 'satisfied' reverie in which – as we will see later – it may not be especially surprising that environmental pollution and other societal problems are generally seen as troubling, but distant, and basically 'somebody else's problem'.

TOWARDS A 'MAKING AND DOING' CULTURE

More optimistically, however, we can see a growing engagement with a 'making and doing' culture. This orientation rejects the passivity of the 'sit back' model, and seeks opportunities for creativity, social connections, and personal growth. In the education sphere, this approach is promoted globally by the LEGO Foundation and its various alliances – which has included some work with me – and is well captured by Guy Claxton's book, *What's the Point of School?*, which highlights ways in which some teachers are rejecting the 'sit back and be told' school culture described above, and instead are setting their students challenges which are much more about making and doing.[11] Students are encouraged to work together to ask questions, explore different strategies of investigation, and create their own solutions. This approach is open about the fact that learning is an ongoing process that everyone is engaged in – teachers themselves might show that they are engaged in a learning project, such as starting to keep bees, or learn a musical instrument. Rather than displaying laminated examples of the 'best answer' on the walls, these classrooms show works in progress, experiments, even things that have gone wrong. They encourage a 'hands-on' approach to learning, and a spirit of enquiry and questioning.

In terms of the media and technologies that we use in everyday life, there has of course been a huge shift towards more interactive, internet-based tools and services. The launch of social media platforms such as Facebook (in 2004), YouTube (2005), Twitter (2006), Instagram (in 2010) and Snapchat (in 2011), to name just a few, has led to huge amounts of interactive and – to varying degrees – creative engagement between people online. In 2017, YouTube had over 1 billion users, watching 5 billion videos every day, and uploading 300 hours of video every minute.[12] Instagram had 700 million users, uploading more than 100 million videos and photos every day.[13] And Facebook had reached more than 2 billion users.[14] Easy-to-use networked tools which enable people to learn about, and from, each other, and to collaborate and share resources, have made a real difference to what people do with, and can get from, their electronic media. The *range* of information-sharing, self-expressive and collaborative things that people do online is extraordinary. Academics, to some extent, have tended to focus on the more 'serious' uses, such as in politics and activism, but of course there are online communities about absolutely everything.

In the non-virtual world, there is a resurgence of interest in craft activities, clubs and fairs,[15] and their DIY technology equivalents involving machines and robotics,[16] as celebrated in the mainstream *Make* magazine and at 'Maker Faires'.[17] Environmental concerns have encouraged people to reduce the amount of stuff they consume, and to find new ways to re-use and recycle. The Transition Towns movement has encouraged communities to work together to find sustainable ways of living.[18] And as we will see, the internet has played an important role in offline real-world activities, as a tool for communication, networks and organization.

DEFINING CREATIVITY

I will use the word 'creativity' – and the phrase 'everyday creativity' – quite freely in this book, in relation to the activities of making which are rewarding to oneself and to others. Attempting to produce a clear-cut and simple definition of creativity can be a diverting and sometimes frustrating task, but we'll start thinking about it here and then come back to it later.

Let's start by looking at how other people define 'creativity'. Mihaly Csikszentmihalyi is perhaps the best-known creativity researcher today. His *Creativity* study was based on interviews with people who were at the highest end of observed creativity – famous creative names, several of whom had won Nobel prizes for their inventions or creations. This seems to put him at the old-fashioned, or at least the elite, end of the scale, but there are perfectly good reasons for this. Csikszentmihalyi has pioneered a sociological approach to creativity, which is actually not at all old-fashioned or traditional: it rejects the classical notion of the creative 'genius' and instead observes how the thing we call creativity emerges from a particular supportive environment. Rather than being a lightning-bolt of unexpected inspiration, he argues, creative outputs appear from individuals who have worked hard over many years to master a particular 'symbolic domain' (physics, poetry, architecture, or whatever) and are encouraged by other supportive individuals, groups and organizations. Csikszentmihalyi is interested in the sociological question of how these things come about – surges of creativity which make a difference to culture, science, or society. He writes:

> Creativity, at least as I define it in this book, is a process by which a symbolic domain in the culture is changed. New songs, new ideas, new machines are what creativity is all about.[19]

This is high-impact creativity, and importantly, it is creativity which is noticed and appreciated by other people:

> According to this view, creativity results from the interaction of a system composed of three elements: a culture that contains symbolic rules, a person who brings novelty into the symbolic domain, and a field of experts who recognise and validate the innovation.[20]

So the inventive individual is only one part of this triad. Creativity in Csikszentmihalyi's formulation needs a particular established context in which to happen, and also needs to be recognized as something significant by other key people working in that domain. As he puts it:

> Just as the sound of a tree crashing in the forest is unheard if nobody is there to hear it, so creative ideas vanish unless there is a receptive audience to record and implement them.[21]

This approach to creativity sets the bar very high, of course. First you have to produce something brilliantly original, that has never been seen before in the world. Then, as if that wasn't hard enough already, it has to be recognized as a brilliantly original thing by other people. Furthermore, they can't be just *any* people, but have to be the movers and shakers, the well-known thought leaders, in the field where you hope to make an impact. (This makes life especially difficult since the established people in any particular area are typically attached to their own high status, and are not necessarily likely to give a warm reception to promising newcomers.)

That's one way of looking at creativity, and it is the right lens for Csikszentmihalyi's analysis of the social conditions which enable recognized, significant innovations to emerge. Other writers on creativity have also followed Csikszentmihalyi's definitions and approach, sometimes in a bid to illuminate 'lower level' creativity. But the lens which is helpful for asking 'How do major cultural or scientific innovations emerge?' is not necessarily the right lens for studying the much more everyday instances of creativity which concern us in this book.

After all, we do typically think of creativity as something which can happen quite routinely, whenever any of us does something in an unexpected but striking and inventive way. We don't *only* say that something is 'creative' when it has been recognized with a Nobel prize, nor do we limit the label to the kind of thing that each of us only does once or twice in a lifetime. Because we are inventive human beings, creativity is something we do rather a lot, and understood in this broad sense it includes everyday ideas we have about how to do things, many of the things we write and produce, acts of management or self-presentation, and even, of course, witty or insightful speech.

When taken down to this everyday level, the edges of what we might call creativity become rather fuzzy, of course. If I managed to bake and decorate a birthday cake which looked like a dinosaur, for instance, I would feel really 'creative'.

And you might agree. But if you had been told that I was a professional birthday cake-maker who had been producing the same dinosaur cake for twenty years, you definitely wouldn't. Between these two poles, my creativity rating might also be affected by, say, whether or not you thought it was 'cheating' to use shop-bought sweets to represent the eyes and scales, and whether or not you suspected I'd looked at pictures of other dinosaur cakes on the internet. It's easy to get bogged down in this kind of thing. But as I said in *Creative Explorations*:

> You could argue endlessly, if you wanted to be rather trivial, about whether one thing 'is' and another thing 'is not' creative. But that's not really the point. The point is that creativity is widely dispersed and, more importantly, is one of the most central aspects of being human.[22]

Most of the research literature *about* creativity, however, does not really take this view. A reasonable summary is provided by Charles Lumsden, who considered a range of definitions from leading figures, and found that 'the "definitions" of creativity I have seen in the literature . . . carry the unique imprint of their progenitors while suggesting some mild degree of consensus: creativity as a kind of capacity to think up something new that people find significant'.[23]

The trouble with this approach, though – as I'll go on to say in chapter 3 – is the strong emphasis on the end product, and the judgement of others. Creativity might be better understood as a *process*, and a *feeling*. In this way of looking at it, creativity is about breaking new ground, but internally: the sense of going somewhere, doing something, that you've not done before. This might lead to fruits which others can appreciate, but those may be secondary to the process of creativity itself, which is best identified from within.

Hold onto these thoughts for now. In a section at the end of chapter 3 I'll be wheeling out a gleaming new definition of creativity which hopefully overcomes these problems.

WHAT THIS BOOK IS AND WHAT IT IS NOT

This book is a discussion about the value of everyday creativity, taking in handmade physical objects and real-life experiences as well as the recent explosion of online creativity. Indeed, it seeks to make connections from one sphere to the other, in the hope that we can learn about recent creativity in social media by looking at what people have said about the values, ethics and benefits of more traditional craft and DIY activities, and perhaps also vice versa. This is generally done through the use of some relevant theories and philosophies – quite grounded and earthy ones, nothing very abstract – and knitted, I hope, into the reality and experience of particular creative activities.

This is *not*, though, a set of case studies about particular craftspeople, artisans, bloggers and YouTube-makers. That wasn't meant to be the point of this book – you can get such material elsewhere, and I didn't want the discussion to be based around a sequence of meetings and anecdotes. Nor is it one of those books which weaves together autobiography with more general insight – although if you want that kind of thing, I can recommend three good books, all published since 2010: *The Case for Working with Your Hands: or Why Office Work is Bad for Us and Fixing Things Feels Good* by the philosopher and motorcycle mechanic Matthew Crawford (published in the US with the slightly shorter title, *Shop Class as Soulcraft: An Inquiry into the Value of Work*); *Made by Hand: Searching for Meaning in a Throwaway World* by Mark Frauenfelder, the Editor-in-Chief of *Make* magazine; and *Why We Make Things and Why it Matters: The Education of a Craftsman* by woodworker Peter Korn.[24] Those three books, along with Richard Sennett's excellent *The Craftsman* – which I also recommend – primarily concern the values, applied intelligence, and feelings associated with making things *by hand*, as well as the need to understand how our material world works so that we can engage with it, fix it, or transform it.[25]

This book is about those things too, to some extent, and includes a few autobiographical bits, but it's more about the value of making stuff more generally. In particular, it includes an emphasis on making and sharing our own *media* culture – I mean, via low-fi YouTube videos, eccentric blogs, quirky music and homemade websites, rather than by having to take over the traditional media of television stations and printing presses – which isn't quite 'by hand' in the literal pottery-making, woodcarving sense, but which I feel is still basically a handicraft which connects us with others through its characterful, personality-imprinted, individual nature, as well as because it's a form of communication.

AND THE *REAL* POINT OF THE BOOK IS …

The other reason why the book mostly doesn't pick over lots of examples of creativity, one by one, is because I wanted to address the broader question of '*Why* is everyday creativity important?' Because I feel that it is incredibly important – important for society – and therefore *political*. And, to be frank about my motives, people don't seem to get this. Presenting this kind of thing in front of academics who see themselves as 'critical' and 'political' scholars, I get the definite feeling that they think I'm doing, at best, a sweet kind of sideshow. Whilst they struggle with 'real' issues such as government regulation of broadcasting, or something to do with political parties, I am enthusing about everyday people making nice objects or clever little videos, which may be pleasant but is an irrelevance in terms of political or social concerns. If it's any kind of issue at all, it's a 'cultural' one: and who cares really if people watch silly entertainment on television or if they make their own silly entertainment; if they grow their own flowers, make their own toys or gloves, or buy them from a supermarket; or if people write their own songs, or buy someone else's.

But I think it's absolutely *crucial*. Even if each of the things made seems, to a grumpy observer, rather trivial. You may note that my examples just above are not the absolute essentials of life – people can survive without silly entertainment, flowers, gloves, or songs, if they have to. But it is the fact that people have made a *choice* – to make something themselves rather than just consume what's given by the big suppliers – that is significant. Amplified slightly, it leads to a whole new way of looking at things, and potentially to a real political shift in how we deal with the world.

One example of how the idea of everyday creativity can be scaled up into something significant, political, and vitally important, is the Transition movement. The Transition movement stems from the idea that – although we are likely to face really huge challenges as climate change grows, and as the oil that we rely on so much runs out – human beings are *creative* and can work well together to do great things. And therefore, if we think imaginatively together, and make plans and ideas for a new enjoyable way of living which doesn't rely so much on the environmentally damaging things, or things we're running out of, then we might be okay. This is an approach based on optimism and creativity, and it could actually work. The movement is taking off, and you can read about it in the books *The Transition Handbook* and *The Power of Just Doing Stuff* by Rob Hopkins, and *The Transition Timeline* by

Shaun Chamberlin, or at the website, www.transitionnet work.org.[26]

The Transition movement is a great illustration of what I'm talking about, then, but so is the less obviously 'political' content of online video and craft sites, and everyday home-made events, untrained attempts at art, humble efforts to make a knitted owl with solar-powered eyes, and anything else where people are rejecting the givens and are making their world anew. This helps us to build *resilience* – one of the key Transition words – and the *creative capacity* to deal with significant challenges.

OUTLINE OF THE BOOK

The book begins by forgetting about the internet at first, and exploring some philosophical, political and practical explanations of the human drive to make things. In chapter 2 this is mostly centred around two Victorian makers and thinkers, John Ruskin and William Morris. In chapter 3, we look at more recent craft and DIY ideas, activities, and motivations. By chapter 4, we arrive at the internet again, and consider 'making is connecting' in online environments. In chapter 5 we turn to the value of having social connections, and collaborative projects, in everyday life, and chapter 6 is about having tools for creative expression and making a difference, and features quite a bit of the philosopher Ivan Illich. Chapter 7 considers some of the critiques of social media systems, and finds reason to disagree with some, but concur with others. Chapter 8 is about the creative process, taking music as a starting-point, and chapter 9 also starts with music as a way to look at do-it-yourself processes and ways to get creative work out there. In chapter 10 we consider the principles that underpin effective 'platforms for creativity'. Finally, chapter 11 pulls things together in a conclusion, where we set out seven key principles of 'making is connecting', and offer some positive ideas about developing and connecting creativity.

This book has a website at http://www.makingisconnecting.org. The site includes videos, additional material, relevant links, and other information. See also David Gauntlett's main site at www.davidgauntlett.com.

2

THE MEANING OF MAKING I: PHILOSOPHIES OF CRAFT

In this chapter, and the next one, we will begin our more detailed study of the idea that 'making is connecting', by looking (mostly) at the offline, non-digital world of people making things for themselves and others. This is the activity that we might call 'craft' – although that phrase is loaded with connotations which will vary between people and between places. Craft might suggest the careful practice of a woodcarver or a ceramicist, a skilled practice of making beautiful objects. The term might be associated with traditional and rather twee items which you might have seen on sale at craft fairs in church halls – corn dollies and doilies at surprisingly high prices. Or it might suggest a newer, cool approach to making things yourself, as seen in the recent rise of knitting, 'craft guerrilla' fairs, DIY culture, and other trendy craft activities.

The term 'craft' is further complicated by its relationship with 'art'. Somehow the two concepts have become separated, so that 'art' tends to mean the truly creative transformation of ideas and emotions into visual objects (or texts, performances, music, or whatever), whilst 'craft' – having been shoved out of that space – ends up indicating the less prestigious production of carvings or pots, by less creative people who just like making carvings or pots. This view is, of course, most unfair. As Peter Dormer has observed:

> The separation of craft from art and design is one of the phenomena of late-twentieth-century Western culture. The consequences of this split have been quite startling. It has led to the separation of 'having ideas' from 'making objects'. It has also led to the idea that there exists some sort of mental attribute known as 'creativity' that precedes or can be divorced from a knowledge of how to make things.[1]

One way to avoid this trap is to reject the positioning of 'art' as superior, and instead to regard its stance as unnecessarily pretentious and exclusive, and therefore rather silly, in comparison to the more earthy, engaged spirit of craft. There is still, of course, the problem that this may not be the majority or dominant view.

In recent years the status of craft has been helped by Richard Sennett's excellent book *The Craftsman* – amongst readers and thinkers, I mean, rather than amongst doers and makers, who may not need such writings to persuade them. Sennett argues vigorously against the second-class status of craft, and is especially good on his core theme that thinking and making are aspects of one unified process. The craftsperson does not do the thinking and then move on to the mechanical act of making: on the contrary, making is part of thinking, and, he adds, feeling; and thinking and feeling are part of making.[2] Sennett emphasizes craft as a unity of body and mind – in particular, working with the hands as a central part of the process of thinking and making – and craft as exploration, a process of 'problem solving and problem finding'.[3] More broadly, in Sennett's hands, craft becomes a process of making personal self-identity, and citizenship.

Sennett treats craft with great seriousness, which is warranted, and welcome, and rather moving. But he perhaps misses some of the dimension of pleasure, even joy. As Ellen Dissanayake has written:

> There is an inherent pleasure in making. We might call this *joie de faire* (like *joie de vivre*) to indicate that there is something important, even urgent, to be said about the sheer enjoyment of making something exist that didn't exist before, of using one's own agency, dexterity, feelings and judgment to mold, form, touch, hold and craft physical materials, apart from anticipating the fact of its eventual beauty, uniqueness or usefulness.[4]

This urgent need to *make*, for the sake of the pleasure and understanding gained within the process of making itself, is identified by Dormer as one of the reasons why craft has been able to survive, and perhaps become stronger, in spite of its detachment from so-called fine art.

> Enough people have wanted to go on making things. Enough people believe they can expand their ideas and knowledge about the world through learning and practising a craft. Some people believe that if you want to truly understand a thing you have to make a version of that thing – a model, representation, or piece of mimetic art.[5]

The two quotations above seem to sum up some essential dimensions of craft: the inherent satisfaction of making; the sense of being alive within the process; and the engagement with ideas, learning and knowledge which come not before or after but *within* the practice of making. These engaging ideals are at the heart of all artistic and creative impulses, and make a mockery of the idea that craft is an inferior or second-class kind of activity. Whilst 'fine art' is more dependent on hierarchies and elites, upon which it depends to validate the work, craft is more about creativity and the process of making at a vibrant, grassroots level: proud of its grounded, everyday nature, and not insecurely waiting for an artworld critic, collector or curator to one day say that it was all worthwhile.

In particular, craft seems to be about a *drive* to make and share things, no matter what anyone says. In a different essay, Peter Dormer writes:

> Making – craft, skill, and the realisation of an object through craft labour – is not a trivial issue for craftspeople. Making is both the means through which the craftsperson explores their obsession or idea and an end in itself.[6]

In this sense, making and connecting is not an option – it is experienced as a necessity. It seems vital and contemporary, but woven into a vision of craft – a connection between humans and handmade objects and nature – which is as old as the hills. Actually, though, as we will see more in the next chapter, the notion of 'craft' which today seems timeless is actually quite new. It began with two Victorian thinkers who hated Victorian times, John Ruskin and William Morris, whose work and ideas occupy the rest of this chapter. Why are we looking at these two long-dead men? The answer lies, as you will see, in their ideas about *creativity* as a part of everyday life, and as a binding force in 'fellowship' – which today we would call *community*. In their own ways, they were saying that 'making is connecting', and their works have much to offer today.

JOHN RUSKIN

Ruskin was born in 1819, making him fifteen years older than Morris. Although we typically picture eminent Victorians as craggy prophets with lots of grey hair and beards, Ruskin got going early. At the point when he published the second volume of *The Stones of Venice*, a book which really impressed William Morris whilst a new undergraduate at Oxford – in 1853 – both were young men (at thirty-four and nineteen respectively).

Ruskin was extremely prolific. He is remembered primarily as an artist and art critic, and as a social thinker, but also produced poetry and fiction, and wrote about architecture, geology, literature, science, and the environment. It is his ideas about art and society, and his critique of the dehumanized model of industrial production, which we will focus on here.

Ruskin's opposition to industrialism, and exploitative capitalism, and his care for the common worker, mean that today we would interpret his stance as 'obviously' a left-wing, socialist kind of position. However, Ruskin is often described as a 'conservative', and indeed he begins his autobiographical *Praeterita* with the declaration, 'I am, and my father was before me, a violent Tory of the old school.'[7]

To modern viewers who tend to place political philosophies – at least as a starting-point – on a left-wing to right-wing spectrum, this can seem confusing – or it certainly does if you assume that the conservatives and Tories must go on the right. In fact, a Ruskin kind of conservatism, which yearns for the (rather distant and idealized) past because of an attachment to the values of communities, local-level organic production, care for the environment, and valuing all workers rather than treating them as parts in a machine, all sounds quite radical and progressive to modern ears – or it does if you see them as a programme for the future, rather than just the mourning of a lost past. That was certainly the attraction for William Morris. As Clive Wilmer notes,

> No political label quite fits Ruskin's politics. . . . His 'Toryism' was such that it could, in his own lifetime, inspire the socialism of William Morris and the founders of the Labour Party; and when he called himself a 'conservative', he usually meant as a preserver of the environment – what we should call a 'conservationist'.[8]

Ruskin's writing was often complex, and unpredictable – not necessarily in a good way. In one lecture he declared, 'For myself, I am never satisfied that I have handled a subject properly till I have contradicted myself at least three times.'[9] Nevertheless, within his massive output there are certain jewels of clarity and vision. One of these is *Unto This Last*, a set of four essays published as a book in 1862, in which the author brings together his ideas to form a powerful moral critique of *laissez-faire* economics – the newly established orthodoxy which maintained that unimpeded individual self-interest should be the driving force of social and economic organization. This, its proponents said, would enable the greatest amount of economic growth, which would be generally good for society even if an unlucky proportion of the population were condemned to inevitable poverty and/or the most menial, meaningless and exhausting work.[10]

This ideology infuriated Ruskin, whose moral and romantic instincts would not allow any system where life was abused and exploited for any purpose.[11] But Ruskin was also making a rigorous, rational argument against the claims of the economists to have established a 'scientific' approach to the cultivation of wealth. The aim of developing a perfect economic system where material concerns are detached from moral ones, and where individual interests are detached from social context, was intellectually wrong as well as morally empty, he argued. This is captured most simply in the assertion, which appears near the end of *Unto This Last*, and is spelled out in capitals: 'THERE IS NO WEALTH BUT LIFE.'[12]

For Ruskin, financial wealth which does not contribute to the stock of human happiness is no wealth at all. He goes on to assert:

> That country is the richest which nourishes the greatest number of noble and happy human beings; that man is richest who, having perfected the functions of his own life to the utmost, has also the widest helpful influence, both personal, and by means of his possessions, over the lives of others.[13]

Ruskin was aware that his critics would try to dismiss him as old-fashioned, sentimental, and failing to take a 'realistic' approach to modern industrial society. *Unto This Last* is therefore a detailed demolition of the prevailing economic philosophies of the day, which ends up suggesting a necessary reorientation of values, even if it does not set out a full social and political programme.

Unto This Last seemed to Victorian society at the time to be a rather shocking and misguided outburst from one of its most celebrated art critics.[14] Ruskin himself notes in the preface that the essays, when published in the *Cornhill Magazine* a year earlier, 'were reprobated in a violent manner, as far as I could hear, by most of the readers they met with'. This was the famous gentleman who had already published five volumes of *Modern Painters*, as well as highly regarded books on architecture and drawing. Why was he suddenly upsetting the establishment with these radical ideas?

RUSKIN ON CREATIVITY AND IMPERFECTION

In fact, Ruskin's social-political views are well grounded in his previous writings on art and architecture, and, interestingly for us, stem from an emphasis on the primacy of human *creativity*. I introduced *Unto This Last*, above, as an instance of rather unusual clarity in Ruskin; another such burst of Ruskin insight and lucidity had appeared eight years earlier in an essay entitled 'The Nature of Gothic'. This was the sixth chapter of the second volume of *The Stones of Venice*, a typically sprawling three-volume discussion of Gothic architecture. This is the Ruskin that caught the attention of the undergraduate William Morris, as mentioned above. He read chunks of it excitedly to his Oxford friend Edward Burne-Jones in 1853, and, as a lifelong fan of this essay in particular, Morris would republish it as a beautiful book by his own Kelmscott Press in 1892, writing in the preface that 'in future days [this chapter] will be considered as one of the very few necessary and inevitable utterances of the century'.[15]

In 'The Nature of Gothic', Ruskin focuses his attention on the defining characteristics of Gothic architecture – finally getting round to specifying why it is special, and why he loves it so much. The reasons, it turns out, are good ones, and not simply a matter of aesthetic choice. Ruskin admires the 'savagery' and 'rudeness' of the Gothic style, not for a masculine, tough reason, but because he sees it as the loving embrace of humanity's imperfections. The craftspeople who contribute to a Gothic building put in *thoughtful* work, even though it is imperfect. To force a craftsperson to make things to fixed specifications – 'with absolute precision by line and rule' – was to make them a 'slave', Ruskin asserted.[16]

In the medieval Gothic style which he favoured, however, 'this slavery is done away with altogether; Christianity having recognised, in small things as well as great, the individual value of every soul'.[17] Ruskin therefore welcomes the collaborative mish-mash, the combined construction of individual quirks and talents, a celebration of imperfection, imagination, and 'do what you can'. Yes, even the apparently laid-back phrase 'do what you can' appears in Ruskin, as he suggests that Christianity says to every Gothic crafter, 'Do what you can, and confess frankly what you are unable to do; neither let your effort be shortened for fear of failure, nor your confession silenced for fear of shame.'[18]

In a much more recent work, *The Sympathy of Things* by Lars Spuybroek, the author – an architect – assembles a hymn to Ruskin's relevance today. In the striking first chapter, 'The Digital Nature of Gothic', Spuybroek suggests that although Ruskin was opposed to machines – because machines were things that repetitively churned out copies of the same object – he would not be opposed to the digital, which is about design and relationships. After all, the Gothic architecture that Ruskin loved was about the relationships of parts, forming a whole complex interwoven network. Spuybroek writes:

> The Gothic is an architecture of *relationality*, of pattern, an architecture that constantly forges new relationships and expresses them in every possible form and shape. The Gothic makes this-place-here into every place, and this-moment-now into always. Maybe not everything-everything, but everything-enough, and maybe not always-always, but always-long enough. Enough so that you start caring about other things. As you see this thing here and now, in fact you are 'seeing' all things, or, as Ruskin says, you are experiencing 'a sympathy' with everything.[19]

'*I believe in things*', he says – referring to a sort of spiritual charge which means that you expect physical stuff to be meaningful.[20] 'To believe in things is to be prepared to be involved.'[21] So the spirituality that Spuybroek picks out from Ruskin is the zingy aliveness of *things*, combined with the real meaning of *work*, which is about intensity and enjoyment. This is distinct from the kind of *labour* that you might do just to get paid. 'Labour is based on the minimum we can do', Spuybroek explains, 'work on the maximum we can give.'[22]

> Work and the objects created through work, in Ruskin's mind, circulate for a larger or smaller part in a *gift economy*, not the market economy of mere supply and demand.[23]

Clearly these ideas are fruitful as we consider much of the work done by creative people using digital technologies – a relational network of exchange, characterized by an engaged intensity, which is *enjoyed*, and is more like gift-giving than unwelcome labour. But now we will zip back from Spuybroek's digital-era Ruskin to actual nineteenth-century Ruskin.

In 'The Nature of Gothic', Ruskin contrasts the noble, creative, imperfect work done by a thoughtful maker against the ignoble desire to see the 'narrow accomplishment' of supposedly 'perfect' work done to a readymade pattern.[24] This brings out the moral choice to be made: 'You must either make a tool of the creature, or a man of him', Ruskin writes. 'You cannot make both.'[25] A human being can be forced to work as a 'tool', following the precise instructions of their master, making things correctly, but they are dehumanized and their spirit is gagged. Or they can be allowed to 'begin to imagine, to think, to try to do anything worth doing' – and this might lead to roughness, failure, and shame, but also unleashes 'the whole majesty' of the individual.

This tips Ruskin into a fiery denunciation of England's new

industrial landscape, where 'the animation of her multitudes is sent like fuel to feed the factory smoke', and where men's creativity and intelligence is suffocated by repetitive machine work – oh, he says, 'this is to be slave-masters indeed'.[26] But he continues with a gentler point of comparison:

> On the other hand, go forth again to gaze upon the old cathedral front, where you have smiled so often at the fantastic ignorance of the old sculptors: examine once more those ugly goblins, and formless monsters, and stern statues, anatomiless and rigid; but do not mock at them, for they are signs of the life and liberty of every workman who struck the stone; a freedom of thought, and rank in scale of being, such as no laws, no charters, no charities can secure; but which it must be the first aim of all Europe at this day to regain for her children.[27]

This contrast between medieval craftsmanship and Victorian industrialism brings Ruskin to a critique of the division of labour – the system of capitalist efficiency whereby complex tasks are broken down into discrete stages, with each worker being responsible for the repeated production of one bit, rather than the whole. This form of organization had been praised by Adam Smith in the very first sentence of his 1776 treatise, *An Inquiry into the Nature and Causes of the Wealth of Nations*, where the process is said to have produced 'the greatest improvements in the productive powers of labour'.[28] Later in the same work, Smith worried that unstimulating specialization may mean that the worker 'has no occasion to exert his understanding, or to exercise his invention, in finding out expedients for removing difficulties which never occur . . . and generally becomes as stupid and ignorant as it is possible for a human creature to become'.[29] These concerns, buried deep in the text, were largely ignored by Smith's disciples.

THE DIVISION OF LABOUR

Today, we recognize the argument against the division of labour as a key element of the Marxist critique of capitalism. Karl Marx's argument that the division of labour led to alienation would be considered fully in the first volume of Marx's *Capital*, published fourteen years after 'The Nature of Gothic', in 1867. Earlier, in 1844, Marx was writing privately that this alienation caused by machine work meant that for the worker, 'Just as he is thus depressed spiritually and physically to the condition of a machine, and from being a man becomes an abstract activity and a belly.'[30] But Ruskin would not have read Marx's work at this time,[31] and makes the same kind of argument in his own way.

Both Ruskin and Marx employ the notion that the male worker who is reduced to repetitive machine work ceases to be 'a man'. But there are interesting differences in how the two thinkers make their similar argument. For Ruskin, the primary crime of the industrial system is that it steals from the worker the opportunity to create a whole object and to put his own creative mark upon it. Marx's critique is motivated by similar concerns, but the master economist uses somewhat different language and emphases; Marx's wage-slave worker is for Ruskin a creative spirit whose voice has been stolen. He writes:

> We have much studied and much perfected, of late, the great civilized invention of the division of labour; only we give it a false name. It is not, truly speaking, the labour that is divided; but the men: – Divided into mere segments of men – broken into small fragments and crumbs of life; so that all the little piece of intelligence that is left in a man is not enough to make a pin, or a nail, but exhausts itself in making the point of a pin, or the head of a nail.[32]

Ruskin anticipates an objection from his reader, that if any particular worker is a great artist who is unable to express himself, due to the division of labour, then he should be 'taken away and made a gentleman', and encouraged to produce beautiful designs which could then be executed by 'common workmen'. But he says:

> All ideas of this kind are founded upon two mistaken suppositions: the first, that one man's thoughts can be, or ought to be, executed by another man's hands; the second, that manual labour is a degradation, when it is governed by intellect.[33]

For Ruskin, the thought and the craft of making, the mental and the physical, were united in the same process. The division of labour was flawed, therefore, not only because it separated the stages of production into meaningless and tedious bits, but also because it separated the intellectual and the physical work which should be united in the process of making:

> We are always in these days endeavouring to separate the two; we want one man to be always thinking, and another to be always working, and we call one a gentleman, and the other an operative; whereas the workman ought often to be thinking, and the thinker often to be working, and both should be gentlemen, in the best sense.[34]

For Ruskin, as Peter Anthony observes, work was vital in terms that were moral and spiritual, connecting 'man' with nature and with God; whereas for Marx its significance was social and economic.[35] Marx's analysis is a critique of a kind of slavery, and Ruskin makes the same point, just as strongly, but it is embedded in a celebration of human creativity and craft, and the moral imperative that this should be freely expressed, individual, and unconstrained. Where Marx has a plan for how to fix this – the revolution which would replace the present system with a communist one – Ruskin's lament is less explicitly prescriptive, and can certainly seem unrealistically nostalgic – as in the wish, above, that we should simply elevate all workers to be 'gentlemen'. Nevertheless, even if Ruskin did not offer a simple manifesto for change, his great contribution was to establish individual, autonomous creativity as a core value which society must nurture, not crush, if it is to retain any moral authority, or quality of life.

WILLIAM MORRIS RIDES IN

It was this emphasis on the power of individually crafted work which caught the attention of the young William Morris. As we have seen, this approach, suggested by Ruskin, is not (simply) a celebration of individualistic 'making things' but rather has profound social implications. It begins with an appreciation of the unconstrained joyfulness which Ruskin saw in the often bizarre, strange and rough ornamentation which individual craftspeople had contributed to Gothic buildings – so this part of the argument could seem just to be an appreciation of individual talents. Or, indeed, could seem slightly patronizing, since much of the time Ruskin doesn't even seem to think that their work was of any great quality – he's just happy that these long-dead workers have done their best, and made their mark. But the argument shifts from the individual to the society – from the simple artist to the 'big picture' – by a logical route: individual self-expression is so vital that if a society creates supposedly rational systems (such as the capitalist division of labour) which do not allow a voice to people's individual creativity, then the whole system rapidly becomes sick and degraded, like a tree in barren soil.

Morris believed this passionately, and developed this emphasis on individual creative expression into a more expansive vision of happy, empowered creative communities. As Viscount Snowden put it in a Morris centenary pamphlet published in Walthamstow in 1934:

> He aimed at a community of fellowship in which all individuals would share in common the joys of creative art.[36]

Morris had been embroiled in medieval fantasies and Romantic literature from an early age. He had read Walter Scott's historical novels before he was seven, played games of knights, barons and fairies, and visited old churches with his father.[37] But as he became a young man, medievalism took on a more developed meaning, in tandem with new research which was building knowledge about medieval life. As his excellent biographer, E. P. Thompson, puts it:

> For Morris, the most important result of the new scholarship was in the reconstruction of a picture of the Middle Ages, neither as a grotesque nor as a faery world, but as a real *community* of human beings – an organic pre-capitalist community with values and an art of its own, sharply contrasted with those of Victorian England.[38]

Although life in medieval England had its share of difficulties and injustices, it was not systematically engineered to degrade the human spirit, or wedded to the notion of self-interest as the inevitable motive of all behaviour. Being able to evoke a clear picture of a way of living so very different to his current reality helped Morris to retain his genuine faith in the possibility of change.

And whilst Ruskin was something of an amateur artist as well as art critic, Morris combined theory and practice much more comprehensively. He mastered all kinds of creative techniques during the course of his lifetime, moving on from painting and drawing to embrace embroidery, woodcuts, calligraphy and book printing, tapestry weaving, and textile printing. He clearly felt that a hands-on engagement with a craft was the only way to truly understand it.

Morris decried the 'profit-grinding society' with its abysmal working conditions and 'shoddy' goods.[39] Like Ruskin, he felt that workers should be able to take pleasure from making beautiful things from the finest materials. Unlike Ruskin, though, Morris was a well-organized entrepreneur and avid multi-tasker, who didn't waste any time in creating a successful business in response to this need. Thus, in 1861, Morris, Marshall, Faulkner & Co. was founded – 'Fine Art Workmen in Painting, Carving, Furniture and the Metals' – producing handcrafted objects, wallpaper and textiles for the home, as well as major commissions for the decoration of rooms at St James's Palace, and the South Kensington Museum (now the V&A), as well as several churches. In 1875, the business came under Morris's sole ownership, as Morris & Co.

Later in life, in 1891, Morris also founded the Kelmscott Press, which used the approach and printing techniques of 400 years earlier in order – as Morris explained to a journalist in 1895 – to give 'a beautiful form' to 'the ideas we cherish'.[40] By this point Morris's craft work had become more of an all-consuming hobby than a commercial venture, and the Press only issued limited numbers of its expensively-made volumes.

'TIME-TRAVELLERS FROM THE FUTURE'

Morris's dedication to the production of high-priced luxury objects, and the lavishly decorated Kelmscott Press books, can seem puzzling since their very high production costs meant they were necessarily only available to an elite. In an 1891 newspaper interview, Morris presented his vision of a socialist society where 'We should have a library on every street corner, where everybody should read all the best books, printed in the best and most beautiful type.'[41] But in his own time, Morris did not seek to begin a 'books for all' publishing revolution, as Allen Lane would do later with affordable Penguin paperbacks.[42] Instead he made exclusive hand-crafted treasures.

A helpful explanation for this anomaly is offered by Tony Pinkney:

> From this standpoint, then, the Kelmscott Press books, however expensive and restricted in social circulation in their own day, are not evidences of medievalist nostalgia and political withdrawal, but are rather time-travellers from some far future we can barely imagine, showing how lovingly artefacts might be crafted in the socialist world that is to come.[43]

Although Morris did not articulate it quite in this manner, this seems an appropriate way of understanding what his high-class business was really meant to represent. Morris's battle was fought on two fronts: first, to prompt a transformation of society, via grand and revolutionary plans, this necessarily having to happen at a point in the future; but second, to modify and disrupt things, in the here and now, by inserting finely-produced material objects, and ethical working practices, into a society accustomed to 'shoddy' products and exploitative factories.

Clive Wilmer, editor of the very good Penguin Classics selection of Morris's work, *News from Nowhere and Other Writings*, similarly defends the author by explaining, on his behalf, that 'the creation of beautiful furnishings and so on is part of a process of *public education*, providing a model of good production methods and pioneering a return to higher standards of design'.[44] The expensive Kelmscott Press books are therefore consistent with Morris's 'all-or-nothing politics' – he would rather show the world the true ideal book, rather than compromise with more affordable models of lower quality.

Once we see Morris's craft work in this light, we can see that his written works – poetry, fiction, and prose – are just other dimensions of the *same* project. So rather than thinking that William Morris was a man who ran a craft business, and who also happened to be a writer of poetry and novels, and who also found time to produce political critiques and pamphlets, we instead come to the realization that William Morris was a man who projected a vision – a vision of great fundamental hope and optimism – through a striking number of different channels. On the one hand it might be a utopian novel, such as *News from Nowhere*, which fast-forwards the reader to an ideal, pastoral world of the future, where Morris would like you to live, or on the other hand it might be a utopian sitting-room, which fast-forwards its inhabitant to a world of well-made, comfortable and attractive domestic objects, which Morris would like you to live in. Along with the political non-fiction writings, they are all 'visionary accounts of an ideal world', as Wilmer puts it, reminding us of the possibility of alternatives: 'To dream of the impossible and disregard reality is to question the inevitability of existing circumstances.'[45]

Today, that spirit is perhaps seen in the higher-quality, carefully-made and relatively more expensive products offered at craft and maker fairs, and online stores, where people who have produced lovely garments and finely-packaged vinyl records have the courage to ask a necessarily higher price for them – because quality and hard work cannot be cheap, but they do command respect. We might think, too, of the crowdfunding site Kickstarter, where 'investors' are invited to buy into the desire of a creative person to make something, and to follow them on the journey. Ultimately, they do typically receive a thing, but the process highlights the journey of design, creation and production, and is the opposite of the standard online-shopping mission to get things very fast and very cheap.

And I do, actually, count LEGO in here – they are a hugely successful multinational company, of course, and LEGO is perceived as a relatively expensive toy. But in all my dealings with the company over many years, I have only seen a huge commitment to quality and creativity in play, and giving people the best quality experience with a creative product, responsibly and ethically produced. Of course, being so big means the company has a lot of power, and there have been missteps along the way: LEGO's relationship with gender issues, for instance, has been tricky, although not always bad. Seeing LEGO products as Morris-like 'visionary accounts of an ideal world' might seem a bit far-fetched, but I do think they are trying, and that has great value.

HOPE AND FULFILMENT

William Morris, then, with both his writings and his finely-made things, offered readers – and customers – a helping hand into the possibility of a new world. The more common approach of Marxist writers tends to be a more hectoring tone of voice – reaching its nadir, perhaps, in Theodor Adorno's writings in the 1930s and 1940s, where the critic seems unable to *believe* that people would be so stupid as to apparently enjoy the appalling sentimental offerings of the popular culture industry. On the one hand, it's a well-meaning stance: Adorno passionately believes that people deserve better. But on the other hand, he just seems disgusted to observe that almost everybody is an idiot.

William Morris takes a kinder approach to everyday life, recognizing that people have to 'make do' within a system which is not of their choosing. Like Adorno, he feared that industrial capitalism diverted people's desires away from the natural love of nature, creativity and fresh air, into 'sham wants' which it could more easily satisfy. But instead of telling them how dumb their lives are, he offers stories, manifestos, songs and objects from a better future, to feed the positive aspirations which he believes still reside in human hearts. It is one of Morris's undoubted strengths, that although he despises and sometimes despairs of modern society, he is unwilling to give up hope. As E. P. Thompson observes,

> 'Hope' was a key-word in Morris's vocabulary. By 'hope' he meant all that gives worth and continuity to human endeavour, all that makes man's finest aspirations seem possible of achievement in the real world.[46]

Morris was also well ahead of his time on the environment and sustainability: he decried the pollution of the industrial age, which he had seen come to swamp London within his own lifetime, and argued that a sustainable relationship with nature would be essential for the continued survival of humanity. He observed that science had become a servant of the capitalist system, in terms of exploitation and profiteering, but was not being tasked to help *alleviate* the impact of industrial processes:

> And Science – we have loved her well, and followed her diligently, what will she do? I fear she is so much in the pay of the counting-house, the counting-house and the drill-sergeant, that she is too busy, and will for the present do nothing. Yet there are matters which I should have thought easy for her; say for example teaching Manchester how to consume its own smoke, or Leeds how to get rid of its superfluous black dye without turning it into the river ...[47]

The notion that one arm of science and technology should be used to fix the environmental degradation caused by the other arm remains controversial, but Morris was 150 years ahead of the current debates.

Having established some of Morris's core values, we will now look in a little more detail at his views on creative cultures.

MORRIS ON MAKING AND SHARING

The distinctive and special thing about today's social media world is that, at its best, it offers users a reasonably equal platform on which to share creative artefacts – such as videos, images and writings – which they have made themselves and which express their own emotions or ideas. If we acknowledge the limits (notably the limitations of access in terms of equipment, and in terms of skills), we can reasonably suggest that this is an ideal which William Morris would have approved of.

For Morris, the sharing of art in a community was one of the fundamentals, part of a society's life-blood. In a lecture in 1877 he declared:

> I do not want art for a few, any more than education for a few, or freedom for a few.[48]

Without the opportunity to make their mark on the world, and in particular on the things around them in everyday life, people's relaxation time would be 'vacant and uninteresting', and their work 'mere endurance', Morris says.[49]

Making one's mark in this way requires some *effort*, of course, but Morris assumes that this work brings its own rewards and so is fuelled from within. He knows that working as a slave to the capitalist system, with no control over one's tasks and no freedom of personal expression, offers no fulfilment at all; but he is just as certain that self-initiated and expressive work is a joy, not a burden, and he assumes people will take to it with vigour.[50]

In 'Useful Work versus Useless Toil', a lecture from 1884, Morris explains that creative work, which he more or less equates with any work worth doing, offers 'hope' – that key word again – in three ways. First there is 'hope of rest' – the pleasurable buzz of a job well done, as one comes to relax after the event. Second, 'hope of product' – the achievement of having made something worthwhile. And third, 'hope of pleasure in the work itself' – a conscious pleasure in the activity, while it is being engaged in, and not 'mere habit'.[51] This point is amplified in the most spirited tones:

> I think that to all living things there is a pleasure in the exercise of their energies. . . . But a man at work, making something that he feels will exist because he is working at it and wills it, is exercising the energies of his mind and soul as well as of his body. Memory and imagination help him as he works. Not only his own thoughts, but the thoughts of the men of past ages guide his hands; and as a part of the human race, he creates. If we work thus we shall be men, and our days will be happy and eventful.[52]

(As in all cases with these Victorian quotes, I hope the reader will forgive the author for his masculine language and read the stuff about a 'manly' existence to mean a full and zesty engagement with the spirit of humanity – which, of course, is both female and male.)

Morris acknowledges that this joyful celebration of work may seem 'strange' to many of his readers, as he knows that in current everyday reality they are trapped on the wrong side of the fence, doing 'slave's work – mere toiling to live, that we may live to toil'. This doesn't change the fact that an alternative exists, and Morris is not easily put off listing desirable possibilities just because their realization in the present world may be difficult to imagine.

Later in the same lecture, Morris turns his attention to the 'rich non-producing classes' who have a taste for pointless objects which are merely intended to reflect and symbolize their wealth. But this is not wealth, the author asserts, it is 'waste'. Wealth is something else entirely:

> Wealth is what Nature gives us and what a reasonable man can make out of the gifts of Nature for his reasonable use. The sunlight, the fresh air, the unspoiled face of the earth, food, raiment and housing necessary and decent; the storing up of knowledge of all kinds, and the power of disseminating it; means of free communication between man and man; works of art, the beauty which man creates when he is most a man, most aspiring and thoughtful – all things which serve the pleasure of people, free, manly, and uncorrupted. This is wealth.[53]

This redefinition of the meaning of 'wealth' echoes Ruskin's 'There is no wealth but life', of course, but Morris's list is interesting – not least of all because, over 100 years before the rise of the World Wide Web, it highlights the collection and dissemination of knowledge, communication between people, and the ability to create and share expressive material, as the true route to pleasure and fulfilment.

EVERYDAY ARTS

Morris understood 'genuine art' to be 'the expression of man's pleasure in his handiwork',[54] and deplored the separation between the professional world of 'art' and the everyday things that people make. Historically he judged the arts to be 'healthy' when they were built upon an intimate weaving together of 'craft' abilities and artistic ideas, the practical and the emotional, and the stimulation of both pleasure and intellect.[55] The artist should be humble, engaged with the everyday, and willing to make things themselves – to get their hands dirty, as it were. As Morris puts it: 'The best artist was a workman still, the humblest workman was an artist.'[56]

Today, the category of 'artist' is even more sharply removed from everyday creative practices, and often seems to be based on having the 'right' kind of art education, the necessary fashionable artworld connections, and a pretentious way of talking about things. Until quite recently, this used to be deeply frustrating for creative people who did not happen to be part of the artworld in-crowd, because they were therefore denied the ability to share their work with others. You could go down the mainstream populist route, and hope to find TV stardom, or at least get anonymous but paid work doing graphics for movies; or you could hope to become the next darling of the artworld, ideally by memorizing some French poststructuralism and applying it to your 'vision' somehow; or nothing. Today, the digital environment means that people don't have to worry so much about labels – art / craft / whatever – and have relatively unlimited channels for sharing stuff they have made. As Clay Shirky has observed, the relevant filters now operate *after*, not before, publication, so at least you can get your stuff out there.[57] It is not guaranteed that anyone will pay attention, but at least work can be shown and shared, and the likelihood of it being noticed is much less dependent on a small number of elite gatekeepers. And the more you openly show and share, the more likely it is that some people will start to take notice, and begin a conversation.

Morris might have had some concerns about the ways in which today's everyday-creative makers offer their work to be profited from, via advertising, by the owners of the big content-hosting websites such as YouTube – an issue which we will return to in chapter 7. But if we leave that dimension to one side for now, the level of free and spontaneous creative sharing should certainly have given him a warm glow. The only healthy art, he said, is 'an art which is to be made by the people and for the people, as a happiness to the maker and the user'.[58] I am confident in saying that this is much more clearly a description of daily activity on YouTube than it is an account of the interactions between the elite inhabitants of the contemporary artworld, such as the people named in *ArtReview* magazine's *Power 100* list.

Finally, a note on individualism. Later in this book, where as mentioned we will have to consider whether sites like YouTube are best understood as hateful 'profit grinding' mills for user-generated content, we will also have to consider whether we prefer the aggregated 'wisdom of crowds' notion of social media, where many users collaborate and contribute to produce the best resources, or whether the individual voice is more important. E. P. Thompson explains Morris's view thus:

> In both *News from Nowhere* and the lectures, the emphasis is upon the communal life. But (as Morris never ceased to

> repeat) true individualism was only possible in a Communist society, which needed and valued the contribution of each individual to the common good; and, in a society which fostered true variety, he knew that different men would choose to live in different ways.[59]

So we do not have to choose between the individual *or* the collective: rather, a diverse *community* of *individual* voices offers a satisfying combined solution.

3

THE MEANING OF MAKING II: CRAFT TODAY

This chapter continues to follow the development of thinking about craft activity and making things. We will look briefly at how the ideas of Ruskin and Morris fed into the Arts and Crafts movement, and an ethos which would appear later in the twentieth century as 'DIY culture'. We will consider how those values can then spread out into a more general philosophy of everyday life. But then we'll try to be rather more concrete again, and consider some of today's popular craft practices, and the recent 'rise' of craft, and look at *why* people in the present day still like to make things themselves. And then at the end of the chapter, we will return to the discussion of the meaning of creativity, which we started in chapter 1, and will propose a new definition of creativity which seems better suited to our purposes.

THE EMERGENCE OF CRAFT

As mentioned in the previous chapter, craft can seem like a timeless practice, rooted in ancient and traditional ways of engaging with the world and building communities. Indeed, those practices may well be ancient – but the word 'craft' itself is relatively new. In the eighteenth century, 'craft' referred primarily to political cunning and a sly, jocular, tricksy approach to social issues.[1] By the time of Samuel Johnson's *Dictionary of the English Language* in 1755, 'manual art; trade' is listed as one of the meanings, along with 'art; ability; dexterity', alongside the earlier usage as 'fraud; cunning; artifice'.[2] At that point, though, craft was not associated with any particular methods or objects, and could be applied to any cultural practices.[3] During the nineteenth century, the notion of 'craft' or a 'craftsman' appeared even less often, remaining pretty dormant until the last quarter of that century, when it sprang into action.[4]

Although dissecting the etymology of specific words is not always the most valuable exercise, Paul Greenhalgh – a former Head of Research at the Victoria and Albert Museum – uses the rather arbitrary gathering of ideas and orientations under the notion of craft to set out its different constituent dimensions. He writes:

> The ideological and intellectual underpinning of the craft constituency is not a consistent whole, but has several distinct threads to it, which have only become intertwined relatively recently. It is these threads, or elements, that I will deal with here. There are three. I will describe them as *decorative art*, the *vernacular*, and the *politics of work*.[5]

The first of these, decorative art, is a broad term which seems to encompass all the 'applied' forms of creativity which have in common the bruised, second-class feeling of being excluded from the category of 'fine art'. The second element, the vernacular, refers to the authentic, natural voice of a community, unselfconsciously communicated through everyday things that people have made. In the third element, the politics of work, the actual crafted objects become secondary to the broader ideals about the conditions in which they are made. This is the political message of Ruskin and Morris, that creative workers must be free to express themselves through the production of whole objects. They have control over their own labour, and contribute to a vibrant and dynamic culture through the creation of their own individual things.

THE ARTS AND CRAFTS MOVEMENT

It was the combination of these three threads that led to the Arts and Crafts movement. This loose grouping of idealistic thinkers and craftspeople built on the ideas of Ruskin and Morris in different ways, but central to the movement was the idea that all creative work was of equal status, and was the means by which human beings could connect with nature, with their own sense of self, and with other people. Making things expressed individual life through the work of the hands, and therefore could not be divided into machine-like steps or repetitive sameness.[6]

The phrase 'Arts and Crafts' was first used in this context in 1887, and the movement burned brightly until the First World War. Although rooted in Victorian Britain, it spread around the world, most notably in the United States, where it connected meaningfully with American notions of self-reliance, individualism, community, and romantic connection with nature. Greenhalgh summarizes its legacy as follows:

> The Arts and Crafts movement, in retrospect, can be seen to be the most successful construction of a theory and practice of ethical art. . . . The *vernacular* was the model, unalienated *work* was the means and *art* was the goal. The larger ideal pulled the three elements into proximity. It was a brilliant formulation: humankind would be liberated through communal creativity.[7]

It is something very much like this vision which inspires contemporary craft enthusiasts today, as well as exponents of social media and online creativity. Although rooted in a seemingly distant age, its message is practical, positive and ethical. (As ever, something which is powerful and true when expressed by a creative user of online tools, can also be nauseating and self-serving when declaimed by the CEO of Facebook; but in the right hands, the point is still okay.) Greenhalgh goes on to say:

> Ultimately, for craft pioneers, the movement was centred on physical and mental freedom. By uniting the work process directly to the demand for a higher quality of life, they had regenerated the idea that craft was synonymous with power.[8]

The American inheritors of the Arts and Crafts movement added the democratic element which today we would call 'DIY culture'. As we have seen, dehumanizing industrial methods were rejected because of a concern for the individual worker, but the Arts and Crafts alternative led to beautiful handmade products that the typical worker could not afford. This terrible paradox is immediately dissolved in the simple phrase: 'do it yourself'.

This solution to the conundrum was helped along by Gustav Stickley, a furniture-maker, craftsman and architect, based in New York. From 1901 to 1916, Stickley published a magazine called *The Craftsman*, which began as a US-based expression of the British Arts and Crafts movement – launching with detailed discussions of the life and work of Morris and Ruskin, in the first and second issues respectively – but over time came to represent a distinct American version of that philosophy. Stickley's belief in 'a simple, democratic art' that would provide Americans with 'material surroundings conducive to plain living and high thinking' was such that he included his designs and working plans for furniture, metalwork and needlework in the magazine[9] – even though this, to some extent, undermined his own business, which was based on selling this stuff as unique finished products. In this sense, Stickley invented, or rather revived, the concept of 'open source' – the system by which software developers today share unprotected code in the belief that others should be freely able to use it and improve it.

This democratic approach is highly consistent with the ideals of the Arts and Crafts movement: craft skills were valued for their own careful, individual, handmade beauty, not because they were supposed to be the skills of an expert elite. William Morris made things to a very high standard, because that gave him pleasure, and because he thought the care and quality of their production would bring pleasure to others too. But he didn't make things to a very high standard because he thought that it made him better than everybody else. 'Do it yourself' is, therefore, part of the original Arts and Crafts message – but processed through American optimism, and communicated in a cheerful and unpretentious way.

DIY CULTURE

Today, the mainstream notion of 'DIY' is associated with everyday home improvement – putting up shelves, assembling flat-pack wardrobes and fixing drainpipes oneself, without professional help. This is a commonplace, suburban kind of phenomenon, popularly seen as a bit boring, and nothing to do with any kind of radical political movement.

When this kind of DIY emerged in the 1960s, though, it was – at least for some – associated with the alternative counterculture. In particular, it was argued that the formal education system had filled students' heads with abstract information, supposedly of some background value for those who might enter the professions, but lacking real-world usefulness.

The philosopher Alan Watts put it like this:

> Our educational system, in its entirety, does nothing to give us any kind of material competence. In other words, we don't learn how to cook, how to make clothes, how to build houses, how to make love, or to do any of the absolutely fundamental things of life. The whole education that we get for our children in school is entirely in terms of abstractions. It trains you to be an insurance salesman or a bureaucrat, or some kind of cerebral character.[10]

This was said during a 1967 symposium, of sorts, which took place on Watts's houseboat moored in Sausalito, California, in which his interlocutors included the LSD enthusiast Timothy Leary, the beat poet Allen Ginsberg, and the poet and environmentalist Gary Snyder. I mention these details to give a flavour of the context in which these ideals developed. It's not the typical bunch of people you'd associate with 'DIY culture' if the phrase 'do it yourself' only reminds you of giant hardware stores.

This critical attitude to schooling, allied with the notion that people can do things better themselves without such institutions, was reflected in the work of John Holt, whose books *How Children Fail* and *How Children Learn* raised public awareness of these new ideas in the 1960s.[11] (Similar themes were also developed by Ivan Illich in the early 1970s, whose work is discussed in chapter 6.) Holt argued that learning was something that humans do naturally from the earliest age, and that any machinery designed to make 'learning' happen as a specific kind of activity, separate from the normal experience of everyday life – as schools intend to do – could only get in the way.[12] This gave considerable support to the emergent home-schooling movement – literally a DIY approach to education, in which learners are typically supported to follow their own interests and explore the world in whatever way they choose. Responding to critics' fears that children would not bother to learn anything if left to their own devices, Holt argued that children should be *trusted* to build their own understandings, and could make their own meaningful connections with knowledge, which would be much more useful and effective for them than the abstract pile of procedures and information that children are told that they will need by schools.

Another key figure in this everyday-life DIY movement was Stewart Brand, who in 1968 launched his homemade publication, *The Whole Earth Catalog*, which was highly successful and influential, and had several further editions up to 1985. Subtitled 'Access to Tools', it offered readers a (mostly mail-order) gateway to all kinds of resources, including information, technical books and courses, as well as physical tools such as those for building, metalwork, gardening and early electronics.

The phrase 'whole Earth', which appears in the title of many of Brand's projects, refers to a thought that he had in 1966, that when NASA released a photograph showing the whole of the planet from space, it would lead to a change of consciousness as people realized their place in a global system of limited resources. One week later, he was thrown off the University of California Berkeley campus for wearing a day-glo sandwich board and selling 25-cent badges which read: 'Why haven't we seen a photograph of the whole Earth yet?' This was reported in the *San Francisco Chronicle*, and picked up by other newspapers, which helped his nascent viral campaign enormously.[13]

The well-illustrated *Whole Earth Catalog*, published two years after that, was eclectic in the extreme, but the things and ideas that it featured shared a common spirit. As it said in its statement of purpose at the front:

> We are as gods and might as well get good at it. So far, remotely done power and glory – as via government, big business, formal education, church – has succeeded to the point where gross defects obscure actual gains. In response to this dilemma and to these gains a realm of intimate, personal power is developing power of the individual to conduct his own education, find his own inspiration, shape his own environment, and share his adventure with whoever is interested. Tools that aid this process are sought and promoted by the Whole Earth Catalog.[14]

Later, Brand went on to be a pioneer of home computing and the internet, and co-founded the online community The WELL – The Whole Earth 'Lectronic Link – which will be discussed in chapter 6, and later still was a proponent of certain technological solutions to environmental problems (as in his 2009 book, *Whole Earth Discipline*).

Across all of Brand's work – with the possible exception of his recent (reluctant) enthusiasm for nuclear power and geoengineering – we see the values of self-reliance, do it yourself and community. And, to be fair, humanity wouldn't be needing the nuclear power and geoengineering if it had stuck to the caring, convivial, small-scale ecological values which Brand has always supported. Significantly, Brand's work helps us trace a direct path from William Morris and the Arts and Crafts movement, to its heir, the countercultural Do It Yourself movement, and on to the internet and social media.

PUNK DIY

A similar-but-different version of the DIY ethos is the 'lo-fi' music and zine culture, influenced in part by the punk scene. This DIY culture is characterized by a rejection of the glossy, highly-produced, celebrity-oriented mainstream of popular culture, and its replacement with a knowingly non-glossy, often messily-produced alternative which is much less bothered about physical beauty, and declares an emphasis on content rather than style.

This ethos is discussed, for example, in Amy Spencer's book *DIY: The Rise of Lo-Fi Culture*. She's an enthusiastic guide. On the first page she says:

> In the face of the bland consumerist pop that dominates the airwaves and the bestselling celebrity biographies that fill the bookshops it is exciting to realize that there are an increasing amount of independent and creative minds who care enough to go against the grain and produce music, art, magazines and literature that is truly unique – whether it is likely to sell or not.[15]

Spencer does not believe that online culture is destined to replace these independently-made objects, because of the excitement associated with creating alternative cultural items that you can hold in your own hands. This is a shift away from the strict meaning of 'homemade' or 'handmade', since the ideal here is to pay a small printer or disc-presser to make you a box of, say, 500 things to sell or give to friends and like-minded souls. Spencer says:

> The internet has enabled DIY culture to become more accessible and less elitist, but, remarkably, it hasn't diminished the enduring appeal of the homemade zine or the 4-track demo.[16]

As a former zine-maker myself, I have to agree that having a box of *actual things* that you have created is quite delightful, and trading in that culture, where you might swap your zine for someone else's self-published comic, which perhaps comes with a 'free gift' of a metal badge or a two-track flexi-disc, that expresses the undiluted enthusiasm of one or two committed creators in the form of a physical object . . . well, to be honest, the internet isn't *quite* the same.

On the other hand, producing boxes full of new physical objects is often bad for the environment, and getting rid of those objects, even to people who want them, is hard work. In the book *Web Studies*, published way back in 2000, I gave my own experience with zines to show how convenient this new World Wide Web thing could be. I said:

> When I was a student, I published a fanzine (or 'small press magazine') with an anti-sexist theme, *Powercut*, which was reproduced by a professional printing company (in exchange for a significant chunk of my humble student finances). Producing and printing the thing was the (relatively) easy part: it was the *distribution* which would eat up my life. I spent hundreds of hours visiting and writing to bookshops, and getting magazines and newspapers to write about it – with ordering details – so that I could spend yet more hours responding to mail order requests. I published

> two issues, and for each one, it took me a year to shift 800 copies. This was regarded as a considerable success in small press circles.
>
> Today, like many people, I can write a review or article, stick it on the Web, then sit back and relax. 800 or so people can have read it – well, *seen* it – within a week. I largely enjoyed the *Powercut* experience, back in 1991–93, but think how much simpler my life would have been – and how much more of a life I would have had! – if Tim Berners-Lee had bothered to invent the World Wide Web just a few years earlier than he actually did.[17]

Amy Spencer notes that zines are more like gifts than commercial products, since they are done for love not money, and argues that unlike mainstream media, the mode of their production is inspiring for readers – showing that you don't have to accept the given culture, and can create your own instead.[18] She highlights the role of 'riot grrrl' zines as central to establishing the principles of 'third wave' feminism, which rejected the victim stance and instead went on the front foot. Rather than just complaining about offensive popular culture, they created its replacement:

> Here women redefined feminism for the 90s and recognised each other as manufacturers of culture, as opposed to participants in a culture that they were encouraged to accept. They were encouraged to reclaim the media and produce their own cultural forms.[19]

They formed bands, and produced zines, which often parodied the conventions of mainstream culture with fake fashion features, and ironic, angry versions of 'agony aunt' columns, alongside more serious material on sexism, domestic violence and body image. The alternative zine movement also led to 'mama zines' offering an alternative to young parents who did not wish to swallow the commercialized vision of parenthood.

Betsy Greer, who coined the term 'craftivism' (meaning – as you would expect – the confluence of craft and activism), makes the point that today it is easy to buy stuff – clothing, music, reading-matter, children's toys, food, or whatever: cheap or expensive versions of any of these things are readily available. But, she argues, there is a resistance, a *political choice*, in not buying those things and choosing to make your own instead.[20] (Or, similarly, to buy or exchange a locally homemade thing from someone you know.) It is in this way that traditional crafts such as knitting, cooking, weaving, sewing and gardening have come to take on a gentle revolutionary dimension.

We've only scratched the surface of DIY approaches and practices here, but the central idea at the heart of them all is a rejection of the idea that you overcome problems by paying somebody else to provide a solution. We've got used to experts, professionals and businesses telling us that the way to do things – whether building a shed, or learning about a subject, or getting entertainment – is to pay other people, who know what they're doing, to do the task for us, because we couldn't really manage it ourselves. DIY culture says that's rubbish: you can do it yourself, and you can do it with more creativity, character and relevance than if you got a generic or 'expert' solution. And, importantly, it *feels good* to do it yourself: it's really good for self-esteem – a crucial dimension of personal psychology – whereas getting it done for you is disempowering, and often frustrating, and less meaningful.

Of course, our time and our skills are usually far from unlimited, so it is often convenient to get experienced people to help us – that's fine, of course, and it keeps the economy going, as people can sell their time and expertise to others. But the DIY point that for many tasks, you *can* do it for yourself, and would feel pride and pleasure if you did so, remains true.

CRAFTING AS AN ATTITUDE TO EVERYDAY LIFE

The DIY ethos, and a passion for craft, are not just about isolated projects, but spill over into everyday life more generally. Suggesting that people can make, fix and repair things for themselves has much in common with sustainability and environmentalism. It also obviously connects with anti-consumerism – the rejection of the idea that the answer to all of our needs and problems can be purchased from shops. This doesn't mean that the crafty person rejects all 'stuff' – on the contrary, having interesting things in our lives, things that we enjoy and which we look after, is enriching. The problem, as John Naish argues in his book *Enough*, is that we keep on wanting to acquire things rather than finding pleasure in the ones we've got. When the basic human brain evolved, gathering stuff continuously was good for survival. Naish quotes Robert Trivers, an evolutionary biologist, who says: 'We've evolved to be maximising machines. There isn't necessarily a stop mechanism in us that says, "Relax, you've got enough".'[21]

So although most people now have some awareness of environmental issues, and may even suspect that having more and more things isn't going to make us happier, we don't tend to think 'I've got enough now.' Instead, we continue to acquire new stuff, rather than making or reusing things, if only for the temporary frisson of opening a glossy new item, or the novelty of an unfamiliar gadget. Even hearing about, for instance, the Great Pacific Garbage Patch – a mass of plastic waste floating in the ocean, covering an area at least the size of Texas[22] – makes us sad for humanity, but doesn't seem to affect individual behaviour.

Perhaps the warm values of craft and creativity can help here, offering a positive vision of making and reusing, rather than the more austere and negative-sounding 'stop that!' message suggested by anti-consumerism arguments and shocking pollution news. Since making and sharing things can make a positive contribution to well-being and a sense of connectedness – as argued throughout this book – then there is much to be gained from shopping less, and creating and recycling more. The human brain doesn't always think like that, however, so we need to make a conscious effort to reprogram ourselves.

This is not just about 'things' of course. The corresponding argument in the field of media and entertainment is that we can gain pleasure, and a sense of connectedness, from the homemade stories, films, animations and reports made by everyday amateur people, on a domestic level, and shared online. There is already more than 'enough' professional material being generated every day. There is a strong argument for having well-resourced and independent news and current affairs programmes, and quality drama and entertainment on film, television and online. But in a healthy society there should be just as much cheerfully unfinanced non-professional material made by all kinds of people, just because they want to, or have something to say, all around the world. (Ideally, though, we'd also be spending less time looking at screens, as indicated in chapters 1 and 11.)

Meanwhile, the notion of craft has been extended into spheres of life which are not really to do with making things – or making media – at all. A notable example is the concept of 'crafting gentleness', developed by Anthony McCann. In his online invitation to consider 'crafting gentleness', he explains:

> The notion of crafting is often associated with activities like pottery, knitting, woodwork, quiltmaking and so on. Engaging in these sorts of crafting can be a great way to remind ourselves that we can make a difference, to remind ourselves that we can learn to listen more carefully to how we make the differences that we make. Crafting materials can be a way to align ourselves to think more in terms of the consequences and effects of what we do, to consider that helpfulness and appropriateness might be friendlier values to live by than rigid rules of right and wrong. By sculpting, shaping, moulding, guiding, building, and by listening and responding as we go, we can become more aware of how we make a difference. Crafting can be a reclamation of the power of life.[23]

The hands-on engagement of crafting and making, then, connects us with broader values, but the crafting orientation becomes one which can be a continuous part of everyday life, regardless of whether or not we happen to have a hands-on craft project. Rather, the gentle crafting spirit comes, ideally, to occupy all interactions with people and with nature:

> Here, crafting activities are understood as reminders that we can become aware of how we always-already make a difference, at any time, in any situation. We are *always-already* sculpting, shaping, moulding, guiding, building. We *always-already* have an influence on how we and others experience life. We can become more aware of how we *always-already* matter. . . . There is nothing more personal, political, or relevant than attending to the . . . character of our own attitude as we engage in crafting our experience and our relationships.[24]

The understanding that we make our own experiences, as well as shaping our material surroundings, is an important one to emerge from craft activity. This idea also arises from the 'slow' movement – the growing feeling that the world is becoming too fast, crazy, and driven by demands and targets and pointless aspirations, and that we have to reclaim a gentler pace.

In Carl Honoré's excellent 2004 book, *In Praise of Slow*, which introduced the slow movement to a general audience, the author shows how the modern impetus to cram as much stuff as possible into our days has a negative effect on our well-being, and also means that we gain less pleasure, and knowledge, from the things that we do.[25] He argues that a 'slower' approach to work, leisure, education, child development, and other areas of life, can dramatically increase the quality of the experiences, even if they are fewer in number. He emphasizes that notions such as 'slow work' or 'slow education' do not represent a shift towards laziness, but are rather about taking a more measured pace, to do things properly, and to appreciate and enjoy them, without a constant sense of rush and the background panic that one isn't getting through things fast enough. So in some ways it is about working harder, and doing things better, by making decisions to reduce the rush.

The link with craft and making is that when one is not just a consumer, guzzling thing after thing, but also a producer, going through the necessarily slower and more thoughtful process of making something, one becomes more aware of the details and decisions which underpin everyday things and experiences, and therefore more able to gain pleasure and inspiration from the appreciation of things.[26]

CRAFT PRACTICES AND THE 'RISE' OF CRAFT

Having discussed craft as a general approach and ethos, we will now look, in a more direct and concrete way, at some of today's craft activities, and why people do them. In the first chapter I mentioned the apparent surge of interest in craft clubs and fairs, alongside the rise of digital technologies and social media. Such trends may often seem to grow or subside, and to some extent are generated in the imagination of the mainstream media, whilst the reality is probably that the human appetite for making things may be reasonably stable across time. Human beings have obviously made things for their own use for thousands of years. The broad recent history seems to be that during the Second World War, in the US, the UK, and elsewhere, the make-it-yourself and 'make do and mend' ethos was especially strong, encouraged by governments and embraced by the people, as a domestic tactic showing the kind of initiative that might help to win the war.[27] But after that period of self-help and austerity, through the second half of the twentieth century, people tended to be more delighted with manufactured goods, and were less impressed by homemade clothing, tools or furniture, which could be seen as cheap and embarrassing.[28] But since the start of the present century – and obviously these are rough and blurred movements, not clear-cut phases – enthusiasm and respect for homemade things has risen again. This is, I think, partly because of the growth in awareness of environmental issues – people are increasingly aware that the manufacturing of endless stuff is not simply a proud sign of humanity's superior powers, but rather has troubling implications – and also because of the rise of the Web as a frequently homemade phenomenon, which can, additionally, connect and support crafters around the world.

Although heavily connected with traditions of craft and making which go back decades, and indeed centuries, this resurgence of activity is often explained – and, to be fair, genuinely *experienced* – as a 'new' phenomenon. For instance, in the 2008 book *Handmade Nation: The Rise of DIY, Art,*

Craft and Design, one of the co-editors, Faythe Levine, writes breathlessly about her excitement at setting up a stall at the Renegade Craft Fair in Chicago, in 2003:

> A lot of us had no clue what we were doing, but there was this exhilarating energy throughout Wicker Park. . . . I knew something big was happening. . . . We were redefining what craft was and making it our own. . . . Without really being conscious of it, we were creating an independent economy free from corporate ties. I quickly realised I was a part of a burgeoning art community based on creativity, determination, and networking.[29]

This exhilaration at being part of an apparently new craft movement may also have been felt by some individuals ten, twenty or a hundred years earlier, but no matter. *Handmade Nation* certainly does seem to document a newly empowered and organized movement – helped, as I've said, by the new visibility of their activities via the internet, which enables the excited enthusiasts in one corner of the world to inspire and encourage similarly energized individuals elsewhere, with a depth and speed that was not previously possible. Special mention must go here to Etsy, a vast and lovely platform where people can buy and sell, but also admire and be inspired by, a massive array of crafted things from around the world. Ravelry, the superb social network for knitters, has also been very influential.[30] As Garth Johnson, who produces the blog extremecraft.com, says:

> It may sound strange that a bunch of people who are trying to reclaim handicraft are using technology to do so, but it's undeniably true. . . . It's the internet that holds the craft world together. Show me a crafter without a website and I'll show you a crafter who will probably have a website

> within six months. The handmade nation wields the internet just as effectively as it does a knitting needle or a roll of duct tape.[31]

For these crafters, the internet is not the new place where craft itself happens – that's what we will be discussing in the next chapter – but is the new vehicle for communicating about (real-world) craft, for showing projects and connecting with others. It means that they have been able to collectively develop a firm and positive sense of shared meaning, and mission, which was probably more difficult to establish when craft activity was more fragmented and isolated.

One such expression of the personal and political meanings of this recent movement is presented, for instance, in the 'Craftifesto', written by Amy Carlton and Cinnamon Cooper, founders of the 'DIY Trunk Show', an annual craft event in Chicago:

> *Craftifesto: The Power is in Your Hands!*
> We believe:
> *Craft is powerful.* We want to show the depth and breadth of the crafting world. Anything you want you can probably get from a person in your own community.
> *Craft is personal.* To know that something was made by hand, by someone who cares that you like it, makes that object much more enjoyable.
> *Craft is political.* We're trying to change the world. We want everyone to rethink corporate culture and consumerism.
> *Craft is possible.* Everybody can create something![32]

These statements show how craft has become more than just individuals making nice things: there is now a sense of community and shared purpose. *Handmade Nation* – which is not only a book but also a 2009 documentary film of the same name – showcases a rich array of craft activity from the United States, including people making clothes, dolls, books, bags, jewellery, prints, footwear, and other things, using a huge variety of techniques and styles. *Make* magazine, and the associated *Maker Faire* events, similarly showcase a huge range of DIY projects, which are often more to do with engineering and technology, but are driven by the same ethos, and often have an ecological dimension, by reusing former junk, or by producing or saving power.

CRAFT MOTIVATIONS

So what explains the activity, and the rise, of crafting? Part of the explanation appears above, in that crafting is now a community and a movement with appealing values, that people want to be a part of. But there are further personal reasons why people choose to be *making things* rather than joining other kinds of friendly-sounding communities. Sabrina Gschwandtner, a knitter who has published both a series of journals and a book called *KnitKnit*, says that she is frequently asked 'Why is handcraft so popular right now?' She suggests that it is 'a reaction against a whole slew of things, including our hyperfast culture, increasing reliance on digital technology, [and] the proliferation of consumer culture'.[33] She notes that sustainability is often a motivating factor. And she says that often,

> people want to see a project through from beginning to end, something they don't get to do in their daily lives. In their jobs, they do one part of producing something and they don't do the other parts. In producing a handcraft project, people can see something from start to finish and then have a material product that they can use themselves or give away.[34]

This is an argument that can apply to a range of crafts: the same point is made by Matthew Crawford to explain why fixing a motorbike is so satisfying, compared with office work, in his book *The Case for Working with Your Hands.*[35]

Other crafters interviewed for *Handmade Nation* provide further explanations. Deb Dormody, who makes and binds her own books, says that homemade things are special because they carry the 'authentic and personal' touch of the person who has made them[36] (which reflects the point made by Ruskin in the previous chapter). Christy Petterson, who makes earrings, postcards, and other things, tells of how she always liked being creative but had been put off doing 'art' because the education system had framed it as 'serious' and 'analytical'. It was only when she happened to find websites such as Getcrafty.com that she felt able and inspired to do whatever she wanted – 'I realised that I had found my people', as she puts it.[37]

Alena Hennessy, who makes clothes and tiles, had previously been an artist working through galleries, but found it limiting and boring. When she tried to break away from that world, the open and sharing community of craftspeople took her by surprise: 'In the craft community, I feel very connected to people whom I have never met in person. I didn't expect to be so inspired by what everyone else was doing. . . . It is very different from a typical gallery art scene: it is a really wonderful sort of collaborative, supportive, noncompetitive network', she says.[38] At a more individual level, Jenny Hart talks about how she had thought that embroidery looked 'tedious' and stressful – 'like it would make me want to pull my hair out' – but she discovered that it was a great way to relax and curb anxiety. She launched Sublimestitching.com to show others that embroidery did not have to be about following complex diagrams, but could simply be enjoyed:

> I don't think our generation really likes to be told what to do. . . . We really like to have a lot of wiggle room for experimenting and being creative, and we like to have our mark on it. Embroidery leaves a lot of room for that.[39]

These motivations, then, all tend to combine personal satisfactions with the pleasure and inspiration of being part of a craft community.

CRAFTING TOGETHERNESS

The crafters featured in *Handmade Nation* are generally those who have become visible, and inspiring to others, through the online and offline networks of craft enthusiasts. And, of course, their views are no less significant for that. But the craft world – unlike the artworld – is a place where fame, and comparative status amongst peers, is meant to be unimportant. In line with this reasoning, a number of books and websites about craft today emphasize the essentially intimate and personal nature of the experience of making. Here, making is still connecting – with materials, other people, and the world – but in gentle and quiet ways, with no need for grand celebratory announcements. One example is the book *The Creative Family*, by Amanda Blake Soule, which offers a powerful and democratic argument for widespread, unspecialized, everyday craft activity. The end products of craft activities here are not widely circulated on websites, are not sold for money, and seek no external recognition, but are hugely important for the reason given in the book's subtitle, *How to Encourage Imagination and Nurture Family Connections*. Soule does actually have a level of online fame, as the creator of the popular *SouleMama* blog, but this book emphasizes the personal and family benefits of everyday creative projects (which is one of the things that her 'adventures in thrifting, crafting and parenting' blog is about).

Despite the 'How to' subtitle – a formula favoured by publishers – the book is far from prescriptive. Instead, it encourages any activities which help families to bond, and appreciate each other, through creative work and play.

> Living a creative life can encompass all areas of our family life – from our hobbies, to the way we connect with nature, to the ways we connect in our community, to the ways we celebrate our days together, and to the ways we celebrate each other.[40]

Soule emphasizes the *process* of creativity, which helps people to learn and bond together. She emphasizes the value of all family members being engaged in creative projects – not just encouraging a child to do a painting (although that's good and fine), but everyone actively having one or two projects on the go:

> I see both my personal creative efforts and the act of engaging creatively with my children as being on the same continuum of creative living – they feed into each other. Being creative (in whatever capacity) is important: important to me, because I feel myself to be a more complete person when my creativity is expressed; important to my children, who witness adults growing, sharing and learning creatively; and important to my family, who grow and connect by creating together.[41]

Actively seeking out opportunities to be creative together is presented here as one of the most important things that families can do. Soule argues that this is good for the well-being of parents, who can continue to explore their own interests and maintain a distinct identity, and for bonding the family together, as well as for the creative development of children. She also highlights the ways in which 'creative living' can play a positive role in local and global communities – whether through direct engagement with particular campaigns, such as those making clothes and blankets for those homeless or displaced people who may need them (like Afghans for Afghans, or the Dulaan Project[42]), or through being mindful of the ways in which creative activities could help or impact local groups, or the environment.

A PROCESS WITH POWER

I read about lots of different kinds of craft activities for this book, including volumes on knitting, embroidery, guerrilla gardening, sustainable technology, homemade electronics, and other things. As it turns out, it may not be the best use of the available space to go through them one by one here, but I can draw out a theme which connects them all: the meaningful and rewarding *process* of making.

In *The Subversive Stitch*, Rozsika Parker writes about embroidery as a craft practice which is two contrasting things at once: on the one hand, it is, and has been, a marker of femininity, but on the other hand, it is, and has been, a 'weapon of resistance' to the constraints associated with the idea of femininity, enabling women to actively produce things in the world – transforming materials into meaningful objects – and to carve out a place for personal thought and self-expression.[43] She argues:

> The processes of creativity – the finding of form for thought – have a transformative impact on the sense of self. The embroiderer holds in her hands a coherent object which exists both outside in the world and inside her head.

> Winnicott's theory of mirroring helps us understand how the experience of embroidering and the embroidery affirms the self as a being with agency, acceptability and potency. . . . The embroiderer sees a positive reflection of herself in her work and, importantly, in the reception of her work by others.[44]

Similarly, in the conclusion to her study *The Culture of Knitting*, Joanne Turney writes that knitting 'offers a means of creativity, of confidence in one's own ability to "do", as well as occupying a space in which one can just "be"'.[45] The process of knitting is rewarding because something both pleasing and useful is produced, and for some because it represents an ethical and political choice – to make some clothing oneself rather than purchase it from the clothing industry, with its often very badly paid workers. Perhaps surprisingly, however, the outcome of the process is relatively unimportant. From her interviews with amateur knitters, Turney finds that:

> The emphasis of the personal, emotional and subjective testimonies of the respondents intimated that knitting was a journey, in which frequently the travelling (knitting) was more important or emotionally significant than the arrival at the destination (knitted object).[46]

A study of quilting by Marybeth C. Stalp reaches similar conclusions. Indeed, she finds a significant tension between the views of quilters' family and friends, and the quilters themselves. For her research, Stalp intensively interviewed seventy middle-aged women who identified themselves as 'quilters', and spoke to many more quilting guilds and groups. She reports that quilters' family members typically found the amount of time spent on quilting to be rather frustrating and difficult to understand, but tried to find value in the activity by praising the usefulness and the number of quilts made.

For quilters themselves, however, this approach could just be annoying. They rarely knew how many quilts they had produced – this was of little interest to them – and found most of their pleasure in the *process*, not the product.[47] They were drawn to quilting as an expressive, creative activity, sometimes to continue or to 'recover' a family tradition of quilting; and as an activity which would give them space to think, to make, and 'to see themselves as part of a larger culture, a community of culture creators with a past and a future'.[48]

These pleasures and connections are not limited to knitting and sewing. The motivations of guerrilla gardeners, to take one more example, can be surprisingly similar. Guerrilla gardening refers to 'the illicit cultivation of someone else's land', as Richard Reynolds puts it, although the land in question has usually not been much cared for by its owner.[49] Guerrilla gardeners plant tulips on roundabouts, vegetables on roadside verges, and daffodils in neglected parks. These non-confrontational activists take pleasure in the secret and anonymous process of their work; their ongoing efforts to make the world a nicer place through small but beautiful interventions; and their sense of connection with the illicit planting community in particular, gardeners and environmental activists in general, and with nature itself. They gain pleasure from what they have done, but it is the *doing it* which really counts.[50]

UNEXPECTED DETOUR: THINKING ABOUT CREATIVITY WITH STAR WARS

When I was first working on all this, I was starting to teach a new module at the University of Westminster, entitled, simply, 'Creativity'. Some taught courses can start off by defining their terms in the first lecture, and move quickly on to consider the issues at stake in more detail. With 'creativity' I didn't think that the basic definition could be that simple, and so instead tried to take the students on a journey where we would modify and tweak our interpretation of 'creativity' as we went along.

In the first week I showed images of various things – a more or less 'random' selection of things for discussion, from the moon landings to a potato masher – and asked the students whether they considered each item to be 'creative' or not. When they said yes or no, a discussion of 'why' or 'why not' meant that we were able to pin down some of the key features of creativity – or at least, a kind of 'gut reaction' to what creativity might look like. This included many of the points that we mentioned in chapter 1: something new, original, or surprising; putting established elements together in a new way; and deliberate and thoughtful (rather than accidental) action. We also tentatively added 'handmade' and 'homemade', the product of individual physical activity, although this seemed rather unstable as a defining aspect.

One of the items I used for discussion was a poster for *Star Wars*, representing the original 1977 movie, and also one for *Star Wars Episode IV: A New Hope: Special Edition*, representing the 1997 reworked version of the film with added computer-generated (CGI) effects. I had correctly assumed that the students would be happy to recognize the original *Star Wars* as a creative product. Even if we acknowledge that it drew upon a number of existing genres and traditions –

such as the Western, Samurai, romantic epic and Second World War movies – and then used them in a new way, it still qualifies easily. The more curious issue was whether George Lucas's tinkering – adding reasonably pointless and not entirely convincing CGI alien creatures, and establishing shots, costing much time and expense, twenty years later – would count as creative. We were split: on the one hand, it would be churlish and absurd to decide that this technically cutting-edge and previously unheard-of level of movie reworking was 'not creative'. But on the other hand, it would be easy to argue that making *Star Wars* originally, from nothing, in a couple of years, was far more creative than spending several more years fiddling with details which made almost no difference to the emotional experience of the story.

This connected again with the 'handmade' debate. The computer-generated elements of the *Star Wars* Special Editions, and the vast amounts of CGI in the three prequel films, *The Phantom Menace* (1999), *Attack of the Clones* (2002) and *Revenge of the Sith* (2005), seemed to lack the charm and tangible appeal of the physical models constructed for the earlier films. Even though the newer films featured very complex digital vistas, with many moving vehicles and details, painstakingly created in a time-consuming process of computer craft work by talented digital artists, viewers were still left with a feeling that this was unlovely digital overkill.

Although this judgement may be unfair, this move away from the more obvious 'handmade' feel, towards a level of glossy wizardry which we find it more difficult to relate to, seemed to contribute to a general feeling that 'creativity' was not really taking place. Of course, adding three less-good films onto the front of a much-loved trilogy didn't really help either.

This, then, added up to a strong vote in favour of loving but not overcomplicated craft work, at a human level, designed to create a response of emotional engagement rather than mere appreciation of technological achievement. These thoughts fed into our ongoing conversation about the meaning of creativity.

Another item I showed to the students for consideration was *Star Wars Uncut* (starwarsuncut.com) – a fan project to remake *Star Wars* in a patchwork of 15-second chunks. As the site explained:

> You and 472 other people have the chance to recreate *Star Wars: A New Hope*. Below is the entire movie split up into 15 second clips. Click on one of the scenes to claim it, film it, and upload it. When we're all done, we'll stitch it all together and watch the magic happen.

The 15-second clips had been made in a wide variety of styles: animation using drawings, cardboard and toys, and live-action video with homemade costumes and props, puppets and pets. The level of 'creativity' on show is quite delightful. (By 2014 these global collaborators had remade all of *Star Wars*, and *The Empire Strikes Back* too, in 15-second home-made bits.)

But surely a low-quality, homemade, shot-for-shot remake of an *existing* hit movie can't count as an especially 'creative' activity, can it? This is the derivative work of fans – which would be nothing if it were not for the original *genuinely* creative effort of George Lucas and his colleagues, thirty-three years earlier. Nevertheless, the work of the 473 *Star Wars Uncut* contributors *does* seem to be a remarkable array of creativity. Particular details, such as an Obi-Wan Kenobi whose beard and hair are entirely rendered in masking tape, or an R2-D2 which is clearly someone's little brother in a dustbin, mean that the viewer cannot help but smile in appreciation.

This brings us back to the problem with the standard definitions of creativity, as mentioned in chapter 1. There, you may recall, we saw that creativity is usually identified by its *outcomes*: things or ideas which haven't been seen before, and which make a *difference* in the context in which they appear. This is the essence of the well-known definition offered by Mihaly Csikszentmihalyi, and is common to others.

But this standard notion of creativity, that it necessarily involves producing something that hasn't been done before – whether we mean in that particular context, or in *any* context – contains the odd problem that you can't identify creativity just by seeing it – or feeling it. In fact, even worse, it means that you can't identify creativity without having a detailed historical overview of everything that's been created already. So it would be possible to do something that you feel is genuinely creative, and which really impresses your friends and colleagues, but which could *still* be discounted from being labelled 'creative' when a pesky old sage turns up and observes that the same brilliant thing was done in 1826.

To be fair, Csikszentmihalyi insists that fully 'creative' creations should have been noticed and appreciated by influential people in the relevant field, and this means that such inventions should, by definition, have entered the historical record. But again, this brings us to an approach where creativity is something that can be confirmed or denied by taking a trip to the library. As Csikszentmihalyi is primarily conducting a sociological study of how a particular phenomenon can arise – where that phenomenon is an achievement or innovation which is widely hailed as a creative breakthrough – it makes sense to have this verifiable external view of creativity.

But outside of that particular context, it might be considered strange that we are unable to say if creativity has happened or not, without turning to subject experts. The

Csikszentmihalyi approach denies that creativity is an experience, a feeling, or a process. Instead, it's all about certified outcomes, produced by people who have probably been hailed as a 'creative genius' in the newspapers. (Csikszentmihalyi himself, being sociological about it, wouldn't agree with the 'genius' line, but would say that they were talented individuals who benefited from being in the right place at the right time.)

CREATIVITY REFRAMED

The focus on celebrated outcomes seems especially misplaced when we consider that Csikszentmihalyi is otherwise famous for the concept of 'flow'.[51] Flow describes the experience where a person is wholly engaged in a task, to the extent that time passes unnoticed, and they forget about demands external to the task, such as the need to eat or make phone calls. Their work is challenging, in a satisfying way – not so much that it causes stress and anxiety, and not so little that boredom appears, but just at the right level, prompting absorbed fascination and the hope of discovery. Csikszentmihalyi reports that this experience is common to all of the super-creative people whom he has interviewed – but it is not exclusive to them. The 'flow' experience is presented as being desirable for, and attainable by, anybody, as they go about their work.

With this device – I am not sure how deliberately – Csikszentmihalyi separates the *feelings* and *experiences* associated with creativity, from the definable hard reality of 'actual' high-powered creativity. Although this is fine for his needs, I would like to suggest that – for the purposes of this book at least – we should reject the 'certified public genius' model of creativity and instead embrace a rather fuzzier understanding which is, perhaps, closer to the 'common-sense' notion of creativity that we might use to describe a friend or colleague who seems to like making things or solving problems in everyday life. This doesn't necessarily mean the kind of people who like to knit or make pottery vases – they might enjoy making the household plumbing work effectively, fixing the car, devising innovative business strategies, or coding. And, incidentally, being 'common-sense' doesn't mean that something is necessarily correct, but it's not necessarily wrong either, and there must be some value in speaking to common experience.

We saw above that the meaning of everyday craft and creative activities was to be found within the *process*, not so much in its outcomes, and so it is important that our definition should reflect this as well. We could put it like this:

> *Everyday creativity refers to a process which brings together at least one active human mind, and the material or digital world, in the activity of making something. The activity has not been done in this way by this person (or these people) before. The process may arouse various emotions, such as excitement and frustration, but most especially a feeling of joy. When witnessing and appreciating the output, people may sense the presence of the maker, and recognize those feelings.*

I'm afraid this is not a compact dictionary definition. That's because it is an attempt to describe something which, by its nature, is difficult to define concisely.

A one-sentence version might be:

> *Everyday creativity refers to a process which brings together at least one active human mind, and the material or digital world, in the activity of making something which is novel in that context, and is a process which evokes a feeling of joy.*

This is slightly less satisfactory, because I had to cut some bits off, but reasonable.

In the longer version, the point about 'presence of the maker', and recognition of the feelings they may have felt in the process of creation, refers to the way in which we may mirror (or feel ourselves to be mirroring) the sense of concentration, or happiness, mourning, or other feeling, which we sense is contained in the clearly 'human' elements of a creative work. This is the handmade imperfection which Ruskin argued makes human craft work so special. And it is what I was referring to above, when I said that 'the viewer cannot help but smile in appreciation' at the cheap homemade details of the *Star Wars Uncut* videos.

The reference to joy, which I kept in both the short and long versions of the definition, might seem curious. It raises the question: would we say that something was 'not creative' if we somehow knew that the process of its construction involved no joy whatsoever? Well, perhaps we would. With no magical smile-inducing spark behind it, the constructed thing is just, well, a constructed thing. And would we refuse to describe a person as 'creative' if their making process was all hard concentration and no flicker of pleasure? Again, yes, perhaps we would. I certainly like it better than the other definition, which – let us not forget – would deny the 'creative' label to people much *more* often.

Of course, the 'joy' does not need to be present throughout. Making things is often an intense, difficult, or frustrating experience. But whether the thrilling zing comes right at the start, with an exciting idea before any planning, or right at the end, when the thing is finally *done*, it's likely to be in there somewhere.

Now, the sensibly sceptical reader might at this point be wondering if I am trying to replace a well-established definition of 'creativity' with my own inauthentic version, like someone sneakily changing the rules in order to win an argument. But I would suggest that my description of creativity lines up well with regular usage. For instance, when we talk about networked digital tools which give everyday people opportunities to be creative, and to share the fruits of their creativity, we are talking about the kind of creativity that I have outlined above. We are *not* talking about the kind of creativity as defined by Csikszentmihalyi, which only counts activity as 'creative' when it has led to outcomes which have had a significant, recognized impact on the relevant field.

And similarly, when we meaningfully say 'this is all very creative', about an exhibition put on by fashion students at the local college, or about a complex marble run made by a father and daughter team, or about handmade toys at a craft fair, or an agricultural machine made by a farmer to make a regular task more efficient, we are again talking about creativity as I have outlined it, and not like the Csikszentmihalyi definition.

Although the word 'creativity' might be over-used in the world today, it is rightly and reasonably used in relation to some significant everyday activities – of the kind I describe in my definition – and this is both meaningful and widely accepted. Nobody would sensibly say that you are not creative unless you have *actually* done something on a par with inventing the helicopter, or founding the radical painting movement of cubism. And the more everyday, emotion-oriented and process-based description of creativity offered by my definition seems to work pretty well in practice.

For example, it enables us to account for the inclination to say that both the original *Star Wars* movie, and the *Star Wars Uncut* homemade remakes of scenes score highly for creativity, whilst the process that generated the *Star Wars* Special Editions is less creative. The Special Editions are an example where the level of discernible joy is insufficient. And we feel warmer about *The Force Awakens*, despite its sort-of 'greatest hits' storyline, because you can somehow tell that these people really loved making it.

And this approach helps to explain why we might want to assert that a selection of amateur videos on YouTube are 'more creative' than an evening's worth of stuff on television. The latter is likely to be polished, very professionally produced, and may be quite imaginative, but it's not quite the kind of thing that the word 'creativity' was made for. Whereas on YouTube, you have a world of people doing amazing, silly, clever, pointless, or heartfelt things, and putting them out in the world for others to experience, *because they want to*, and that seems to be much more like what 'creativity' is meant to be all about.

Creativity is something that is *felt*, not something that needs external expert verification. I rest my case, for now, although we'll come back to this later.

4

THE MEANING OF MAKING III: DIGITAL

In the preceding two chapters we have looked at some of the philosophy and practice of craft – the careful, thoughtful process of making something with the hands. Producing something for the digital sphere might be thought of as the *opposite* of the physical, material process of craft work. The early terms used to characterize the internet, such as 'virtual reality' and 'cyberculture', underlined the notion that this activity is ethereal and not 'real'. The newer notion of 'the cloud' – the virtual space where online programs and processing as well as content are increasingly located, seemingly 'up there' and away from earthly computing machines – gives a similar impression.

But in my experience, making things to share online is very much a craft process. You start with nothing, except perhaps for some basic tools and materials, which contain no prescription and seemingly infinite possibilities. When I started making websites, in 1997, I had to do it by typing the HTML code into a plain text editor (which in my case was

Notepad, the very basic text editor which has been included in every version of Microsoft Windows since 1985).[1] This is known as 'hand coding', a term which is meaningful beyond the simple fact that you use your hands to type, which of course is common to many computer functions. 'Hand coding' points to the delicate process of building up the code bit by bit, testing it from time to time to see if there are any bugs – tiny imperfections which typically stop the whole thing from working. It's a process you feel your way through – starting with a few ideas, and maybe a couple of rough sketches, you start to put the thing together, see how it goes, take a step back, make some changes, and see how it looks. This may lead to some new ideas, then you change things a bit, keep on going, until it's done. You also have to make all the individual graphics (titles, logos, buttons and pictures), again starting with nothing, trying out ideas, seeing what looks right, making all the visual bits and bobs the site will need as you build it from the ground up.

You use keyboard and mouse, but this activity is obviously not 'hands-on' in the normal craft sense – you can't *literally* press your fingers into the craft material, the equivalent of the clay or wood or paint, because it's all digital. But you can certainly leave your metaphorical fingerprints all over the thing you're making; indeed, it's hard not to. The personality of the maker always comes across in the finished thing. So this process is like craft in the tinkering, weaving, 'from the ground up' experience of making something; and it's also like craft in that the maker imprints some of their character upon the work, and its audiences are likely to sense their 'presence' – that sense of connection which we installed in our definition of creativity at the end of the previous chapter.

In the twenty years since I started tapping bits of HTML into Notepad, the tools have changed, but the process is pretty similar. Nowadays, helpful 'what you see is what you get' software means that the tinkering is less often interrupted by crashes or totally unexpected results, but it's still tinkering, and it's still building from the ground up, and you still need to make the necessary components (such as graphics) elsewhere and then pull them into your website workshop. And the same principles apply if you're not making websites at all but are, say, making online video, which again is a messy process of creating a range of material which you then cut, select and edit to craft a finished object. As with physical handmade crafts, you end up with a 'polished' end product, which may have a 'simple' appearance, but behind it there are hours of intricate, tentative and difficult work.

So this chapter continues our discussion of craft, and the meaning of making things, into the digital realm – and in particular to the internet and social media, where today's creators have the opportunity to easily share their work with other internet-connected people all around the world.

The online world is, of course, vast. There's no point trying to describe all of the creative things that happen there, because there's just so much of it. It's not even like we're interested in just one *kind* of creativity, such as online poetry, photography, or politics (even though you couldn't do justice to any of them in a book chapter either). As it happens, as mentioned in the previous chapter, I edited a book called *Web Studies* – published in 2000, followed by an all-new second edition in 2004 – which did indeed attempt to capture all dimensions of online creativity: 'everyday Web life, art and culture, Web business, and global Web communities, politics and protest', as it said on the back cover. But of course, all you could really get were some snapshots of interesting bits of the Web, and their implications.

So here, we'll start with something both very simple and very complex, a social media 'platform' from which we can learn something about others: YouTube.

MAKING AND CONNECTING ON YOUTUBE

YouTube is by far the best-known and most-used online video platform. You are sure to know this already, as YouTube has become ubiquitous on the internet, and in popular culture generally. Launched in 2005, it quickly came to dominate online video, with its straightforward interface and simple tools for sharing and embedding material. Just four years later, YouTube was serving more than 1 billion videos every day, and hundreds of thousands of videos were being uploaded by users daily.[2] By 2017, the platform had over 1 billion users.[3]

In the earliest days of YouTube, around 2005–7, I have to admit that it didn't strike me as a central place for participatory culture – probably because I was equating video with television. If you're interested in everyday people coming together online, making and sharing and connecting, then a site of televisionish clips doesn't sound very promising, as television is necessarily rather professional and complex, rather than handmade and simple, and not at all easy to produce. It also seems to be about watching rather than about communicating. The television model is what we were trying to get *away* from.

Of course, I was wrong. Well, mostly wrong: videos are odd entrants in the 'communal allotment' of social media – as I described it in chapter 1 – since each item tends to be a self-contained and 'sealed' package, which means that other users cannot easily add bits to, or re-edit, a posted video. (Technically, it is perfectly possible to download a YouTube video, in lower-than-original quality, and re-edit it, but this is a much more complicated process than, say, editing a Wikipedia page, which can be done in a matter of seconds.) However, if we relate this to the 'allotment' metaphor, adding videos to YouTube is like adding plants to the garden; and then those items can be nurtured by others (through likes and links) and responded to (through comments and further videos). Contributing diverse plants to a shared garden is a perfectly good form of collaboration: we don't actually need to be pruning, feeding and fussing over individual plants together. So it's still a social media community, but with the level of mashability being set one notch higher.

As for the worry that videos are an unnecessarily professional and complicated type of building-block for online interaction: it turned out that I was feeling uneasy about something which obviously wasn't bothering other people. The online community seem to be pretty forgiving about formal quality issues – and I had to remind myself that being a perfectionist isn't actually a *good* thing. I received a memorable lesson on this point when, for some reason, I found myself watching a video by Chris Anderson showing a radio-controlled blimp that he had made at home. There are quite a lot of public Chris Andersons – including a jazz pianist, an athlete and the guy who runs the TED conference, none of whom are *this* Chris Anderson. This is the one who wrote *The Long Tail* and was at that time Editor-in-Chief of *Wired* magazine. In other words, he's someone who should be a master of social media, who is concerned with excellent design, who is a well-known professional.

The very striking and delightful thing about his blimp video was this: it was *messy*. Not, I should say, that it was uninteresting, or foolish, or that his radio-controlled blimp thing was not impressive.[4] His homemade blimp was surely very clever, and the video conveyed a perfectly reasonable sense of what the thing looked like and how it operated. But the video was not at all professional in its execution: the handheld camera was shaky, the autofocus wasn't always right, and in particular the audio was very rough, with Anderson apparently unconcerned by the crashes and shouts which his children were making in the background of his languid, unscripted commentary. Anderson clearly wanted to share his blimp-making work with the blimp-making community (yes, this is a particular hobby, with its own community of enthusiasts, and Anderson in this case seemed to be speaking to them, rather than to the broader audience – such as the readers of his best-selling books). But he was not going to spend ages cutting together the best shots, or re-recording the audio, for a more polished presentation. And the important point is that, as a viewer, I *did not mind*. It was *fine*. I liked the unshowy, rough-and-ready nature of the whole thing. It was liberating. Then I remembered that I had also recently looked at YouTube videos on sewing – to make a toy for Finn – which were educational but simply done, and I hadn't been bothered by the low-fi recording; and I had watched a terribly ropey video of Clay Shirky doing a talk, apparently filmed by someone in the audience, and I hadn't really minded that either. I do normally like things to be presented nicely, but this focus on content rather than style conveyed the powerful, inclusive, happy message that 'anyone can do this'.

Here we find ourselves to be modern versions of John Ruskin, whom we met in chapter 2. Ruskin asserted that it is better that objects made by people should bear the marks of the effort of making them, rather than being polished but impersonal. Writing in 1849, he said that things made by people should exhibit 'the vivid expression of the intellectual life which has been concerned in their production'.[5] Such creations 'become noble or ignoble in proportion to the amount of the energy of that mind which has visibly been employed upon them'.[6]

This view appeared in *The Seven Lamps of Architecture*, where each of the 'lamps' represents a guiding principle for architects and other creative workers. This one is part of 'the lamp of *life*', where Ruskin argues that the joy of workers' creativity should be visible in the things they produce. Developing this theme three years later in his essay 'The Nature of Gothic', Ruskin suggests that a slick production is nice if you can get it, but is not the most important thing:

> If you are to have the thought of a rough and untaught man, you must have it in a rough and untaught way; but from an educated man, who can without effort express his thoughts in an educated way, take the graceful expression, and be thankful. Only *get* the thought, and do not silence the peasant because he cannot speak good grammar, or until you have taught him his grammar. Grammar and refinement are good things, both, only be sure of the better thing first.[7]

Here we must forgive Ruskin his Victorian tone, because he is at least trying to be nice, and of course is saying that we should put aside snobbish notions about the appearance of things, and instead appreciate the intellectual effort that they embody. In this scenario, I'm afraid, Chris Anderson, author of *The Long Tail* and former Editor-in-Chief of *Wired*, is 'a rough and untaught man', and a 'peasant', but one with something to say. Ruskin continues:

> So the rule is simple: Always look for invention first, and after that, for such execution as will help the invention, and as the inventor is capable of without painful effort, and *no more*. Above all, demand no refinement of execution where there is no thought, for that is slaves' work, unredeemed. Rather choose rough work than smooth work, so only that the practical purpose be answered, and never imagine there is reason to be proud of anything that may be accomplished by patience and sand-paper.[8]

In modern terms, Ruskin is saying that spending hours on overwrought postproduction is unnecessary, and deadens the human connection that we would otherwise make with the work. Thus I could see thought, life and inspiration in the video produced by the blimp-making peasant, Chris Anderson, which encouraged my own creativity; whereas a more 'professional' quality of video would only have reinforced the feeling that video-making was not something that a 'rough and untaught' person such as myself could participate in.

And so I started making videos for YouTube. In fact, this story has two strands, because on the one hand I started making 'personal' home movies, since the birth of our son Finn (and, later, daughter Edie) had given us something really worth preserving in moving pictures; and also, having started to get the hang of digital video-making, I began to produce work-related videos about some of my academic projects and research. These appear on separate YouTube channels, giving me the dual experience of being a domestic amateur on one channel and a public academic on the other. Chris Anderson's noisy, shaky videos gave me the confidence to make my own, although in practice I can't help trying to make the videos look and sound as good as I can, so the reality is not as liberatingly rough-and-ready as promised. And the same amount of effort goes into both categories of video, even though a personal video showing highlights from Finn's first year has only been viewed 75 times, whilst a worky one called 'Participation culture, creativity, and social change' is at 25,000.

For either type of video, I don't just think of it as a 'video' – it's a 'YouTube video'. Within a couple of years of its existence, the site's very name had become descriptive of a particular kind of audiovisual artefact: the short, fast, online video. This is the case even though being a 'YouTube video' says nothing really about the content. But YouTube is a particular kind of thing – a platform of possibilities.

YOUTUBE AS ARCHETYPE OF THE DIGITAL CREATIVE PLATFORM

Social media applications which encourage people to make and share things are often not very specific *tools*, as such, but are broad *platforms*. The word 'platform' is both the technically correct term for this kind of thing, but also the right common-sense word to describe the kind of stage which they offer for creative performance. Platforms of this kind tend not to assert a preference for particular topics or styles of material. Rather, they encourage users to express their creativity in whatever way they choose – within a particular framework, and general type of content. YouTube is now a very well-established platform, and so makes a decent case study through which to consider the places where digital craft work happens.[9]

YouTube is perhaps a bit unusual as a platform in that the core content, the videos themselves, can involve a lot more work – and a greater range of *types* of work – compared with, say, writing a blog post or a tweet, which just involves some typing. Some types of YouTube video, such as the direct-to-camera talking videos and videogame-capture-with-voiceover videos produced by many of the most successful YouTube 'stars', are basically quick to do, especially if errors, spontaneity and things-going-wrong are part of the charm. They still need thought, preparation and imagination, though, and frequently some editing. Other kinds of video typically involve the filming of many parts, editing, subtitles, perhaps music, and even when done in a 'fast and dirty' style are not actually that quick to make. Apart from that caveat, however, YouTube is an archetypal digital creative platform in three key ways.

1. A framework for participation

First of all, it offers a framework for participation. The key element here is the invitation to users to upload their own videos. For the first five years YouTube actually limited their length to just 10 minutes. Then the length restriction was dropped, but the ways in which people tend to watch YouTube means that everything is still, ideally, short.

So, some things are set: YouTube is primarily a place for videos, and in particular, short videos. But everything else is open. Whilst early contributions to the site seemed to be mostly youthful skateboard stunts and amateur music videos, the range soon blossomed, and YouTube is now, of course, a home for poets, engineers, medics, teachers, and a vast multitude of others, and the content is now an incredible array of material in diverse styles, on an enormous range of topics, including performance, education, video journals, sport, technology, family life, and how-to guides and discussions on everything from car maintenance to breast-feeding.

This highlights the sense in which YouTube is essentially 'just' a platform for creativity. In an unglamorous formulation, it is a database website, which invites people to add data as files, comments, tags and links between different bits of information (notably user profiles and video content). Without the responses of users to this open invitation, YouTube would be nothing – there would literally be (almost) nothing there. YouTube could solicit material from existing media companies – as it has done, forming partnerships with numerous well-established corporations – but there is much evidence that YouTube's huge popularity, and dominance in the online video field, is due to its emphasis on establishing its framework as one which primarily supports a *community of participation and communication* amongst everyday users, rather than elite professionals.[10]

(The YouTube community focus is discussed in point 3, below.)

One view of such a platform is that it is a (commercial) service offered to users, who know what they are dealing with when they use it, and who are basically pleased that it gives them a stage on which to share their thoughts and their creative work, and a network through which they can connect with others, for free. A much more negative interpretation is offered by critical theorists such as Mark Andrejevic and Christian Fuchs, who see the user activity, freely 'given' by people as they upload videos and conduct community activity on the site, to be a new form of exploitation.[11] YouTube is a business built on the labour of unpaid video-makers around the world. In addition, as users move around YouTube, willingly indicating their interests and preferences through their searches, clicks and likes, they generate valuable data which is gathered by the corporation and used for commercial purposes. To these critics, this is 'immaterial labour', which is autonomous (you go on YouTube as a free choice) but creates an 'exploitable surplus' (valuable data). The extent to which you see this as primarily sinister and worrying is perhaps a matter of personal preference (and we'll be discussing this more in chapter 7).

A less damning perspective is offered by Virginia Nightingale, who suggests that the companies that own online platforms such as YouTube and Instagram act as the 'patrons' of collective creative activity, retaining some power and control, but also welcoming the imaginative work of users.[12] Whichever way you look at it, the trade-off between having a free online environment for sharing material, on the one hand, and providing a corporation with some useful data – and the opportunity to show us a few adverts – on the other, is one which millions of users seem to be more-or-less comfortable with, although that doesn't necessarily mean it's the perfect solution.

2. Agnostic about content

Second, within this framework, YouTube is entirely agnostic about what contributions can be made (apart from some precautions about pornographic and potentially offensive or abusive material). The platform is there, on offer, but the opportunities for innovation in content are left open to the users. Some people have used it in ways that mimic established forms or styles, such as the music video, the interview, the comedy sketch, or the product review 'show'. A number of these individuals aspired to enter the mainstream media, and some have done so when their YouTube popularity has brought them to the attention of the traditional industries. Some have developed a particular kind of YouTube stardom which is its own genre, with daily posts about their lives and interests. There are also the hugely popular YouTube stars who make a new form of entertainment based on amiable, witty, or wild voiceovers to video game play. Others post examples of their professional practice – such as demonstrations of training or consultancy styles, or architectural 'walk-through' videos – in order to attract clients. Musicians and other artists use YouTube as one tool in their spread of ways to share their work, and perhaps their creative process, with others, partly to build an audience and partly to get feedback.

Other contributors are entirely unconcerned about reaching a broad audience, and use YouTube to share family videos with friends and relatives. And some create what Patricia Lange has called 'videos of affinity', which are simply-produced recordings, with little or no postproduction, created purely to connect with a community of friends and acquaintances.[13] These kinds of videos can seem trivial to those who expect online video to aspire to 'TV standard' productions, but any such criticism is clearly misdirected since, as Clay Shirky has explained, when online material seems pointless or baffling, the explanation is usually: 'It's simple. They're not talking to you.'[14] These are just quick, reasonably transient ways to make a simple connection. The artist Martin Creed has mentioned that one of his motivations for making creative work is – counter to the idea of the grand artistic statement – rather just 'to say hello',[15] and these 'videos of affinity' sit, even more modestly, in that tradition.

3. Fostering community

Third, YouTube is more than a video archive: it is, and keenly positions itself as, a community. The platform actively encourages users to make comments, to subscribe, to 'like', to follow creators and friends, and send messages, and to make videos responding to other videos.

These are not – or certainly not entirely – tacked-on 'social networking' features. Rather, as Jean Burgess and Joshua Green have shown, the users who have managed to become 'YouTube stars' have done so by embracing the community, and by acting as community members themselves. They have typically risen to the top of YouTube visibility not by acting as aloof stars, but by being community *participants*. They invite and respond to comments on the platform, make links with others, and refer to community comments, responses and events within the videos themselves. They are actively embedded within their online community.[16]

Burgess and Green draw an interesting contrast with stars from mainstream media who have tried to build a following on YouTube, often unsuccessfully. The researchers observe:

> However charming . . . or silly the content of their videos might be, what all the entrepreneurial YouTube stars have

> in common is the fit between their creative practice and the dynamics of YouTube as a platform for participatory culture.[17]

Engagement in the community is not just a route to online stardom, of course. Henry Jenkins suggests that YouTube offers 'strong social incentives' to make and share, and that users are inspired by 'the emotional support of a community eager to see their productions'.[18] He also suggests, quoting Yochai Benkler, that participation in an online culture such as YouTube's can 'make their practitioners better "readers" of their own culture and more self-reflective and critical of the culture they occupy'[19] – a claim which perhaps applies more in some cases than in others.

There is also the gift-giving dimension to YouTube's community: users give and receive homemade video 'gifts' for reasons which are to do with feelings and attachments, rather than economics. The notion of the gift economy helps us, in particular, to understand the rewards for participation – such as 'status', 'prestige', or 'esteem', which have no (immediate) economic value.[20]

In sum, then, YouTube is a platform which offers a *framework* for participation, but which is *open* to a very wide variety of uses and contributions, and basically *agnostic* about the content, which means it has been adopted by a wide range of users for a diverse array of purposes. People use YouTube to *communicate* and *connect*, to share knowledge and skills, and to entertain. They use the *community* features of the site to *support* each other and engage in debates, and to generate the characteristics of a '*gift economy*'. Whilst it is true that the majority of visitors to YouTube are viewing, not producing and participating, there are still literally millions of users who engage with this creative platform every day, and whose relationship with professional media has been fundamentally shifted because of the knowledge that they can be the creators, and not just receivers, of inventive audiovisual productions.

MOTIVATIONS FOR MAKING AND SHARING

This discussion of YouTube so far has been relatively 'top-down' – a look at what happens when a business or organization establishes a platform and invites people to contribute to it, and make social connections upon it. Now I'd like to dig a bit deeper into *why* people make and share stuff online. For some platforms this is reasonably straightforward, because the amount of *effort* is low, and the social rewards and connections make it worthwhile. So Facebook, for instance, only requires simple and momentary inputs (adding a status update, or a link, or a photo), and in return you get to be part of an active social network, where people might make comments on your stuff, and you can comment on theirs, leading to a sense of mutual engagement and community, as well as an opportunity to try to impress like-minded people with your interests and activities.

In a similar way, Instagram provides an easy and quick way for people to show others what they are doing, where they have been, or things they are proud of – including friends and family. They may also wish to share the aesthetic qualities of the appealing or inventive images that they have made. Or all of these things.

This regular, easy sharing of everyday personal stuff cultivates what Leisa Reichelt has called 'ambient intimacy'. In a blog post, she explains:

> Ambient intimacy is about being able to keep in touch with people with a level of regularity and intimacy that you wouldn't usually have access to, because time and space

> conspire to make it impossible. Flickr lets me see what friends are eating for lunch, how they've redecorated their bedroom, their latest haircut. Twitter tells me when they're hungry, what technology is currently frustrating them, who they're having drinks with tonight.[21]

Reichelt acknowledges that some people believe that they would find all this information to be just unwanted trivia and 'annoying noise'. But the success of social networking platforms shows that people do get something from the regular sharing of ordinary fragments of everyday life.

> There are a lot of us . . . who find great value in this ongoing noise. It helps us get to know people who would otherwise be just acquaintances. It makes us feel closer to people we care for but in whose lives we're not able to participate as closely as we'd like.[22]

With services of this kind, there is not really a big question of 'why do users go to the *trouble* of doing this?', because it's all quite easy, and producing the content is not time-consuming. The motivation and the reward are basically the same thing: to be part of an active community, part of a conversation, and to feel somewhat more connected to people we know. Possibly also – but not necessarily – to come into contact with some new people.

Other online creative activities, though, take more *effort*, which makes the question of motivation less straightforward and more intriguing. Preparing a single video for YouTube, for example, might take several hours, or a few days. Writing a blog is also rather time-consuming and quite hard work. So why do people do these things, putting their creative work out into the world with no financial incentive? Some people do get income from blog-writing, or video-making, it's true, but most of the content out there does not directly bring in money and is made for other reasons. So what are those reasons?

Let's start with blogs. Some blogs are everyday scrapbooks, or a diary of a holiday, for instance, which are not especially difficult to produce, and which connect their authors with their friends and family in a way which is similar to the social networks mentioned above. But some blogs require more work, and are produced by committed individuals who want to share some aspect of their enthusiasms, or creative practice, or parenting, on a regular basis.

In the first edition of this book I piled up a set of stories, responses to online queries, as well as more formal academic research, about why people wanted to create blogs and similar online content. I'll summarize that material here. If we begin at the more anecdotal level, we heard from David Jennings, an educational consultant from London, who produced a blog where he wrote about an item from his record collection, one a day, every day. He explained that it was about the love of music, and the pathology of collecting. It was done as a public blog in order to compel himself to keep going, and 'to give real attention to the things I've collected, one by one, rather than just piling them up'.[23] The project also connected him with other people, who often stumbled across the blog when searching for information about a particular track, and would share memories, feelings and musical associations of their own. We also considered Amanda Blake Soule, author of the long-established *SouleMama* blog, who explained that the blog helped her to store parenting memories and hold onto special moments.[24] It was also clear, from feedback, that her blog was a comfort and support to others.

A bundle of other responses from social media indicated that people created blogs and other online content in order to entertain or teach others; to show off creative work, and get feedback; to create a diary or record; to be part of discussions and part of a community; to be a maker rather than just a consumer; to collaborate; and to be heard.

This all reinforced the idea that people spend time creating online content because they want to feel active and recognized within a community of interesting people, and because they wish to express or display aspects of themselves and their interests. But the theme of *recognition* came through a little more strongly than we might have anticipated: people want to lay down signs of their existence and their ideas, and they want this to be *noticed*. This is not surprising, but it adds a significant note to our general picture of what's going on. The 'sharing' and 'connecting' themes sound warm and benign; seeking recognition is not necessarily very different, but it includes a harder edge, a kind of demand – 'notice me!' – which we have to acknowledge as well.

The academic studies about motivations of bloggers told the same story.[25] Partly, we found, people make these things and share them because *they want to* – the process of making the thing, and knowing that others may encounter it, brings its own pleasures. Partly it is because they want to connect and communicate with others, and to be an active participant in online dialogues and communities, both giving and receiving ideas, feedback and support. And partly this output expresses a wish to be noticed, recognized, and heard.

These motivations follow on from – and are part of a continuum with – the motivations for engaging in hands-on craft activity discussed in the previous chapter. We can see that online, like the crafters offline, people like to be able to make and manage a whole thing, seeing it develop from first idea through to completion. In some cases they enjoy collaborating during the process. And they certainly like to share the process of making, as well as the finished thing, with others. They feel that they can express themselves in an 'authentic and personal' way, and connect with a like-minded community. These are all things that were cited as motivations for engagement with physical crafts and making. In the previous chapter, Rozsika Parker made a very good point about how embroidery could have 'a transformative impact on the sense of self'. Here is part of her argument again, but with references to embroidery replaced with references to blogging:

> The experience of blogging and the blog affirms the self as a being with agency, acceptability and potency. . . . The blogger sees a positive reflection of herself in her work and, importantly, in the reception of her work by others.[26]

This absolutely makes sense. We could equally insert 'website-maker', 'music producer' or 'YouTube video creator', of course. These motives, qualities and desires are in many ways timeless, then, but the internet provides a platform for sharing and exchange, with unique properties of accessibility and reach.

In other words, for centuries people have liked to make things, and share them with others, in order to communicate, to be part of a conversation, and to receive support or recognition; but the internet has given us a forum where people can do this without gatekeepers, without geographical restrictions, and in an organized way that means we can find like-minded people easily – so that we can share ideas and enthusiasms with people who actually care about the things that we care about, and are likely to have meaningful, informed responses.

BEYOND THE SCREEN

In this chapter, the online making-and-connecting hub I've mentioned most often is YouTube. But as we've noted already, YouTube is in a sense an odd illustration of the anti-television, hands-on, making-things principle, since it is about people making and sharing *video clips*, and so although it may involve all kinds of creative activity at the *production* stage, what you *consume* is not unlike more television-y stuff. Of course, making videos is often a physical, hands-on, real-world process, and the online community culture around the videos involves all kinds of sharing and communication which are much more interactive and two-way than the standard television experience (within which I include, of course, the supposedly more interactive, but fundamentally one-way, *digital* television experience). Furthermore, there are many other social media platforms about making and sharing things which are not at all television-y, such as general and specialist knowledge (Wikipedia), photography (Instagram), knitting (Ravelry), microfinance for third-world entrepreneurs (Kiva), or any creative project needing funding (Kickstarter).

In the early days of the Web, much of the popular appeal was about how you could do familiar tasks more efficiently – shopping, banking, chatting and information-finding, for instance. Since then, we have seen the rise of more services that are about being social, doing unfamiliar things, and engaging more in real life, in the places where you live.

One long-standing example is Meetup.com, which enables people with shared interests to meet up locally, taking the standard idea of the virtual community – people who have something in common, who wouldn't have known about each other if it wasn't for the internet – and then throwing in the novel idea that they might actually get together for a coffee. There are many more community-based skills-sharing networks, where people can learn to do things such as screenprinting, bike mechanics, home audio production, jewellery casting and DIY electronics (for examples, just search for 'skill share' and the name of a place).

A notable recent development has been the rise of Men's Sheds, which began as a movement in Australia (mensheds.com.au) and is now booming in the UK (menssheds.org.uk) and elsewhere. The idea is to help primarily retired men – who may be experiencing isolation, loneliness or depression, after a lifetime of work – to connect with each other through activities based in a 'shed' where they can make and do things for themselves or for the community. 'Through collaboration, problem solving and decision-making, a men's shed can considerably enhance the initiation and implementation of projects, and improve the lifestyle of many men', says the Austalian website, which provides help and resources for finding or starting a shed. The UK site quotes a man called Bill, aged sixty-seven: 'It gives me a reason to get up in the morning and for two days a week I feel I'm gainfully employed. I really feel good working with and helping other men who often feel isolated in the community. I would need a very good reason not to come.'

Initiatives such as these were possible before the Web, of course, but were more difficult to organize, and in particular were liable to draw in more outgoing, gregarious kinds of people, whilst leaving others isolated. The internet gives such individuals a simple way of hearing about – and developing a sense of comfort and familiarity with – groups, activities, meetings and projects, making it considerably easier to overcome the emotional and psychological hurdles to participation.

Making and sharing things online, engaging with people who (at first) you don't know anything about, anywhere in the world, can be very rewarding. Any kind of meaningful creative 'project' is good to have, as we will see in the next chapter. And those initiatives which bring people into *real-life* contact with others can be especially helpful for happiness and well-being – as we will see.

5

THE VALUE OF CONNECTING: PERSONAL HAPPINESS AND SOCIAL CAPITAL

In the previous chapters we considered the value of making things. In this one we will look at the importance of friendly social connections. It might be easy to think of this as a rather trivial matter: 'friendly social connections' may be nice to have, but they are hardly the stuff of important social science, economics, or social policy. But surely the very opposite is the case: without human empathy, communication, trust and general-purpose goodwill and friendliness, society would very quickly dissolve in a horrible apocalypse of never-ending misunderstanding, crime and conflict.

Looked at in that sense, we can see that the value of social connections has been rightly explored by social scientists for over a century in their many and diverse studies of social cohesion, the family, religion, 'deviance', economics, social policy, politics, war, terrorism, and other topics. In this chapter we will narrow this field, and look first at the recent studies of happiness, which suggest that individuals are more satisfied when they are part of social networks. Then we will consider the literature on 'social capital' – a sociological term for shared values and connectedness – which shows that we are all, collectively, better off as a society when we are active parts of the social fabric.

HAPPINESS STUDIES

The last couple of decades have seen a sharp rise in scholarly interest regarding the topic of 'happiness'. This is partly because serious academics have finally become willing to engage with a term which previously would have been seen, outside of literary and philosophical studies, as too 'fluffy': the sensible researcher of previous generations would have discussed 'scales of social satisfaction', or 'trust', but would generally have avoided admitting that they were concerned with human happiness. This is perverse, of course, because the question of how to have happy people in a happy society addresses every caring politician's dilemma and has links with every social problem.

When people are asked about what would increase our happiness, it is common to think that 'more money' must be at least *part* of the answer. Indeed, richer people tend to think that they need more additional income than poorer people do.[1] However, as happiness researchers have found, people are very bad at predicting what will *actually* make them happy – beyond the instant-hit burst of excitement that they can imagine when various possible treats are suggested to them.[2]

Meanwhile, the idea that money is not actually a route to happiness has been a well-known and seemingly popular one for some time. In one of his best-known parables, Jesus argued that 'It is easier for a camel to go through the eye of a needle than for a rich man to enter the kingdom of God' (Matthew 19:23–4). The Beatles echoed the sentiment in their 1964 hit *Can't Buy Me Love*, and indeed the insignificance of money in the quest for happiness underpins numerous pop songs, such as *Love Don't Cost A Thing* by Jennifer Lopez and *The Best Things In Life Are Free* by Luther Vandross, movies from *Citizen Kane* and *It's a Wonderful Life* to *Trading Places* and *Iron Man*, and in particular romantic comedies – for instance, from the many possible examples, it is the 'message' of *Notting Hill*, *Two Weeks' Notice* and *About A Boy*, all of which happen to star Hugh Grant.

CAN'T BUY ME HAPPINESS?

As it turns out, Jesus, the Beatles and Hugh Grant all seem to be right about this one. Indeed, the starting-point for much contemporary happiness research is the observation that almost everybody thinks that they would be happier if they had more money, but that studies demonstrate that this is simply not the case – with the exception of the very poor. In general, when people get more money, they soon get used to it, and return to much the same level of (dis)satisfaction that they were at before.[3]

There is a good old Marxist argument which says that when religions, movies, or pop songs suggest that money doesn't make you any happier, this is a form of propaganda – designed to persuade the impoverished and exploited that their desire for a greater share of society's wealth is misplaced. The news that more money wouldn't make us any happier appears to contradict that. But there are two things worth noting here. First of all, as mentioned above, increased income *does* make a significant and sustained difference to those people who previously were very poor, living below subsistence level. Secondly, it is *relative* income which makes people more or less happy – if we are getting much less than other people, we are much less happy.[4]

Correspondingly, and rather disappointingly, these same

statistics indicate that if an individual became rich, they would only be happier if their position was reasonably unique; if *everyone* became much better-off, they wouldn't all become much happier. This is not a pessimistic hypothesis, but rather can be observed as a matter of historical record: during the twentieth century in America and Europe, for example, the general standard of living rose dramatically. But recorded levels of happiness stayed remarkably constant.[5]

Because people are unrealistic as they imagine their possible futures, and fail to realize that they would simply get used to having more money, they tend to spend more and more time working – which doesn't actually make them happier – and correspondingly less time doing other things. Research in social psychology has suggested that this is part of a broader phenomenon: that human beings tend to focus on the wrong things – superficial things – when thinking about future possibilities. This is expressed in striking terms by David Schkade of the University of California, San Diego, who summarizes his research in this area with the assertion: 'Anything you can focus on isn't as important as you think.'[6]

One of Schkade's curious case studies is to do with people moving to California. Lots of people dream of making California their home. This is not some Beach Boys-inspired propaganda, but a plain fact: opinion polls have consistently shown that it is the state that most Americans would like to move to.[7] Each year, more than a million people move into California from other states. But also each year, more than a million people move out of California to make a life elsewhere. Something draws them in. But also, something pushes them away. Schkade and his colleague Daniel Kahneman argue that the people who dream of moving to California are victims of a 'focusing illusion': they have zoomed in on an appealing detail – a sunny climate – at the expense of the bigger picture, which in this case is everything else in life.[8]

The researchers supported this by conducting a survey in California, and in the Mid-Western states of Michigan and Ohio. This found that people in the Mid-West were just as satisfied in their lives as the people who lived in California. However, when asked to predict how happy *other people* would be, participants across the board thought that the Californians would be happier. And indeed, Californians were personally happier about their climate. But otherwise, their lives had not been taken onto a better, more magical plane, just because the sun was shining. And crucially, nobody really thought that the weather was that important. They rated other factors such as job prospects, personal safety and social life as being much more significant for their own happiness, and of course this was reflected in the fact that Californians and Mid-Westerners did indeed have remarkably similar levels of self-reported happiness.

This explains the people moving out of California, as well as those moving in. Those moving in, this research would suggest, may be mistakenly fixated on the dream of all that sunshine, and not really thinking about the other things that matter to them in life. Whereas those moving out are likely to be people who have tired of the famous Californian obsession with body image, or who pine for the homely charms of the state they grew up in, or who want a more secure environment for their families. Of course, people move for all kinds of reasons, but the Californian-sunshine 'focusing illusion' illustrates nicely our ability to get overly excited about 'quick hits' and forget what really matters.

HAPPINESS UNDER THE MICROSCOPE

If only we knew which things would *actually* make us more happy – not just in the short term, but as a long-term quality of life kind of factor. But now we do – thanks to the new 'science of happiness', which draws upon economics and psychology. From economics, it takes the idea that you can look at data about a range of social or economic inputs and draw statistical inferences about what has positive or negative results. Unlike traditional economics, though, it does not assume that human behaviour is *necessarily* driven by money and self-interest. From psychology, it takes the idea that people's inner states are important, and that personal experience can, in broad terms, be assessed and measured. This emergent field also draws usefully upon neuroscience, sociology and philosophy.

Rather than taking happiness as a poetic or romantic concept, the 'new science' takes the presence or absence of happiness as a hard-nosed empirical fact. Measuring levels of happiness is not difficult: you simply ask people to attach a number to it themselves, with a question such as 'Taking all things together, would you say you are very happy, quite happy, or not very happy?' This isn't deep, but works fine as a survey question, and produces comparable empirical data on how happy people say that they are. This is, then, a fact, rather than a feeling – although it is made up of self-reports about feelings – and when we match it up with other empirical data we find that it is a fact with consequences. For example, it has been found that happy people live longer than less happy people. This is not because the unhappy people are unhappy about some third factor which is contributing to their early demise. Rather, people with otherwise comparable circumstances seem to be sustained if they have a sunny disposition.

One especially memorable analysis, known to experts as 'the nun study', led by David Snowdon, shows this vividly. The study tracked an unusually homogeneous group – a set of American Catholic nuns. In the 1930s, when new nuns joined the School Sisters of Notre Dame, they were asked to write an autobiographical sketch. Some sixty years later, researchers looked at 180 of these handwritten accounts, written when the women were on average twenty-two years old, which had been kept on file. Rating their autobiographies for amount of 'positive emotional content', they found this to be a strong predictor of longevity. Of those who were alive in 1991, more than half of those who had written the least cheerful accounts – more than half a century earlier – would die before the end of the decade, whereas those who told a more contented story in their youth had significantly longer lives, with only one in five of nuns in the happiest quarter not making it through the same period.[9] In other words, it seems that happiness, regardless of other factors, means you live longer.

GREATEST HITS OF HAPPINESS

Richard Layard, well-known as an economist and now one of the leading authorities on happiness, has drawn upon numerous studies and datasets to produce what he calls the 'Big Seven factors affecting happiness'. These are:

- Family relationships
- Financial situation
- Work
- Community and friends
- Health
- Personal freedom
- Personal values[10]

Layard explains that the first five of these are listed in order of importance, with personal freedom and personal values being additional crucial factors. He observes that except for health and income, these seven factors 'are all concerned with the quality of our relationships'.[11] Happiness therefore has a lot to do with the social bonds and connectedness that concern us in this book. So let's look at each of the relevant factors in turn.

First of all, it is perhaps no surprise that family relationships appear to have the very strongest relationship with reported levels of happiness. In spite of all the jokes that are commonly made about marriage as a kind of prison or limitation on happiness, data consistently shows that married people are happier than unmarried people, and that the ending of a marriage is generally unmatched as a source of unhappiness. For instance, Layard uses data from the World Values Survey, which covers 90,000 people in forty-six countries, and asks people to self-report on their own happiness as well as many other features of their life. From these statistics we can discern that becoming separated from a spouse has an impact on happiness four times greater than that of a one-third drop in family income. It is worse than becoming unemployed, having a significant decline in health, or living in an undemocratic dictatorship.[12] This strong finding in favour of 'marriage' should not be taken to be an affirmation of heterosexuality, of course – many countries have now introduced same-sex marriage, or civil unions, on a similar basis, and the benefits of these public affirmations of commitment are likely to be exactly the same.[13] As Layard explains:

> The main benefits of marriage or cohabitation are obvious: you give each other love and comfort; you share resources, gaining economies of scale; you help each other. . . . Married people are healthier and live longer. . . . We need other people, and we need to be needed. Increasingly, research confirms the dominating importance of love.[14]

This need for social bonds follows through into the third item on Layard's list, the importance of work. Becoming unemployed has a huge impact on happiness, which is only partially explained by the difficulties caused by the corresponding drop in income; it is the loss of social relationships and self-esteem associated with work which hits especially hard. Whilst any work tends to provide some sense of purpose, and social connections, the data also shows that work should be *meaningful* in order to add to our happiness. As Layard reports:

> Perhaps the most important issue is the extent to which you have control over what you do. There is a creative spark in each of us, and if it finds no outlet, we feel half-dead. This can be literally true: among British civil servants of any given grade, those who do the most routine work experience the most rapid clogging of the arteries.[15]

All of these things – relationships, self-esteem, meaning – also go to explain why retired people are no more happy than working people: they have gained lots of leisure time, but may have also lost a lot of social connections, and the feeling of making some kind of difference.[16]

Fourth in Layard's 'Big Seven' factors affecting happiness is community and friendship. As we will see more below, feeling a part of a helpful and trustworthy community can give a huge lift to people's general sense of contentment. This theme is perhaps magnified at the more macro level, where the ways in which governments connect with personal and community life add up to the measures of 'personal freedom', such as corruption, accountability and effectiveness of government services. These again have a significant impact on happiness.

You might think, for instance, that local government

decision-making processes could not have much to do with happiness, except perhaps that we would be very happy not to have to hear about them. But that is only because we have become used to having no control in that area – it seems boring because it is out of our hands. A study by Bruno Frey and Alois Stutzer was able to show that actually, where people had power in this sphere, it affected the mood across the whole population.[17] Their research looked at Switzerland, which is divided into twenty-six cantons, and where policy issues are frequently decided by referendum – but to varying degrees. In the cantons where citizens had the most rights to referendums, compared with those where these rights were least, people were 11 per cent more likely to describe themselves as 'completely satisfied' with their life. Living in a place where it was relatively easy to get the signatures necessary to trigger the mechanisms of direct democracy had this clear and sizeable impact on the happiness of the people in that canton – not just on the people launching referendums, but the whole population.[18]

Finally, on Layard's list of factors affecting happiness, there is 'personal values', in other words our inner self and philosophy of life. One of the most consistent findings of happiness research, for instance, is that people who believe in God are happier than those who do not. It is possible that happy people are more likely to believe in God, rather than the belief causing happiness, at an individual level, but Layard asserts that 'since the relation also exists at the national level, we can be sure that to some extent belief causes happiness'.[19] A study by the Pew Research Center in the US (nothing, in fact, to do with church pews) seemed to find a similar connection between religion and happiness – although the finding may be more to do with the social bonds of church *attendance*. 'People who attend religious services weekly or more are happier (43% very happy) than those who attend monthly or less (31%); or seldom or never (26%)', they report.[20] They also note that this correlation 'has been a consistent finding in the General Social Surveys taken over the years'.[21] Even amongst those of the same religious faith, actually *going* to church makes a very significant difference to reported levels of happiness. Church attendance may reinforce faith, which, as noted above, makes people happier, but it additionally involves regular participation in a local network of goodwill and community, which – as we have also seen – is a strong propagator of happiness.

GET A PROJECT

Looking at Layard's 'Big Seven', we might think that all we needed to do to attain a super level of happiness would be to align a reasonable number of these factors around ourselves and simply wait for the happiness to flow in. If we move to an especially democratic canton in Switzerland, get married, turn up regularly at work and church, invite some friends round, and get some decent medical and financial advice, we should be able to score 100 per cent happiness.

However, although all of these things might help to *support* our efforts, happiness does not follow from passive participation. Similarly, the idea that you can be happier if you merely lower your expectations, doesn't really work. People need something to strive towards. Richard Layard puts it very nicely: 'Prod any happy person and you will find a project.'[22] As Tibor Scitovsky argued in his 1976 book *The Joyless Economy*, individuals in modern societies tend to have reasonable amounts of money and free time, but this is no good if they are simply bored. Traditional economics has tended to be blind to such issues, since it would assume that gains in money and leisure are inherently positive.[23]

However, happiness researchers such as Sonja

Lyubomirsky and her colleagues Kennon M. Sheldon and David Schkade are able to point to a number of studies which demonstrate that goal-oriented activities are a major contributor to happiness.[24] Indeed, comparative studies have shown that the intentionality of *choosing* to do a particular activity adds considerably to the pleasure, when compared to pleasant changes in circumstance which have merely happened.[25] And, unlike most things that give a boost to happiness – even marriage – the pleasure of working on projects does not fade over time.[26] You could say that this statistic is a little unfair, as people can readily create new and stimulating projects for themselves, whereas exciting new marriages, or delightful new homes, say, cannot be generated easily, and come with costs. But such is the nature of projects: relatively easy to create, and a source of pleasure, even when you haven't really done much about them.

Happiness, then, is about close relationships, community and well-being. It cannot be determined by a certain level of material comfort. Instead, it stems from having meaningful connections with others, and meaningful things to do. A 2016 book, *Happiness Explained* by Paul Anand, emphasizes the role of 'human flourishing' in levels of happiness, and identifies four crucial elements for individuals and society to achieve this – fairness, autonomy, community and engagement.[27] Fairness is to do with the impact on our satisfaction, and quality of life, in a society with evident injustices and inequalities. There is perhaps growing recognition that stark economic inequalities are bad for everyone, the argument made powerfully by Richard Wilkinson and Kate Pickett in their 2010 book, *The Spirit Level*.[28] In 2017, Kate Raworth's *Doughnut Economics* used a memorable metaphor to show that humans on planet Earth need to work out a way to exist within the ring of the doughnut – representing a safe and just space for humanity – between a social foundation that no one should fall below, and an ecological ceiling of planetary pressure that we should not go beyond.[29] This is vital for fairness, and even more essential for sustainability – literally for continued tolerable life on this planet.

Anand's other three elements – autonomy, community and engagement – are directly related to the themes we have already discussed: ability to select projects and direct one's own actions; meaningful connections with others; and a lively sense of being part of something. Personal projects are especially valuable if they are not contained at the individual level but involve some form of sharing, cooperation, or contribution to other people's well-being. As Richard Layard says:

> A society cannot flourish without some sense of shared purpose. The current pursuit of self-realisation will not work. If your sole duty is to achieve the best for yourself, life becomes just too stressful, too lonely – you are set up to fail. Instead, you need to feel you exist for something larger, and that very thought takes off some of the pressure.[30]

This means we need to broaden our focus from individual happiness to activities within the social fabric more generally. This brings us to the discussion of 'social capital', which is the focus of the rest of this chapter.

SOCIAL CAPITAL AND COMMUNITIES

The happiness research, discussed above, has indicated factors which typically make *individuals* happier, and which can often be encouraged or stimulated at government level, thereby helping society as a *whole* to be happier. For instance, support can be given to couples and families – in the form of centres and activities for parents and children, and relationship support – and the benefits of marriage have been extended to same-sex couples.[31] Governments also obviously play a crucial role in the stability and legislation of work; support for and prevention of ill-health; and in levels of freedom and active democracy. So, although the government can't 'make you happy' *per se*, it can give support to some of the structures that might help to foster individual happiness.

A slightly different way of looking at similar issues is found in the literature on 'social capital'. This discussion also begins with individuals, in the sense that social well-being is a responsibility of us all, and then it tends to reach towards a more inclusive, participatory, community-based view of the solutions. 'Social capital' has become a buzzword amongst policy-makers and think-tanks since the 1990s, so there is again a question of what the state can do to support social capital – but also an idea that social capital might help the state. The 'happiness' and 'social capital' studies are not mutually exclusive fields: the research mentioned above which suggests that collaboration and social projects are good for happiness, for instance, could also be absolutely central to social capital scholars making their case.

Compared to 'happiness', 'social capital' is a less self-explanatory term, and – as is often the way with academic jargon – is understood differently by different writers. Before we look at the different approaches, I will try to outline the meaning of the term in a general way. It started life as a metaphorical mirror of financial capital: just as a supply of money can enable you to do things that you otherwise could not do, a stock of social relationships will also make it easier to do things that otherwise you could not. These relationships are central to the smooth running of a society. L. J. Hanifan, who seems to have been the first person to use the term, wrote in 1916:

> The individual is helpless socially, if left to himself. . . . If he comes into contact with his neighbour, and they with other neighbours, there will be an accumulation of social capital, which may . . . bear a social potentiality sufficient to the substantial improvement of living conditions in the whole community. The community as a whole will benefit by the cooperation of all its parts, while the individual will find in his associations the advantages of the help, the sympathy, and the fellowship of his neighbours.[32]

Hanifan's notion of 'social capital' failed to capture the general imagination at that time, and remained generally invisible for several more decades. Indeed, those who started talking about social capital from the 1980s onwards may well have been ignorant of this earlier usage. However, Hanifan's outline of social capital is remarkably close to its accepted use today. It is worth clarifying that social capital (being about social networks and relationships) is distinct from other forms of non-financial capital that people might talk about these days, such as human capital (individual expertise), physical capital (equipment) and cultural capital (individual cultural knowledge). The thing that these different forms of capital all have in common – the thing that makes them 'capital' rather than just 'know-how' – is that they are all used to create further capital.

Generally, the social capital writers are concerned with social relationships based on cooperation, reciprocity, goodwill and trust, oriented towards a society that's nice for everybody to live in. Inevitably, they generally have to admit that there is a 'dark side' to social capital as well: even the most brutal, selfish, antisocial person tends to have social networks, and indeed they can achieve their goals much more efficiently if they have a good stock of social relationships. The advocates of 'social capital' would be in favour of mutually supportive community groups of enthusiasts with shared interests, but the Ku Klux Klan is a mutually supportive community group of enthusiasts with shared interests.

So although social capital can seem like a wonderful 'happy glue' for society, solving all its problems, its functions are not *necessarily* always wholesome, kind and ethical. Nevertheless, the social capital literature does seem to suggest a path towards a better society, which we should not dismiss just because there are – as always – possible antisocial applications of the idea.

WHY WE'RE LOOKING AT SOCIAL CAPITAL

To be clear: the reason why you're reading about social capital in this book is because the social capital research is all about the value of people doing things (making and connecting) in communities, versus what happens when they don't.

By the end of this chapter, it will hopefully be clear that people doing stuff together in communities is really valuable for a number of reasons, whereas when they don't – when they remain isolated, strangers to their neighbours, not communicating – then society enters a downward spiral. That doesn't just mean 'a bit less friendly', but really *falling apart*, with higher levels of crime, distrust, depression and illness.

The social capital literature doesn't directly and completely prove that 'making is connecting', but it does show the value of connecting through doing things together. The additional job of showing that creative activity is better for this than anything else is hopefully done in the other chapters.

THREE APPROACHES TO SOCIAL CAPITAL

In the past two or three decades, scholars have taken an interest in three different perspectives on social capital in particular. These are based on the ideas of Pierre Bourdieu, James Coleman and Robert Putnam. The first two are part of the background story, and I wrote a few pages on them for this book – but then needed to make the book a bit shorter, and so now I've cut those out and put them on the book's website instead (www.makingisconnecting.org). So here we'll cover Bourdieu and Coleman rather briefly, and then discuss Putnam – the king of social capital writers, and the key source for most discussions of the topic today – in more depth.

French sociologist Pierre Bourdieu (1930–2002) was interested in the ways in which society is reproduced, and how the dominant classes retain their position. He wisely observed that this could not be explained by economics alone, and developed a model based on cultural capital, and social capital, as well as economic capital. Cultural capital refers to the ways in which people would use cultural knowledge to undergird their place in the hierarchy (most easily pictured as pretentious displays of middle-class taste).[33] Social capital, meanwhile, refers to the advantage gained 'by virtue of possessing a durable network of more or less institutionalized relationships of mutual acquaintance and recognition'.[34] This definition, in itself, is similar to other definitions, such as those that we will see below, and Hanifan's approach above. But where other writers see social capital as a fundamentally heartwarming network of social connections, Bourdieu uses it to explain the cold realities of social inequality. Here, social capital is a way of showing how the middle and upper classes make sure that their spheres remain exclusive. Although distinct from economic capital, and operating in a different way, it is inseparable from it. Clearly, this relates to a real phenomenon in social life: studies continue to show that social mobility remains something of a myth, and that tomorrow's wealthy professionals are most likely to be the children of today's wealthy professionals.[35] But social networks are not *always* just the exclusionary tool of elites, and so Bourdieu's approach to the concept of social capital is rather limited and deterministic.

Around the same time, in the late 1980s and early 1990s, the American sociologist James Coleman (1926–95) was also writing about social capital. Coleman also linked social capital with economics, but in a different way. He wanted to combine the insights of sociology and economic theory, seeing social capital as a way of adding a human and more collective social face to the overly rational and individualistic models of traditional economics. Coleman's approach leads to a broader view of social capital, where it is not seen only as stock held by powerful elites, but notes its value for all kinds of communities, including the powerless and marginalized.

He proposes a model in which social capital is one of the potential resources which an actor can use, alongside other resources such as their own skills and expertise (human capital), tools (physical capital), or money (economic capital). Unusually, though, social capital is not necessarily 'owned' by the individual but instead arises as a resource which is *available* to them.[36] So, for example, if you live on a street where you can rely on your neighbours to look out for your children, then you have access to a form of social capital which other people, in less trusting or well-bonded streets, do not. Furthermore, this is not a resource which you could give or sell to your friend on the other side of town. To get access to it, she would have to move into your street (or one like it) and establish some relationships with her neighbours – all of which would take time and effort – because social capital is a resource based on trust and shared values, and develops from the weaving-together of people in communities.

Coleman also highlights the role of social capital as a source of useful everyday information, and of norms and sanctions, which can facilitate certain kinds of actions, but can also be restrictive.[37] In particular he singles out 'one effect of social capital that is especially important: its effect on the creation of human capital in the next generation'.[38] This 'human capital', such as a secure sense of self-identity, confidence in expressing one's own opinions, and emotional intelligence, enables young people to become better learners, and so helps them to be more successful in the education system and in society. This human capital emerges out of social capital, because this kind of development depends upon *relationships*, most obviously within the family (or other support network).

In this model, then, social capital – in any context – relies on people looking beyond themselves and engaging in supportive or helpful actions, *not* because they expect a reward or immediate reciprocal help, but because they believe it's a good thing to do. Coleman himself seems to struggle against the gravitational pull of traditional economic theory, and is barely able to accept this conclusion. Nevertheless, he usefully highlights the significance of social capital as part of a potential solution for marginalized learners, and its importance in parenting, for people of any social class.

ROBERT PUTNAM AND ALEXIS DE TOCQUEVILLE

Bourdieu and Coleman are well-known within academic circles, but Robert Putnam is perceived as the popular, public face of 'social capital' theory. A professor at Harvard University's John F. Kennedy School of Government, Putnam's article 'Bowling alone: America's declining social capital' was published in the *Journal of Democracy* in 1995, and, surprisingly for an academic article, shot its author to fame – or, at least, fame amongst journalists and policy wonks – as he was invited to meet President Clinton and other influential officials. Putnam then turned his short article into a substantial and thoroughly-researched book, packed with data, also entitled *Bowling Alone*, and discussed it on a tour of numerous venues and radio stations across North America and Europe.

Putnam's work is often described as 'neo-Tocquevillian', suggesting that he is reviving the spirit of Alexis de Tocqueville, the nineteenth-century French author of *On Democracy in America* (published in two volumes, 1835 and 1840). This book is well-known in the United States, and in a sense forms part of American mythology. For this reason it is worth delving into this bit of backstory, for a short while, in order to help us understand the impact of Putnam's argument.

Alexis de Tocqueville was a civil servant and social thinker, from an aristocratic background, who travelled across the United States in 1831. In his book, which draws upon the experiences of this journey, he seems to assume that a large democracy with such levels of freedom and equality in the eyes of the law should produce an anarchic level of individualism, and general chaos. (This seemingly high level of freedom and equality was relative, of course, being limited to white males.) However, de Tocqueville seems compelled to report that, contrary to his expectations, he found an impressive level of community spirit and mutual support at all levels of American society.

He notes that American citizens 'enjoy unlimited freedom of association for political purposes', and observes that this seems to *also* encourage civil associations, a term which covers all the non-governmental, and not explicitly political, clubs and organizations, including charities, religious groups, bee-keepers' associations, volunteer fire brigades, sports clubs, parenting groups, and so on. De Tocqueville marvels at how 'Americans of all ages, all conditions, and all dispositions constantly form associations' for a huge range of purposes,[39] and he emphatically 'admires' this capacity.

It is easy to see how American readers will have swelled with pride, through the nineteenth and twentieth centuries, at this famous European assessment of their civic connectedness and community spirit. De Tocqueville was especially impressed that Americans, as he saw it, did not pin their hopes on individuals, and did not ask or wait for the government to act on their behalf – as he asserts the English or the French would do – but instead have 'carried to the highest perfection the art of pursuing in common the object of their common desires and have applied this new science to the greatest number of purposes'.[40] He asserts:

> Nothing, in my opinion, is more deserving of our attention than the intellectual and moral associations of America. . . . As soon as several of the inhabitants of the United States have taken up an opinion or a feeling which they wish to promote in the world, they look out for mutual assistance; and as soon as they have found one another out, they combine. From that moment they are no longer isolated men, but a power seen from afar, whose actions serve for an example and whose language is listened to.[41]

Despite its grand tone, this observation is not to do with American political associations, which the author is also aware of and impressed by, but with all other shared social or cultural needs or interests. He writes that 'the art of associating together' is essential if civil society is to be maintained. Modest connections create the conditions which enable more substantial ones to grow:

> The greater the multiplicity of small affairs, the more do men, even without knowing it, acquire facility in prosecuting great undertakings in common.[42]

This apparent American capacity to form mutually supportive groups and associations seems quite wonderful and has become part of America's proud story. This helps to explain why, 160 years later, a Harvard professor's book about civic engagement became so widely discussed – as it suggested that de Tocqueville's dream society was rapidly collapsing.

PUTNAM'S *BOWLING ALONE*

Robert Putnam's argument is that this healthy tendency of Americans to make connections and form associations, between people who otherwise would not have known each other, was collapsing in the latter half of the twentieth century. Like de Tocqueville, Putnam does not have a special interest in people organizing for political purposes: any kind of association is considered to be valuable, whether social, sporting, religious, musical, hobbyist, or whatever. The bowling league is one example of just such an association.

Putnam's memorable title, however, can create some confusion. The phrase *Bowling Alone* suggests a remarkable degree of isolation, as we are apparently invited to picture individuals going out on their own, to roll a lonely ball down their local ten-pin alley. Have people – or specifically, Americans – really become so disconnected and friendless? Well, no. The *Bowling Alone* website seeks to clarify, right at the top, by saying: 'We are bowling alone. More Americans are bowling than ever before, but they are not bowling in leagues.' In other words, they are actually *not* bowling alone. Not at all. They are going out as groups of family and/or friends – and, as it says here, they are actually doing so more than ever. The thing that has declined is the bowling league, a more competitive structure where teams compete against each other. You could certainly wonder whether this is a real loss. Although the team relationships, and even inter-team rivalries, were likely to be friendly, the bowling league obviously required a level of sporting prowess, since teams would almost inevitably want to win. By contrast, the purely 'social' bowling that has more-or-less replaced the league competitions is less to do with bowling aptitude, and more to do with having fun and spending time together. So it's not 'bowling alone' at all.

We cannot conclude from this, of course, that Putnam is all wrong and that American associational life is healthier than ever. Putnam's headline example is easily misunderstood, and weirdly equates being with family or friends with being 'alone'. This perhaps points to the way in which Putnam mourns older forms of association while not entirely recognizing newer ones. Nevertheless, Putnam has data on his side, as we shall see. And the bowling league example is not entirely arbitrary. As John Field explains, league bowling serves in Putnam's discussion as:

> a metaphor for a type of associational activity that brings relative strangers together on a routine and frequent basis, helping to build and sustain a wider set of networks and values that foster general reciprocity and trust, and in turn facilitate mutual collaboration.[43]

Thus, bowling, or singing, or railway modelling, are all activities which may not have a direct impact upon society in themselves, but when people meet up to engage in their shared enthusiasm, this provides really valuable social glue, bringing people together and fostering relationships of trust and reciprocity. This is what 'social capital' is, for Putnam.

He writes that the essence of social capital theory is that 'social networks have value', because social contacts are a resource which boosts the 'productivity of individuals and groups'.[44] He defines social capital as:

> connections among individuals – social networks and the norms of reciprocity and trustworthiness that arise from them.[45]

Therefore social capital is not merely about the *willingness* to be socially helpful or community-minded, but relies on the actual existence of functioning networks accompanied by actually existing expectations.

Putnam then makes a distinction, which he attributes to Ross Gittell and Avis Vidal, between *bridging* social capital and *bonding* social capital. Bridging social capital draws people in, and embraces diversity, making links between different people and groups. Bonding social capital, on the other hand, is more exclusive, tying together people who are already similar, or have interests in common. Both forms have their uses, and it is not necessarily that one is 'better' than the other. Bonding social capital is that which binds together a bunch of rich white men in their golf club, for instance – the kind of exclusive elite connection that Bourdieu was concerned about – but it is also bonding social capital which connects an ethnic minority group in a particular area of a city, providing vital social and psychological support, and help with finding shelter, advice and employment. Bonding social capital can be pictured as a tight-knit circle of comrades; whereas bridging social capital has its arms outstretched, to welcome people in. We should note, incidentally, that it's not a matter of one or the other: different groups or communities might have some degree of *both* kinds of social capital.

In *Bowling Alone*, Putnam marshals his data not only to demonstrate that associational life in the United States has declined, but – crucially – also to address the questions 'Why?' (in other words, what has caused this decline?) and 'So what?' (does this matter, and what are the consequences?). First let's briefly list some of the declining activities which Putnam analyses – these have typically all fallen dramatically since the middle of the twentieth century. In political participation, he finds that citizens may be reasonably interested and well informed, but their behaviour shows a sharp decline in electoral voting, attending public meetings and engagement with political or civic organizations, especially in terms of face-to-face meetings. In terms of the non-political civic associations which so fascinated de Tocqueville, such as hobby clubs and voluntary groups, Putnam finds a sharp decline, with people increasingly joining organizations such as Greenpeace, to which they donate money but never meet up with other supporters – 'mail-order membership', as Putnam ruefully calls it.[46] In terms of religious participation, American religious belief remains strong – as is well-known – but church attendance is down, and churches are less well connected with the wider community.

All of these examples are likely to be somewhat familiar to the modern reader, and could potentially be explained by suggesting that the American public have shifted towards a less formal culture, where people like to 'hang out' in a loose but friendly way – which should still be high in social capital – even though the rather stiff-sounding gardening associations or choral societies have waned in popularity. Surprisingly, though, Putnam's data shows that even informal socializing has dropped, and he presents a clear picture of much less open and outward social connection, and much more family-based staying-in. I discussed this and other details of Putnam's findings in some depth in the first edition of this book; in the present edition I've made some of it more concise, so that we can get onto the meanings of it all.

THE CAUSES OF COLLAPSING SOCIAL CAPITAL

If social capital is in decline, if people are connecting less with others, we have to ask: *why?* How did this happen? Putnam considers a range of possible causes, and arrives at four main factors that he says have caused the decline in civic engagement and social capital. The first of these is generational change, where the explanation seems to be that the experience of the Second World War cemented the centrality of community, solidarity and self-sacrifice, in a way which subsequent conflicts and causes have not. Another factor is the growth of suburbanization, commuting, and sprawl: rather than living and working in their local communities, people increasingly travel some distance from home to work, which reduces their engagement with the community that they live in, and also takes up time in the day, leaving less time for friends and neighbours, and community engagements. Putnam also finds that everyday pressures – 'pressures of time and money', the demands of work and general expectation of busyness – have also made a significant contribution.

The other factor identified by Putnam, and second only to 'generational change' as the most significant, is: television.[47] This is largely for the straightforward reason, which we discussed briefly in chapter 1, that it 'privatizes' leisure time, keeping people at home, on their sofas, for literally several hours every day on average. 'Nothing else in the twentieth century so rapidly and profoundly affected our leisure', Putnam notes. 'In 1950 barely 10 percent of American homes had television sets, but by 1959, 90 percent did, probably the fastest diffusion of a technological innovation ever recorded.'[48] Since then, Putnam's data shows, people became less likely to switch on to watch a particular selected programme – as they typically did in the earlier days of television

– and more likely to have the TV on anyway. Household life would be directed towards a television set, and their connection with the outside world would become filtered through the television. Drawing on his diverse and substantial sources of data, Putnam finds that 'Nothing – not low education, not full-time work, not long commutes in urban agglomerations, not poverty or financial distress – is more broadly associated with civic disengagement and social disconnection than is dependence on television for entertainment.'[49] And, in a surprising and disturbing killer blow, he finds that people don't even really enjoy it: 'Like other addictive or compulsive behaviours, television seems to be a surprisingly unsatisfying experience. Both time diaries and the "beeper" studies [when a beeper prompts participants to record how they are feeling at particular more-or-less random moments during the day] find that for the average viewer television is about as enjoyable as housework and cooking, ranking well below all other leisure activities and indeed below work itself.'[50]

Putnam does not seem to be one of those TV bashers who would find ways to attack popular culture because they had a general disdain for young people's interests, or modern life in general.[51] On the contrary, Putnam gathered data from a broad range of sources and considered a very great number of possible causes for the particular phenomena that concern him. Television does not seem to have been targeted, but rather it *emerges* as a significant cause from Putnam's investigations, published in 2001. Since then, the late twentieth-century phenomenon of a family sat around a television set may have waned, but only because of its displacement by the arguably more individualized and isolating experience of family members – whether in different rooms or the same room – looking at different screens, with a wider range of niche interests and entertainments to occupy them.

THE CONSEQUENCES OF COLLAPSING SOCIAL CAPITAL

Next we have to consider whether this decline in social capital actually matters. Turning to this 'So what?' question, Putnam says:

> An impressive and growing body of research suggests that civic connections help make us healthy, wealthy, and wise. Living *without* social capital is not easy, whether one is a villager in southern Italy or a poor person in the American inner city or a well-heeled entrepreneur in a high-tech industrial district.[52]

His evidence demonstrates that social capital has a considerable impact in a wide range of areas. For example, local environments are both cleaner and safer where there is a higher level of civic engagement. Putnam has even mapped which US states are more or less 'pugnacious' – measured by the proportion of people who agree with the statement 'I'd do better than average in a fist fight' in the DDB Needham Life Style surveys – and found that states high in social capital are less pugnacious. To put it another way, wandering into an area with lower social capital means that people are somewhat more likely to fancy the idea of beating you up.[53] Similarly, the problems of crime and violence in inner cities, his data suggests, cannot be read off from economic factors alone but are most serious where there is a lack of 'community monitoring, socializing, mentoring, and organizing'.[54] When we look at child development, we find that it is heavily influenced by the levels of trust and goodwill, and supportive networks, within their family, school and community. Indeed, as we have seen already, health and happiness for people of all ages are linked with social connectedness.

Social capital is not a supernatural force, of course, and Putnam identifies particular ways in which social capital leads to these positive results.[55] For instance:

- It enables citizens to resolve problems more easily;
- It helps communities to advance because members know that they can rely on each other;
- It fosters awareness of the ways in which our fates are interlinked, and encourages us to be more tolerant, less cynical, and more empathetic.

Since Putnam assembled his landmark book in the late 1990s, we have come to think of the internet as a major, mainstream way of connecting people, as discussed in chapter 4. But can the internet rebuild the broken networks of social capital, and somehow replace the helpful warmth and cohesion of Putnam's face-to-face community associations?

CAN THE INTERNET BUILD SOCIAL CAPITAL?

When Robert Putnam was writing the book, *Bowling Alone*, in the late 1990s, the internet and the World Wide Web were not entirely new, and everybody seemed to be talking about them. It was at that time that I edited a book called *Web Studies*, which documented a wide range of ways in which the internet was connecting people and enabling the creation of new types of culture, entertainment, knowledge-sharing and self-expression.[56] But of course, internet-based technologies were clearly *not* as embedded in people's every-day lives as they are today. In 2000, less than half of the UK or US populations were internet users, and the internet was slow; YouTube would have been unwatchable then, and wasn't launched for another five years.

Nevertheless, by the late 1990s there was a growing awareness that online communities were not necessarily just about hobbies and information, but could also be strong sources of genuine support for new parents, or people with similar illnesses, the divorced or bereaved, or teenagers wondering if anyone else feels like they do. Howard Rheingold's famous 1993 book, *The Virtual Community*, painted a picture of the author's engagement with an early online community, The WELL (The Whole Earth 'Lectronic Link), which was full of heart, kindness and mutual sympathy.

Right near the start of the first chapter, for instance, Rheingold describes the following powerful case, which I quote at some length:

> Jay Allison and his family live in Massachusetts. He and his wife are public-radio producers. I've never met any of them face-to-face, although I feel I know something powerful and intimate about the Allisons and have strong emotional ties to them. What follows are some of Jay's postings on the WELL:
>
> *'Woods Hole. Midnight. I am sitting in the dark of my daughter's room. Her monitor lights blink at me. The lights used to blink too brightly so I covered them with bits of bandage adhesive and now they flash faintly underneath, a persistent red and green, Lillie's heart and lungs.*
>
> *Above the monitor is her portable suction unit. In the glow of the flashlight I'm writing by, it looks like the plastic guts of a science-class human model, the tubes coiled around the power supply, the reservoir, the pump.*
>
> *Tina is upstairs trying to get some sleep. A baby monitor links our bedroom to Lillie's. It links our sleep to Lillie's too, and because our souls are linked to hers, we do not sleep well.*
>
> *I am naked. My stomach is full of beer. The flashlight rests on it, and the beam rises and falls with my breath. My daughter breathes through a white plastic tube inserted into a hole in her throat. She's fourteen months old.'*

Sitting in front of our computers with our hearts racing and tears in our eyes, in Tokyo and Sacramento and Austin, we read about Lillie's croup, her tracheostomy, the days and nights at Massachusetts General Hospital, and now the vigil over Lillie's breathing and the watchful attention to the mechanical apparatus that kept her alive. It went on for days. Weeks. Lillie recovered, and relieved our anxieties about her vocal capabilities after all that time with a hole in her throat by saying the most extraordinary things, duly reported online by Jay.

Later, writing in Whole Earth Review, Jay described the experience:

'Before this time, my computer screen had never been a place to go for solace. Far from it. But there it was. Those nights sitting up late with my daughter, I'd go to my computer, dial up the WELL, and ramble. I wrote about what was happening that night or that year. I didn't know anyone I was "talking" to. I had never laid eyes on them. At 3:00 a.m. my "real" friends were asleep, so I turned to this foreign, invisible community for support. The WELL was always awake.

Any difficulty is harder to bear in isolation. There is nothing to measure against, to lean against. Typing out my journal entries into the computer and over the phone lines, I found fellowship and comfort in this unlikely medium.'[57]

This section alone seems to singlehandedly answer the question of whether you can build social capital online. Clearly, you can. And online networks of this kind would potentially be powerful both in terms of bridging capital – bringing diverse people together, with no geographical limitations – and bonding capital – creating a strong 'in-group' spirit as they share both knowledge and emotions.

Robert Putnam seemed to accept this:

> Communication is a fundamental prerequisite for social and emotional connections. Telecommunications in general and the Internet in particular substantially enhance our ability to communicate; thus it seems reasonable to assume that their net effect will be to enhance community, perhaps even dramatically. Social capital is about networks, and the Net is the network to end all networks.[58]

Of course, all online networks and communities need to be carefully tended, like gardens, by their members, to fulfil their potential. As it appears to be relatively easy for anonymous people online to slide into intolerance and abuse, the power of online communication is only a good thing if wielded wisely.

SUMMING UP ON SOCIAL CAPITAL

This focus on the need to boost social capital in society – whether through online communities, real-world making and connecting activity, or in other ways – seems well-meaning and fruitful. Of course, positive community networks should operate on top of – not *instead* of – a solid level of government-organized social, health and welfare services. As we have seen, voluntary community engagement is a good thing, and is rewarding for participants and their neighbourhoods, but it should be built *above* the baseline of necessary services – not as a money-saving replacement for them. The point of Putnam is to highlight the value of social connections, and connected social projects – not to offer a right-wing excuse for slashing public services.

We also need to be mindful, especially in today's world, to have a balance of bridging and bonding capital. As I write in 2017, supporters of Donald Trump, divisive new president of the United States, and Brexit, the UK's divorce from the European Union, feel themselves to be full of bonding capital – looking after 'their own' – but are frighteningly light on bridging capital – offering the hand of friendship to people of diverse backgrounds.

There is now a significant body of literature on social capital, and we've only scratched the surface here.[59] At the end of his overview of a wide range of social capital theory and research, John Field makes a good, clear argument for the value of the general concept:

> What social capital brings to social theory is an emphasis on relationships and values as significant factors in explaining structures and behaviour. To be more precise, it contributes new insights by focusing on 'meso-level social structures' such as family, neighbourhood, voluntary associations and public institutions as integrating elements between individuals and wider social structures. Moreover, it allows social scientists to examine the role of these meso-level structures in a systematic way since it has a structural dimension (networks), a behavioural dimension (participation) and a cognitive dimension (norms).[60]

In particular he emphasizes that social capital is not only a theoretical tool for thinking about the importance of social connections and civic engagement: rather, there is 'abundant evidence that social capital actually affects the outcomes of social behaviour' and is therefore a powerful force in its own right.[61]

Both the happiness research and the social capital research have provided clear evidence that having friendly social connections and communication, and working together with people on shared projects, is not merely pleasant-but-optional 'icing on the cake' of individual lives, but is absolutely essential both for personal well-being and for a healthy, secure, trustworthy society. Both spheres of research tend to concern geographically-based lives rooted in physical communities, but they have obvious implications for online social activity as well.

In the next chapter we'll move on to discuss the ideas of 1970s philosopher Ivan Illich, who was also concerned with the qualities of a good life – and who also didn't talk about the internet, since it hadn't really been invented yet – and then steer back towards digital media for the second half of that chapter, and the one after that.

6

TOOLS FOR CHANGE

So far in this book we have considered the qualities of 'making things' and have found, amongst other things, that individually crafted items are expressive of a personality, and of a presence in the world; that everyday creativity is central to the health of a society; and that making and sharing your own things, rather than accepting mainstream manufactured or broadcast things, is positive in both political and emotional terms. We have seen evidence that personal creative projects are good for individual happiness, and that when people organize to make things together, it can transform the quality of life in communities. Hopefully that means I have laid some pretty solid groundwork for this chapter, which is possibly (even) broader in scope, and primarily concerns the work of Ivan Illich.

Here we encounter a level of argument which might tie things nicely together, because it's *big*. For Illich, making is not just an act which might brighten your day, or which might help to develop a social connection. What I take from Illich is that *making changes everything*.

So let's explore that.

Ivan Illich (1926–2002) was born in Vienna, studied in Italy, and worked as a parish priest in New York City. Following a position in Puerto Rico, and travels across South America, he set up a cultural and political institute in Mexico. This was followed by further travel and some university positions in the United States, Mexico and Germany. In other words, he had a complex biography, and somewhat nomadic existence, with few possessions. More importantly for us, Illich became known in the 1970s for his radical notion that overdeveloped institutions were crushing the life out of society.[1]

Whilst big, uniform systems may have been developed with the intention of helping people on a broad and democratic scale, Illich argued that they always reach a point beyond which they cause more harm than good. Schools, for instance, are originally intended to provide an *education* – of course – but once they are established into a institutional system they become machines to deliver *schooling* – conformity to rules, and memorization of a set body of knowledge without necessarily learning or understanding – which is then measured as an end in itself. Therefore, Illich suggests, the institution of school makes people stupid, institutionalized medicine makes people sick, and the institution of business ruins the planet. This sounds gloomy, then, but his solutions, based on more individual and community-based engagement, helpfulness and creativity, may be of interest.

DESCHOOLING

Illich first became well-known for a book called *Deschooling Society*, published in 1970. As the title suggests, it is primarily a critique of the compulsory education system, and as such formed part of a challenge to established models of education, alongside the work of other thinkers, such as John Dewey, John Holt and Rudolph Steiner. But *Deschooling Society* also brought to the public's attention the key seeds of Illich's more general argument about large institutions – and the ways in which people could reclaim a more local, healthy and useful way of doing things based on convivial, supportive and relevant interactions between people.

The problem with schools, according to Illich, is that they train students to be dependent on the 'treatment' offered by big institutions. Schools aim to create people who can do well in school tests, but not people who can think for themselves. Perhaps their cruellest manipulation is that they lead people to believe they are *unable* to do things for themselves and that the big institutional solution – the one offered by schools, hospitals and government departments – is the only legitimate one. He says:

> Rich and poor alike . . . view doctoring oneself as irresponsible, learning on one's own as unreliable, and community organisation, when not paid for by those in authority, as a form of aggression or subversion.[2]

This creates a double problem for the poor, who already experience a lack of power over their circumstances, but then, in addition, are schooled into a way of thinking which represents 'a loss of personal potency'.[3]

The solution, Illich says, is not to change the detail of what happens in schools, as replacing one compulsory education machine with another one would not address the problem. On the contrary, we need to create 'a new style of educational relationship' between people and their environment,[4] based on helping people to learn about things that they want to learn about, when they want to do so – rather than bribing or compelling people to acquire a particular stack of information at a particular predetermined time. He writes:

> A good educational system should have three purposes: it should provide all who want to learn with access to available resources at any time in their lives; empower all who want to share what they know to find those who want to learn it from them; and finally, furnish all who want to present an issue to the public with the opportunity to make their challenge known.[5]

Illich outlines a number of ways to achieve this, including skill exchanges (where people can seek others to learn skills from, and can offer to share their own expertise), peer matching (where people can find others with similar interests, so that they can learn together), and new forms of libraries (containing all kinds of 'educational objects'). Rather than education being something that has to be forced upon young people by government, education is here a lively, *chosen* activity which occurs naturally across 'learning webs' of enthusiastic individuals and groups. Illich easily solves any funding issues by assuming that the finance from the existing school system can be redirected towards supporting these schemes, which means that there would be a huge pile of money available to support facilitators, computers, equipment and learning spaces.

The idea that we should simply drop the whole carefully planned institution of education – to be replaced by the apparent anarchy of people just learning about whatever they want to learn about, whenever they want to – seems shocking, and perhaps even ridiculous, precisely because we have learned to accept the natural superiority of a uniform and imposed system. As Illich says:

> School has become the planned process which tools man for a planned world, the principal tool to trap man in man's trap.[6]

Rather than trusting each other to be supportive and helpful, and instead of relying on friendliness and goodwill, we create systems and laws which aim to remove uncertainty and chance, but at the cost of both meaningful human relationships and ordinary usefulness. The helpless, bored child asks her teacher, 'Why do I have to learn this thing now?', and the answer might be 'Because it will be good for you', or 'Because you've got a test on it next week', or simply 'Because I told you to'. This prepares her for a lifetime under other institutions which also provide 'Because I said so' as an explanation for required compliance.

This might seem to be a simple-minded critique of the necessary instruments of social organization. We might object that society needs some systems to preserve basic law and order, to offer support services to the needy, and to ensure that children receive an education – because left to their own devices, we fear that they might not get one. But we do not (necessarily) have to take from Illich that all social organizations and institutions must be disbanded. His point is more that these institutions become too big, and take on a life of their own, where the means become the ends. Therefore we should seek to develop small, local approaches, focused on people's needs, rather than the big bureaucratic operations which inevitably become focused on the needs of their own bureaucracy. Most crucially, I would say, Illich highlights the *loss of joyfulness in everyday experience* that comes with an overplanned system.

TOOLS FOR CONVIVIALITY

In his next book, *Tools for Conviviality*, Illich developed these ideas further. The planned systems, such as the one for education discussed in *Deschooling Society*, are here cast as 'tools' – because a tool is anything used to produce some thing or effect: a means to an end. Therefore, for Illich, the term 'tool' describes hammers and brooms, as well as cars and power stations, and schools and hospitals.[7] This broad use of the term enables him to pull together everything that is designed to do something, whether that is to dig a ditch or to create an 'educated' or 'healthy' person.

Tools for Conviviality was intended to be a pamphlet, for people to discuss, where Illich could set out his 'general theory of tools'.[8] The word 'conviviality' is carefully chosen. It does not refer to drunkenness, of course. 'Conviviality' for Illich is a meaningful kind of communication and engagement between people – people who are friendly, meaningfully connected and alive in the world:

> I choose the term 'conviviality' to designate the opposite of industrial productivity. I intend it to mean autonomous and creative intercourse among persons, and the intercourse of persons with their environment; and this in contrast with the conditioned response of persons to the demands made upon them by others, and by a man-made environment.[9]

So conviviality is about being vigorously engaged in relationships, conscious of values and meanings; and it is about having the capacity to communicate yourself directly, and to create the things of your world yourself. Illich is interesting on the material world – things and objects – because he does not simply argue that we should do away with all 'stuff' (which can seem to be the implication of some critiques of modern consumer societies). For Illich, the things and objects we have in our lives are significant, but there are important questions about where they came from, the role that they play, and what meanings they embody:

> People need not only to obtain things, they need above all the freedom to make things among which they can live, to give shape to them according to their own tastes, and to put them to use in caring for and about others. Prisoners in rich countries often have access to more things and services than members of their families, but they have no say in how things are to be made and cannot decide what to do with them. Their punishment consists in being deprived of what I shall call 'conviviality.' They are degraded to the status of mere consumers.[10]

Conviviality is therefore about having the power to shape one's own world. Illich makes it clear that individuals *must* retain this power – society must not seek to drain it from them. This is, then, a moral position, akin to that of Morris and especially Ruskin, whom we discussed in chapter 2. As before, I do not mean it is associated with moralism – the wish to impose particular traditional values – but rather that Illich's argument is powered by a moral belief that this kind of zesty freedom is crucial to the well-being of society, an irreducible core of what is necessary. As he explains,

> I consider conviviality to be individual freedom realized in personal interdependence and, as such, an intrinsic ethical value. I believe that, in any society, as conviviality is reduced below a certain level, no amount of industrial productivity can effectively satisfy the needs it creates among society's members.[11]

Conviviality therefore also represents the joyfulness which is so easily lost when we try to organize human interests into systems and institutions. Illich makes it clear that human beings, and their societies, are quite adept at producing bad tools – or rather, we create tools with good intentions, but when scaled up, the bureaucratic process becomes an end in itself, and the tool goes bad. A society needs tools – tools that can be controlled and used to good purposes – but they cannot be allowed to become too big and powerful, or we become enslaved by them.

Nevertheless, we can create good tools if we are careful, and try to be aware of the positive and negative potentials of any instrument. As the title suggests, *Tools for Conviviality* sets out Illich's vision of how society needs tools which encourage individual creativity, enabling people to give shape and character to their own lives, rather than those tools which tend to impose a mass sameness. Therefore this is about individuals being able to make their mark on the world, rather than only have the world stamping its mark upon them.

ILLICH AND TECHNOLOGY

Illich does not want to dispose of all industry and technology, although he admits that it is now 'difficult to imagine' a modern society where scientific progress and industrial development are balanced in harmony with human needs.

> Our vision of the possible and the feasible is so restricted by industrial expectations that any alternative to more mass production sounds like a return to past oppression or like a Utopian design for noble savages. In fact, however, the vision of new possibilities requires only the recognition that scientific discoveries can be useful in at least two opposite ways. The first leads to specialization of functions,

> institutionalization of values and centralization of power and turns people into the accessories of bureaucracies or machines. The second enlarges the range of each person's competence, control, and initiative, limited only by other individuals' claims to an equal range of power and freedom.[12]

This is a model which, for instance, connects directly with debates about the World Wide Web which have been pressing ever since the Web became publicly visible (about twenty years after the publication of *Tools for Conviviality*). On the one hand, the Web could be used to centralize a lot of power in one place – we might think of Google here – and to draw people, via attractive toys, to reduce their individuality to the level of a database – we might think of Facebook. These are concerns which will be discussed in the following chapter. More optimistically, the Web could be used – as its creator, Tim Berners-Lee, intended – to increase people's knowledge, and their connections with other people; to extend their ability to have an influence upon the things and environments in their lives; and to enable them to do more things for themselves.

Illich does not talk about computers or electronic networks in any amount of detail[13] – but *Deschooling Society* includes an interesting technological fantasy in the chapter presciently entitled 'Learning Webs'. Illich notes the amount of money which had been poured into providing television services in Latin America in the 1960s, and speculates on the possibilities afforded if this had been spent on tape recorders instead. One in five adults could have been issued with a tape recorder, and 'the money would have sufficed to provide an almost unlimited library of prerecorded tapes, with outlets even in remote villages, as well as an ample supply of empty tapes'.[14] It is these empty tapes which are key. Rather than the wall-to-wall content of television, produced for mass consumption, the emptiness of the tapes waits to be filled by the diverse voices of the people.

> This network of tape recorders, of course, would be radically different from the present network of TV. It would provide opportunity for free expression: literate and illiterate alike could record, preserve, disseminate and repeat their opinions.[15]

Where television would only spread 'institutionally produced programs' giving a voice to the establishment, and their sponsors, the tape recorders would enable people to express themselves, learn, and share knowledge.

Followers of Illich were surprisingly quick to translate these ideas into the world of information technology and networks. For instance, Illich's arguments struck a chord with the Homebrew Computer Club in San Francisco, who in the mid-1970s were starting to play with computer technology as a tool for freedom. The Club fuelled the passions of several future technology stars, including Steve Jobs and Steve Wozniak, the co-founders of Apple, and Lee Felsenstein, who designed the first mass-produced portable computer, the Osborne 1.

As early as 1973, Felsenstein and some friends worked on a project, *Community Memory*, directly inspired by Illich. The project initially linked just two terminals, one in a record shop and one in a library, to a central computer. It was the first public computerized 'bulletin board' system, and the terminal at the record shop end was literally positioned next to their *actual* bulletin board, where people would post messages about meetings, accommodation and gigs. The electronic version was originally intended to be a means of sharing countercultural information and resources, but soon developed into a place for all kinds of culture and chat.[16] Its creators described it as:

> An actively open information system, enabling direct communication among its users with no centralised editing or control over the information exchanged. Such a system represents a precise antithesis to the dominant uses of electronic media which broadcast centrally-determined messages to mass passive audiences.[17]

This was probably the first attempt to create a 'tool for conviviality' in direct response to *Tools for Conviviality*, and also of course now looks like a very early model for digital social media – in particular the open communication, social networking, and tagging of content so that others can find it.

Clearly, for Illich, the tools we have available to us are crucial to the character of our existence. The best tools are not merely 'useful' or 'convenient' additions to everyday life, but can unlock possibilities and enable creative expression, which are essential components of a satisfactory life:

> A convivial society should be designed to allow all its members the most autonomous action by means of tools least controlled by others. People feel joy, as opposed to mere pleasure, to the extent that their activities are creative; while the growth of tools beyond a certain point increases regimentation, dependence, exploitation, and impotence.[18]

Convivial tools are those which can be freely used, by those who wish to employ them; which do not require particular qualifications; and which 'allow the user to express his meaning in action'.[19] In Illich's terms, an online service would be a convivial tool – and therefore part of the solution to the problems faced by modern societies – insofar as it offers the opportunity for free and unconstrained expression and sharing of ideas and culture. If such a service is moderated by an institution, or is unnecessarily complex, or requires specialist knowledge, proprietary codes or licences, or cannot be freely shared, it becomes an 'industrial tool', and part of the problem.

Such tools – whether good ones or bad ones – are not just accessories, but are a fundamental part of everyday social interactions. As Illich argues:

> Tools are intrinsic to social relationships. An individual relates himself in action to his society through the use of tools that he actively masters, or by which he is passively acted upon. To the degree that he masters his tools, he can invest the world with his meaning; to the degree that he is mastered by his tools, the shape of the tool determines his own self-image. Convivial tools are those which give each person who uses them the greatest opportunity to enrich the environment with the fruits of his or her vision. Industrial tools deny this possibility to those who use them and they allow their designers to determine the meaning and expectations of others.[20]

THE POWER OF ILLICH

I have quoted Illich quite extensively in this chapter, in the hope of conveying some of the passion of his argument. His writing feels earthy, and engaged with real things – actual social relations, real communities, hands-on creativity. Much 'revolutionary' or would-be society-changing writing considers social forces with academic or economic detachment, and implies that a new bureaucratic machine, preceded by a big battle, could be the solution. Illich, to his credit, clearly has no appetite for either fighting or bureaucracy, and is much more interested in unlocking the potential of individuals and communities, and trusting them to be loving, sharing and imaginative. Being opposed to big systems, he thankfully does not wish to provide a planned or centralized solution. Indeed, Illich does not assume that he could predict what a future happier society would look like, exactly because he knows that it should rightly emerge through diverse, non-centralized creative acts:

> Industrial innovations are planned, trivial, and conservative. The renewal of convivial tools would be as unpredictable, creative, and lively as the people who use them.[21]

The idea that a person should be enabled to 'express their meaning in action' has the feeling of rough reality, and movement; and the line which makes a particular link between joy and creativity ('People feel joy, as opposed to mere pleasure, to the extent that their activities are creative') is warm, memorable and powerful. Furthermore, Illich's clear opposition between convivial and industrial tools gives us a straightforward means to assess the quality of new innovations (although there would always be debate about their qualities, and some haziness where new tools offered some possibilities of both kinds).

Certainly, when we think about new (or old) forms of media, the extent to which they enable free and creative self-expression is, I think, absolutely crucial. On the one hand this seems obvious – and therefore barely worth writing about. But, on the other hand, a concern for individual everyday creative autonomy is frequently *not* raised as a critical dimension when new technologies, applications or toys are being evaluated. Often, video games and online applications are launched with hype about their 'interactive' or networked 'collaborative' features, but are actually more-or-less closed worlds which do not enable the users to make their mark on the system, and consequently deny them the opportunity to 'express their meaning in action'.

TINKERING AND GENERATIVITY

A similar point was made by Jonathan Zittrain, of Harvard Law School, in his 2008 book *The Future of the Internet and How to Stop It.*[22] Despite the implication in the title, Zittrain didn't want to stop the internet, but sought to avoid a future internet where everything has become proprietary and fixed and non-tinkerable. Zittrain coined the notion of 'generativity' – which is basically the right and the opportunity to be creative – and 'generative technology' – which is technology that enables you to do whatever you want to do with it, to create stories and ideas and uses for yourself. 'Generativity' is therefore a version of Illich's 'conviviality', as applied to technology, and means basically 'Does it want you to do your own thing, or does it want you to do *its* thing?'

Zittrain has a nice example to illustrate this approach, which is, again, from the early days of Apple Computer. In the first edition of this book I retold some of this history, because it charmingly involves computers soldered together by hand and enclosed in handmade wooden cabinets – in 1976! – and it gave me an opportunity to write a long nostalgic footnote about my childhood spent writing games in BASIC on my Commodore Vic-20, a home computer of the early 1980s. You don't need all that now. But the key bit is about the Apple II, which was really the first mainstream personal computer produced by the company, in 1977. Zittrain says:

> The Apple II was quintessentially *generative* technology. It was a platform. It invited people to tinker with it. Hobbyists wrote programs. Businesses began to plan on selling software. Jobs (and Apple) had no clue how the machine would be used. They had their hunches, but, fortunately for them, nothing constrained the PC to the hunches of the founders.[23]

Zittrain's point is that the Apple II, and other early home computers, offered a huge open door to creativity and innovation. Programming the computer for yourself was not a 'behind the scenes' activity, performed by qualified professionals, but was what the machine *assumed* you were going to do when you took it out of the box.

Over time, this level of openness and generativity led to a problem – unhelpful users were able to bring about viruses, spam and identity theft. These unwelcome innovations led to a desire amongst some of the weary public for a 'clean', quality-controlled and therefore censored version of computer systems and the internet – and it is this desire for a locked-down replacement for one of humankind's greatest inventions which is the 'future' that Zittrain wants to 'stop' in his confusing book title.

This may have seemed especially troubling in 2007, when Apple had just launched the iPhone as an entirely locked-down device which nobody could add programs to, except Apple itself. Zittrain notes that Jobs even highlighted these restrictions at the iPhone launch, boasting: 'We define everything that is on the phone.' In fact, this changed quite quickly, with the launch of the App Store a year later in 2008, which has enabled much diverse creativity from developers who have created literally millions of apps for the iPhone and its bigger sister the iPad, which followed in 2010.[24]

We can still complain that to create apps for an iPhone or iPad, you need a separate computer and developers' kit, and ultimately your software must be reviewed and approved by Apple itself before it can go anywhere. Apple typically approves most apps within five days, but this gatekeeping process is the very opposite of the well-established open-publishing ethos of the internet and the World Wide Web.[25] The whole point about the internet was meant to be that you could make and innovate there *without* having to get permission from anyone. This model of the multinational corporation as gatekeeper and protector, to whom content creators are subservient, is a control-freak reversal of the generative ideal of computers, the internet and the Web.

You could say that these details are not great hardships, are unsurprising, and protect consumers. But as Zittrain would remind us, it's all about the spirit of the thing. The anticipated standard user of the gadget is not expected to innovate with it.

But then there's a retort back to that, which is that directly programming the device itself, right out of the box, is not the be-all and end-all of creativity. The App Store offers numerous outstanding creative tools which enable people to make music and animations and films and artworks which were almost unimaginable in the 1970s. You can also use apps which teach you to code in a much more helpful and enabling way than the austere computers of my youth. And if you do want to create new apps for Apple devices yourself, the Apple Developer site, dedicated to that purpose, is falling over itself with helpfulness and warm invitations.[26]

PRESERVING THE OPEN, CREATIVE WEB

In terms of the World Wide Web and the internet, we should be worried about technologies or services which build walls around certain parts of our social digital world, or which seek to control or 'curate' the internet for us, or which – at their most insane – suggest that we won't need to look at anything beyond that offered by their own platform. In other words, we need to be worried about Facebook.

The creator of Minecraft, Notch (Markus Persson), famously cancelled a potentially lucrative collaboration with Facebook with the observation, 'Facebook creeps me out'.[27]

It's not a surprise that the super-tinkering creator of the world's most successful open collaborative playspace would be unimpressed by Facebook. I realize that some of you find Facebook a useful way of communicating with friends and you don't want me being 'snobbish' about it. But Facebook's 'walled garden' – even if it has wide walls and many of your friends inside – is all wrong.

When Tim Berners-Lee invented the World Wide Web, the idea was that any piece of online information could link to any other piece, simply and easily, anywhere in the world, enabling the maximum sharing of ideas and experiences. As he explained in his testimony to the US House of Representatives Subcommittee on Telecommunications and the Internet, back in 2007:

> The success of the World Wide Web, itself built on the open Internet, has depended on three critical factors: (1) unlimited links from any part of the Web to any other; (2) open technical standards as the basis for continued growth of innovation applications; and (3) separation of network layers, enabling independent innovation for network transport, routing and information applications.[28]

The Web grew at a fantastic rate because this arrangement meant that there were no gatekeepers, and nobody had to ask anybody for permission to share what they had to say. Berners-Lee notes that today we are so familiar with these characteristics of the Web that we can easily overlook them as 'obvious' or 'just unimportant'. But of course they are not. They have enabled the Web to become the outstanding resource that it is – something which does indeed seem to be forgotten by those who seek to present a 'simpler', top-down, 'consumer'-oriented version.

Explaining the role of the World Wide Web Consortium

(W3C), which he directs, and the general importance of open standards, Berners-Lee said:

> The special care we extend to the World Wide Web comes from a long tradition that democracies have of protecting their vital communications channels. We nurture and protect our information networks because they stand at the core of our economies, our democracies, and our cultural and personal lives. Of course, the imperative to assure the free flow of information has only grown given the global nature of the Internet and Web. As a Federal judge said in defense of freedom of expression on the Internet: 'The Internet is a far more speech-enhancing medium than print, the village green, or the mails . . . The Internet may fairly be regarded as a never-ending worldwide conversation.'[29]

That is why the Web is – and must remain – a universal platform: 'independent of any specific hardware device, software platform, language, culture, or disability', as Berners-Lee says.[30]

The attractiveness of the Web for many people is very much to do with the fact that you can join the conversation – whether at a light level (such as commenting on blogs, or posting pictures on Instagram) or a deeper level (by creating your own site, network or service). It only remains a convivial tool while these possibilities are obvious and centre-stage. If the Web becomes a place where people are not typically creative, where the anticipated mode of engagement is consumption rather than creativity, then it will have become an industrial tool, and its positive potential will be destroyed.

CONVIVIAL TOOLS EVERYWHERE

Of course, the World Wide Web is not 'the solution' to the problems and social needs outlined by Ivan Illich. Indeed, the idea that a combination of electronic hardware and software, applied on a global scale, could be the answer to our problems might seem laughable. But, of course, the Web is not just technology – most importantly, the Web is *people*. Diverse, interesting, creative people, sharing their ideas and pictures and information and stories.

Illich felt that human beings flourish through warm, supportive, personal friendship connections. The Web helps to create these, although when conducted *only* through a screen we might be concerned that this is not the warmest and most natural form of connection. But as we saw in chapter 4, there has been growth in online tools that help people to make connections in real life. And as we saw in chapter 3, people will always want to create networks and experiences around the process of making things, because they like to see and to share the whole fruits of their own creativity, and to feel connected to other inventive people, and to feel part of meaningful, productive social processes which have a past and a future. This urge appears to be timeless and enduring, but we do need to encourage the conditions and tools that will help it to grow.

7

ONLINE CREATIVITY NEEDS BETTER PLATFORMS

So far in this book we have generally seen social media as a good thing. In this chapter we'll consider some of the more critical views. Some of them are relatively predictable, and seem to come from those who have not sought to engage with the culture, and/or have rather inflexible views about its obvious badness; but others, such as the critical philosophical argument made by Jaron Lanier, and the economic critique by Jonathan Taplin, are more worrying.

First of all, let's recall the positive arguments for social media. This is not a definition or a list of the primary features – the kind of thing which appeared briefly in chapter 1 – but rather the reasons why social media tools can be especially helpful for people making and connecting:

- Services such as YouTube, WordPress and Instagram provide users with easy-to-use platforms which enable them to place their creative work (such as videos, songs, writing, or photography) online.

- These services are typically free (or inexpensive) to use.
- Being part of a big, popular platform makes it easier for your work to be found by others.
- The commenting and community facilities enable others to engage with and respond to the content, and help to build relationships, and possibly collaborations, between creators.

Before today's social media services, you could do most of these things online yourself, but it was often expensive or difficult. People like me, in the 1990s, made our own websites by hand, creating both the content and the framework of layout and graphics that contained it. We could interact with others – generally by email – and could even add their work to our sites, manually. But setting up a database-driven platform is not something I'd try to do myself. Therefore the availability of easy, connective and free social media tools sounds like the perfect solution.

FREE PLATFORMS AS EXPLOITATION OF LABOUR

Social media platforms give us a place to share our stuff, and discuss it with others, for free. But this situation can also be stated in rather less cheerful terms: social media companies provide no content themselves, but instead become highly-valued and (in some cases) profitable businesses off the back of the creativity of their users. In this view, the site owners are the lazy, greedy factory owners, whose wealth is built upon the hard labour of thousands of creative workers. These workers generate value, which the owners exploit by selling advertising opportunities, alongside their work, to other businesses.[1]

This does indeed sound like exploitation, and is true from

a macro point of view. But from the point of view of individual users – well, then there are two ways to look at it. For many people, social media platforms are places to communicate and exchange everyday creativity – the kind of thing this book is generally concerned with. For them, this activity is non-commercial anyway. They never hoped or expected to be able to make any financial gain from sharing their photo, video, poem, or witty remark – that's really not the point. In most cases it would be unrealistic to expect any money for sharing this thing, and indeed it's a financial *advantage* that they don't have to pay to have their work hosted online.

Then there's a different group – artists such as musicians and film-makers who a few decades ago could make a living from sales of their creative work. The major social networks have had a huge impact on that – as we will see later. But first let's focus on everyday users exchanging creative bits and pieces in their spare time.

These users are likely to recognize that sites such as YouTube, Instagram and Facebook are able to exist because they are funded by advertising, and typically accept this as part of the deal. In the research for our 'Digital DIY' project in 2016 we interviewed more than 120 makers, many of whom spoke about the value of knowledge and skills-sharing enabled by platforms such as YouTube, and not one of them mentioned advertising. That doesn't mean that ads are not sometimes annoying, but overall and on balance, they are not perceived as a big problem.[2]

I don't mean to support or celebrate advertising: it's not part of my vision of an ideal society. And I certainly don't agree with Chris Anderson's unlikely thesis, in his book *Free* – discussed further below – that a seemingly endless supply of advertising money means that more or less everything can become free.[3] As the means by which, in a capitalist culture, companies are able to offer 'free' services to users, it's a system which people seem to think is okay, although the incredible monopolies of Facebook and Google, which exist to sell people's attention to advertisers, should make us anxious.

The critical argument here can be put in different ways. The writer and consultant Nicholas Carr has said:

> By putting the means of production into the hands of the masses but withholding from those same masses any ownership over the product of their work, Web 2.0 [/social media] provides an incredibly efficient mechanism to harvest the economic value of the free labor provided by the very, very many and concentrate it into the hands of the very, very few.[4]

This formulation seems to pose the problem rather well – although it's not quite correct, as none of the well-known social media services tries to take *ownership* of work away from its creators; typically, the user keeps copyright and all other rights over their work, but provides the site with a licence to reproduce it.[5] And, as I've said, the 'free labour' which is 'harvested' is happily and voluntarily given by users who *want* to share their creative stuff as part of the regular conversation of everyday life. They have no thought for 'economic value' except, perhaps, that they may be glad that sharing their creative work online is not costing them money. So making them sound like slaves in a workhouse is a rhetorical device which doesn't, I think, line up with most people's own experience. After all, if they felt that they were being punished or exploited, they would simply do something else.

Toby Miller puts a similar case much more grandly:

> The pride with which gullible 'MIT-like/lite' subscribers to digital capitalism and the technological sublime wel-

> come the do-it-yourself elements to YouTube is part of the managerialist, neoliberal discourse that requires consumers to undertake more and more tasks for free or at their own cost.[6]

This argument seems to rest on the assumption that making media to share with others is a job of work – a 'task', as he calls it – which is onerous and tiresome. Miller's apparent anger that people would be 'required' to do this 'for free' only makes sense if your view of creative work is incredibly two-dimensional, so that you think that the 'work' of making a video to share with your friends is no different from the 'work' of coal-mining or street-cleaning. It makes sense in the old media model: for instance, if a commercial television station got me to work as a camera operator on a drama series, but refused to pay me, that would indeed seem unfair. But when applying these expectations to YouTube, I think Miller has made a category error. The creative social acts which we see the results of on YouTube are not the equivalent of work, which you would reasonably expect to get paid for. They are more like the act of putting together a photo album, to show to friends, or the act of recording some music that you have composed, so that you can replay it to a fellow enthusiast. If you asked your friend, or some third party, to pay you money for this experience, you would seem rather wacky. And if your friend told you that your creative endeavours made you a 'gullible subscriber to the managerialist, neoliberal discourse', then you might be understandably perplexed.

Of course, it is indeed the case, as noted above, that services such as YouTube do make money by hosting a broad and deep body of content which the content creators often do not get paid for. So the economic value generated by this mass of videos is indeed kept by YouTube. (To be fair, we should note that creators of much-viewed videos can join the YouTube Partner Programme and participate in a revenue-sharing scheme; but this will not be very profitable for the majority of users.) The 'exploitation' argument appears to make sense on the macro level, where we note that YouTube has copies of millions of videos and is (generally) keeping all the money it makes from showing them to eager viewers.

But if we switch back to the micro level again, each *individual* video has a very small value indeed. For instance, by the end of 2015, YouTube had 1.2 billion videos in its library, and took advertising revenue of around US $4.2 billion in that year.[7] So on a crude calculation, the average video is worth $3.50 a year (£2.80 in the UK), or 29 cents (23p) a month. It's not a lot. As a video-maker, I don't mind YouTube keeping that amount. And I'm glad I don't have to pay for hosting videos online myself, which would cost me *more* than that amount. (Since you ask, I do pay £35 a month for the hosting of my websites by a reliable and secure company, without any adverts – as I have done for twenty years – but for videos it's better for everyone if I just stick them on YouTube.)

Furthermore, YouTube has mostly lost money during its lifetime, due to the cost of running such a bandwidth-hungry service. Today it just about breaks even.[8] It will probably become more profitable as time goes on. But delivering literally hundreds of millions of hours of video to people *every day* is not an inexpensive business.

In any case, I have here joined Miller in mistakenly treating everyday users' YouTube videos as economic objects. As already noted, that's surely not the point. Sharing videos with friends, and interested others, on YouTube *really is* parallel to singing songs around the campfire in the evening, when the day's labour is done. Maybe my singing voice is beautiful and I could, if I wanted to, print tickets and ask the people around the fire to pay me a fee, but that would completely change the atmosphere and our sense of mutual understanding. Not every aspect of life has to be 'monetized' – even though there is usually someone, somewhere, trying to extract economic value from any activity.

It's worth noting as well that *between* those people sharing things online with no thought to money at all, and those who want to be paid for their creative works, there's a third zone of people who are happy to put things on YouTube, at no cost and for no direct financial reward, because for them it is a way to build their reputation and recognition which may pay off in a different way later on – when the people who have seen them on YouTube have the opportunity to buy their book, concert tickets, or whatever. Again in such cases, those people are using YouTube but not being badly exploited by YouTube.

In the Toby Miller article I was discussing, he appears to say that the opportunity to share homemade videos with the millions of YouTube users is only the same as the claim that 'You are the star!' made by the host of the old TV show *Candid Camera*.[9] But, for very obvious reasons, these are really not the same thing at all. Are we really going to say that all the people who offer their hand-crafted videos of information and entertainment on YouTube are just the same as the chumps trapped like zoo animals in an old prank show on television? That's just insulting. People exchanging their creative work online are not idiots. Meanwhile, though, Google and Facebook are not off the hook.

DRAINING MONEY FROM THE CREATIVE ECONOMY

In the first edition of this book I followed the above with a discussion of the way that Marxist critics such as Mark

Andrejevic and, more recently, Christian Fuchs have argued that commercial social media services are actually built on a *double* exploitation. First of all it is argued, as discussed above, that they thrive on the unpaid labour of content creators. Secondly, they exploit the 'labour' of all users of free platforms who generate data about their interests and activities as they click around Facebook, watch videos on YouTube, or search on Google. It's true that this does happen – the platforms do make vast profits by putting together all this personal data that they have captured, to show you highly-targeted advertising. It is literally their business model – that is absolutely what Facebook is built to do. But the talk of exploited 'labour' can undermine rather than support this argument. People don't experience their time spent looking at Facebook or YouTube as 'labour' – it is pleasure and recreation, or it might be exploring their serious interests, but it is not 'work'. And the economic value of that activity is, at an individual level, miniscule, and they could not sell it in any other way. So the 'exploitation of labour' argument, originally used much more powerfully to describe the treatment of workers by factory owners, gets bogged down in arguments about whether this kind of language is, you know, silly.

Meanwhile, though, there is actually a devastating case to be made about what the social media giants – notably Google and Facebook, plus Amazon, which is in a different business with similar effects – have done to the creative and cultural economy. That case is powerfully made in the 2017 book *Move Fast and Break Things* by Jonathan Taplin.[10] Before becoming a university professor, Taplin was a tour manager for Bob Dylan, and a film producer for Martin Scorsese, among other things. He is not a digital luddite, though – indeed, he was also an entrepreneur with an online streaming video service, albeit in 1996, ten years too early.

Essentially, the picture that develops from Taplin's experience and research is this. In the latter half of the twentieth century, there was an entertainment and cultural system where people spent money on the things they enjoyed, and advertising also played a role, supporting a system where creative and cultural industries nurtured talent – at least to some extent – and enabled those artists to make a living. We also already know – although Taplin doesn't talk about this so much – that those businesses were ungenerous, and while the big stars became millionaires, middling successes often struggled financially because the music and movie businesses were much more keen on profits and luxurious executive lifestyles than they were on really helping artists and paying them royalties. At the same time, though, those businesses did take on quite a lot of risk, investing in a range of potential talents in the hope that the rewards from the hits would exceed the losses from the flops. So it was a dynamic system with money flowing around in it, and if an artist could become reasonably well known, they could make a good living.

Taplin contrasts this with the change in recent years, where Google and Facebook have arrived like a massive electromagnet and diverted all the money in that system to themselves. The money now comes from somewhat different sources, because these companies have led people to understand that they don't need to pay for creative work because that can be paid for by advertising. This started in earnest in 2004, the year in which Facebook was launched, and Google raised US $1.67 billion in its initial public offering. In the eleven years between 2004 and 2015, Taplin asserts, 'a massive reallocation of revenue – perhaps $50 [US] billion per year – has taken place, in which economic value has moved from the creators of content to the owners of monopoly platforms'.[11]

Note the two key parts of this huge shift. The first is that the money is diverted away from the people who make stuff to the people who merely enable that stuff to be distributed. And the second is that these platforms are effectively monopolies. Both of these things are bad. Although some alternatives exist, Google is basically the one place that people search for stuff, and its YouTube is the one place for online video; and Facebook is not only the one place for informal social networking but it also owns the best-known place for messaging, WhatsApp, and the popular place for picture-sharing, Instagram. Monopolies are worrying because they enable single companies to be much too powerful, stifle innovative competition, and, in this case, ensure that people who actually make creative stuff get a generally raw deal. We might think that this is just what happens in capitalism, but actually, as Taplin shows, monopolies have always been feared – and regulated – by the defenders of functioning capitalist democracies, because monopolies screw it all up. As Taplin observes:

> It wasn't supposed to be this way. The Web's supposed low barriers to entry should have allowed a very competitive landscape, but it never happened. . . . It turns out the internet is very good at creating winner-takes-all scenarios. The growth of monopoly creates a system that does not function the way classical economists believe market economies should.[12]

It's easy to think that Facebook and Google are merely supporting themselves by showing us some ads, which is what magazines and commercial TV have been doing for decades, and to think that they are doing well financially because a lot of us enjoy the useful services of Facebook and Google. But it's less benign than that, as Taplin articulates clearly.

Gathering as much intimately detailed data on you as possible is the creepy heart of their business model. The success of Facebook is a direct consequence of the fact that it has 'built a massive database of the consumer preferences of two billion people'.[13]

Since the 1990s I have loved Tim Berners-Lee's vision of the World Wide Web – a place of freely interconnected ideas, built out of people's passions – and, I guess I loved it so much that I was insufficiently concerned about the ways in which some businesses were finding ways to capitalize on it. The story of Google in its early days – the tale of some plucky geeks who just wanted to make a really good search engine, and, later, a range of other great free tools for users around the world – was beguiling. But meanwhile, as Taplin puts it:

> The goal of Tim Berners-Lee and Stewart Brand – to construct a new platform for democratic communication – had been co-opted by a new cadre of libertarian *übermenschen*, a group of men who believed that they had both the brilliance and the moral fortitude to operate outside the normal strictures of law and taxes.[14]

They mostly *are* men, he's not wrong, and their apparent belief that their massively profitable companies are the solution to social problems is no secret and is indeed part of their marketing. They have developed extremely close relationships with the governments which might otherwise be expected to be regulating them, and developed tax-avoiding regimes which do not suggest that they have a strong sense of contributing to the greater good.

Is this new situation worse than the old situation? To some extent, I would say, Taplin is oversentimental about the old order. As a friend to some of the minority of artists in the 1960s and 1970s who got selected by record and movie companies and benefited from that system, he mourns its loss. He says that Google and Facebook have swept in and grabbed all the money that used to flow around that system, which was flawed but much less badly flawed – and that's basically true. He goes on to say that this shows that Google and Facebook have become the new 'gatekeepers' – which is not quite right. The internet does still enable an essentially gatekeeper-free way for people to put creative work out there, and for the networks of millions of users to collectively select their favourites, even though this process is inevitably imperfect too. *Getting noticed in the first place* is very hard, and the algorithms and filters of Google and Facebook are supremely significant and powerful in this regard. Nevertheless, gatekeeping has definitely shifted away from a tiny elite towards a more democratic and accessible system.

But Taplin is still rightly angry that these people can't make decent money from sales of their creative work. Here's a striking point:

> [Today, broadly speaking,] the only way that musicians can get paid is the same way they got paid in the seventeenth century: rent a room, lock the doors, and make people pay to get in. By 2020 there will be six billion internet-enabled smartphones in the world, and how can it be that the arrival of digital networks composed of billions of music fans has not been a boon to musicians?[15]

Taplin's argument is powerful and worrying because he builds upon solid, practical knowledge, and concern for the livelihoods of real people – and creative makers in particular. He describes the current situation very well, which is therefore depressing, but he is not without hope. 'I think big changes could happen', he writes, 'if we approach the problem of the monopolization of the internet with honesty, a sense of history, and a determination to protect what we all agree is important: our cultural inheritance.'[16] A similar wish to unlock potential, combined with practical anxiety, infuses the work of Jaron Lanier.

JARON LANIER: CREATIVITY UNBOUND

Jaron Lanier was one of the original digital pioneers, and led the field in virtual reality – a term which he is said to have coined – in the 1980s. He is a musician and philosopher, as well as being a computer scientist, and has created all kinds of things from early computer games to cutting-edge medical simulations, and advanced internet applications. In other words, he *really knows what he's talking about*. And you would expect him to be a kind of leading-edge techno-enthusiast. The fact that he isn't, and that he's worried about a particular way in which the Web has developed, means he's instantly intriguing.

Lanier set out his concerns about how the Web was shaping up – in particular the idea of Web 2.0 and social media – and what this means for online creativity and self-expression, in a 2010 book entitled *You Are Not a Gadget*.[17]

TEMPLATE IDENTITIES

The standard positive view of social network services such as Facebook is that they have made it much easier for people to express themselves online, and to communicate aspects of their identities. That was certainly my view, before I read *You Are Not a Gadget*. Explaining the benefits of such easy-to-use sites to my students, I would recall the early days of the Web, in the 1990s, when individuals would use basic tools such as Microsoft Notepad to make their 'personal homepages'. These handcrafted websites were often messy, informal and self-indulgent. As I mentioned in chapter 4, that's certainly how I started: as a rather late early-adopter, in 1997, I learnt how to make an HTML page with Notepad, and lay it out using invisible tables – that's how you got a neat grid-like layout, back in the day – mostly by looking at the source code of other people's pages. (Eventually I got a book, of the *HTML for Dummies* variety.) This was quite laborious, although at the time it was a geeky challenge, and contributing to the internet – contributing to the *actual internet*, with your stuff visible to people *around the world* – seemed wildly unusual and rewarding.

Since those days – well, actually, *during* those days – personal homepages became derided as places where lonely people would write poems about their cats, or post pictures of their favourite biscuits. They came to be seen as rather pointless, narcissistic sites, which in any case were hard to find and didn't help people to link with friends except when they explicitly added links to each other's homepages. And because making graphics yourself was not the easiest thing in the world, homepages were often decorated with random images swept up from around the Web, a mix of garish colours, corny animations, and – horror of horrors! – blinking 'under construction' messages.

So, fast-forward a decade or two and compare this with Facebook, where almost any moderately literate internet user can create a profile. This is so easy to do, and results in a nice, neat set of boxes of pictures and information – it's clearly an improvement. But, Lanier argues, it's not. He puts individual creativity, and self-expression, above all else – and therefore concludes, with a surprising but clear logic, that the diverse, hand-crafted personal homepages of the 1990s were *much* more preferable than the formulaic, template-driven expression of identity pushed by Facebook. It doesn't matter if they were messy, or had an unexpected tone of voice, or lacked a uniform mode of navigation – on the contrary, those are the things that made them *unique* and *special*.

Now, you might object that templates are simply *helpful*. Design templates help users to present what they want to express clearly, avoiding mess or usability problems, and support them to make their material look presentable without having to study the nuances of graphic design. Blogging tools used by writers, such as WordPress, and sites where musicians can share their work, such as Soundcloud, help their users to present the fruits of their creativity in a clear, straightforward and shareable way, by offering a choice of templates (which can be customized to some extent). Whereas those 1990s personal homepages often looked awful, and could be difficult to use, and even the flexibility of MySpace was frequently abused by people who just seemed to want to make a mess. But remember that Lanier is concerned about how individual *identity* is expressed online. We should always be willing to spend a bit of time making a characterful and personal representation of our identity, he implies – we can't allow our very *selves* to be reduced to a template.

This is one of Lanier's key concerns: that digital systems reduce everything to the level of simple bits of information, so that they can be processed. Sometimes, this is fine and necessary: for instance, when we file a tax return, we reduce our working activity to a set of numbers in a database; but everybody knows the difference between real life and the numbers in a tax return. However, he says:

> the order is reversed when you perform the same kind of self-reduction in order to create a profile on a social networking site. You fill in the data: profession, marital status,

> and residence. But in this case digital reduction becomes a causal element, mediating contact between new friends. That is new. It used to be that government was famous for being impersonal, but in a postpersonal world, that will no longer be a distinction.[18]

When we reduce our humanity to fit in with the requirements of a machine (or a database, or a piece of software), Lanier warns, we lose something of ourselves.

To illustrate the point, he tells the story of how European missionaries preserved some aspects of indigenous musical cultures, but 'de-alienated' them – keeping the more familiar sounds, which they would have been most comfortable with, but removing the strange and alien elements that would be necessary for the most rich and meaningful experience to be preserved. He goes on to say:

> Something like missionary reductionism has happened to the internet with the rise of Web 2.0 [/social media]. The strangeness is being leached away by the mush-making process. Individual web pages as they first appeared in the early 1990s had the flavor of personhood. MySpace preserved some of that flavor, though a process of regularized formatting had begun. Facebook went further, organizing people into multiple-choice identities, while Wikipedia seeks to erase point of view entirely.[19]

The uniform nature of Facebook profiles keeps things simple and predictable; but, Lanier reminds us, human beings are worth cherishing because of their rich, distinctive, individual natures, not because they are simple and predictable. 'We shouldn't seek to make the pack mentality as efficient as possible', he writes. 'We should instead seek to inspire the phenomenon of individual intelligence.'[20]

Lanier is concerned that the enthusiasm for online 'collaboration' might sweep away distinctive creative voices:

> There is no evidence that quantity becomes quality in matters of human expression or achievement. What matters instead, I believe, is a sense of focus, a mind in effective concentration, and an adventurous individual imagination that is distinct from the crowd.[21]

I discussed this at some length in the first edition of this book, but ultimately I think the whole issue is rather a red herring. As we saw in chapter 1, writers such as Clay Shirky and Charles Leadbeater had enthused about the power of online platforms to enable people to collaborate.[22] They showed, correctly, that the internet was really good for organizing mass activities where many people could pitch in – as evidenced by Wikipedia, created by hundreds of thousands of people adding many millions of little contributions. This led to the question of whether the same kind of process could lead to mass-collaboration artworks, such as symphonies, poetry, or films. And maybe this will occasionally be done. There have already been, for instance, various mass-collaboration films, assembled from little bits made by different people.[23] But these are essentially novelties. On the whole, everyone knows that 'designed by committee' is not a compliment, and with good reason. We still cherish individual creative voices in creative works.

Wikipedia is rather different. The mass-collaboration process that created Wikipedia worked brilliantly to create an encyclopaedia, because an encyclopaedia is the classic kind of project to be worked on in this way, with millions of people all contributing their bits of knowledge to make up a valuable whole. Their work is highly fragmentary, but that's fine because an encyclopaedia is something you only look at in discrete chunks, and it's not intended to be a work of imagination, or to take you on an emotional journey.

Thousands of people are unlikely to contribute meaningfully to single creative projects. But, if we shift focus, millions of people *do* contribute to the production of whole *landscapes* of creative work. You don't usually get mass collaboration on particular songs, comedy sketches, or beautiful photographs, but what you do get is millions of people – or groups – creating such works and then placing them in the collaboratively curated online landscape. They also work collaboratively – or at least, as on Wikipedia, multiply and simultaneously – on identifying, sharing and commenting on items of note.

PAYING THE CREATIVES

Another strand of Jaron Lanier's critique is about creators getting paid – or rather, not getting paid – for their work. This is in the same area as Jonathan Taplin's critique of monopoly platforms, discussed above, but has different angles. Lanier sees 'Web 2.0' or social media platforms as representing an ideology which says that everything should be 'free' whilst obscuring the losses, costs and profit-seeking motives. For businesspeople, this approach means that online services can be funded by advertising, or other ways to shield the consumer from the direct cost, and for consumers it means that they should reasonably expect to get all creative stuff for 'free'. The consumer point of view is a combination of the old hacker belief that 'information wants to be free', and the spirit of the file-sharing music downloaders in the early 2000s, who argued that the music industry was a vast, greedy profit-machine which deserved a bit of Robin Hood-style redistribution.

The business point of view is represented by Chris Anderson's 2009 book, *Free: The Future of a Radical Price*, which I've mentioned in passing above, and which I'll say a little more about here. Let's start with a bit of background. In 2006, Chris Anderson published *The Long Tail*, an intelligent and readable 'big idea' book, which pointed out that the internet made available the 'long tail' of items – such as music, films and books – which are not currently popular (and therefore not considered to be worth stocking in a shop or library with limited shelf space).[24] Although these things are not in great demand, he pointed out, there will always be someone *somewhere* who wants one, and the number of such items that can be sold on any one day is roughly the same as the number of current 'hit' products likely to be sold on the same day. So a service like iTunes or Amazon can shift just as many almost forgotten, unloved, back-catalogue items as it sells 'Top 10' hits, as it is not limited by high street shelf space. Whilst this latter point made *The Long Tail* a successful business book, it was also good generally on how minority or niche interests could find a home on the internet, and full of interesting examples. We will revisit it in chapter 9. Chris Anderson is also a keen 'maker' – I happened to mention his YouTube video about a radio-controlled blimp in chapter 4. So his follow-up book, *Free*, was quite keenly anticipated. Naïve readers, such as myself, without really thinking about it too much, imagined that it might show us ways in which all kinds of things which we had previously had to pay for, could suddenly become free.

But any commercial item worth having has to be paid for somewhere along the way – and, as it turned out, Chris Anderson didn't have an alternative to that. The book is littered with eye-catching boxes with headings such as 'How can a car be free?', 'How can a textbook be free?', and 'How can air travel be free?' But the answers are either things you've come across before, or – and perhaps this is worse – are things that are more *annoying* than anything you've ever come across before. So, for instance, a 'car can be free' on a familiar system modelled on mobile phone subscriptions, where you get the hardware 'free' at the start but pay a monthly subscription for many months, which at some point covers the cost of the device.[25] It's not free, then, for the old-fashioned reason that you're actually paying for it.

Air travel could be 'free', Anderson suggests, with a slightly more radical version of the Ryanair model, where the price of the ticket is very low, but there are numerous additional costs for such high-living luxuries as taking luggage, drinking water, or going to the toilet; supplemented by income from intrusive and constant advertising and gambling opportunities.[26] So, in a curious double-whammy, you can spoil the planet's environment by travelling within a contained environment which is already maximally horrible itself.

The 'free textbook' example is rather better, since it suggests a model where the textbook *really is* given away free online, but the company makes money by selling handy chunks of it – in the form of easily-printable PDF chapters, MP3 audio chapters, and even flash cards – to students who want a quick fix of the material rather than dealing with a relatively unwieldy online book.

None of these examples is terribly noble, then. The 'free car' offer simply hides the hardware cost within a monthly subscription, and the flight example replaces a straightforward ticket cost with a range of half-hidden 'additional' fees, plus obnoxious ads and gambling promotions. And the textbook example seems to suggest that the genuinely free knowledge offered online should be presented in an inconvenient manner, so that people who want a better experience can be enticed to pay for a more user-friendly version.

Meanwhile, the consumer idea of online Robin Hoodery – why should we poor peasants have to give money to your bloated, prosperous music industry? – collapsed on the hurdle of regular logic, when it turned out that those greedy record companies ceased to be able to support anybody, if nobody was putting money into the system. Today there is a sort-of 'free' model around musicians, which suggests they can still make money from gigs and merchandise, whilst giving music away for nothing (or, at least, not expecting it to be their main source of income). This has indeed, apparently, proved to be a solution for certain artists.[27] But this seems to be only a very small number of them, who were already famous from the old order, or who had a rare lucky break.[28] This is all discussed further in chapter 9. Furthermore, like the other 'free' examples, it seems a rather tawdry solution – why can't a talented musician make a reasonable living from recorded music? Who decided that music recordings had the status of air, which only a greedy and selfish creator would seek to charge money for, whilst an honourable musician's income should more properly be raised via an unhealthy and environmentally damaging journey around the world's stadiums, selling £60 tickets and £30 T-shirts, with an income top-up via corporate sponsorship?

Let's recap at this point, as things can be a little confusing in this new world. There are the people who are saying that stuff online should be freely given away to the citizens – so they must be the anti-capitalists, the people's heroes, right? And there are those who say that it's only reasonable to charge people money for the fruits of creative labour – and so, being money-chargers, they must be the capitalists, yes? But actually, it's not like that, and it's *almost* the other way round.

Jaron Lanier, a musician himself, is understandably distressed that many musicians cannot make a living by selling music any more. But he doesn't weep for the music *industry*. He's not sad that music-biz executives cannot throw wild parties on private jets any longer. Instead, he has a characteristically gentle, humanistic view, that creative people have a right to be paid for their work – living as we do in this kind of society, where people can usually derive an income from the things that they produce. It's not about sticking up for capitalism, however. On the contrary, he is angry that all the money in the system has gone to content aggregators and advertising-distributors: faceless companies which are the opposite of individual creative people.

The solution, he suggests, would be an easy-to-use, widely accepted micropayments system, in which people would pay a little bit of money when they wanted to access a video, song, article, knitting pattern, or whatever, and the money would go directly to the creator of the item. This is not a new idea, and it's just the kind of thing that the internet could make possible. But now that we have become used to a lot of valuable stuff being available for free online, nobody wants to really pay for it.

We might wonder why early internet pioneers did not embed and popularize a system to direct money to creators. The answer, in a sense, is heartwarming, in that the universe of internet users has turned out to be much more creative than anticipated. According to Lanier, in the 1980s, the dominant view was that a system rewarding individual contributions would be elitist, since the makers of creative or expressive material would only ever be a small minority. Today, we know that the interest and capacity for creative expression is widespread, but now it's too late, and the income derived from the dissemination of this material is going to the platform owners, aggregators and advertising brokers (such as Google and Facebook).

To be fair, we should note that this part of Lanier's complaint is similar to that made by people like Andrejevic, Miller and Fuchs, whom I found, earlier in this chapter, to be less convincing and somewhat exasperating. So why am I happy to agree with Lanier, making much the same point? The difference may lie in their tone and spirit. Toby Miller, in particular, seemed to have no sympathy for everyday people making and sharing creative material on social media platforms – they were like the 'gullible' suckers queuing up to be on *Candid Camera*, he said. Jaron Lanier, however, understands them, is one of them, and is on their side. Rather than 'critical' posturing, he's genuinely worried about our current situation and wants to work towards fixing it.

A different way of distributing money more fairly towards the creative people behind creative works is offered by crowdfunding platforms such as Kickstarter and Patreon. These alternatives will be considered in chapter 9.

SOCIAL MEDIA FUTURE: HUMAN, CREATIVE, SUSTAINABLE?

To sum up, then: Jaron Lanier reminds us of the *human* dimension, and the risks, of dealing with computer-based systems. The idea that data, 'information', can take on a life of its own, and perhaps become a 'hive mind' greater than the sum of its parts, might seem appealing, and can make sense for the sifting of information or the organization of tasks. If taken into the sphere of more creative thought or expression, however, it is more likely a new and terrible form of alienation. 'Information' is nothing until processed by human minds, where *meaning* is created. And an over-enthusiasm for combining and aggregating things in digital systems is more likely to create a 'mush' than it is to create something distinctive and amazing – because you need *people* to work on and develop the ideas of others, in the delicate art of creating and making meaningful things.

Lanier can seem to be opposed to all social media, but actually he's perfectly happy with social media tools which allow expression of the individual voice. The systems or services he doesn't like are those which try to reduce the person to the level of the machine, or self-identity to the fields in a database; or which force us to simplify our self-expression, or want to 'mush' it together with the work of others at the cost of distinctiveness and individuality.

I would agree with that. One of the things this discussion has revealed is that social media and the preceding notion of 'Web 2.0' are quite broad terms which take in a number of things, from a list of particular online services to a number of ideologies – some of which are rather vague. This doesn't mean that 'social media' is meaningless – just that we have to be clear what we're talking about.

Lanier is right that the special, valuable, distinctive thing about the internet is that it enables the sharing of diverse, individual voices and their creative offshoots. ('Individual' doesn't have to mean one person, of course – it can also mean the distinctive work of a group of people who operate as a unit.) Before the rise of social media platforms, there was perhaps more individuality and worthwhile 'strangeness' online, but the difficulties of setting up an online presence meant that many people did not avail themselves of this self-expressive opportunity, and the world of separated sites was rather individualistic. Social media have brought us easy-to-use tools which mean that people can place their creative work on collective sites, and can group, rate and comment on other people's items, helping other like-minded users to find other things that they might be interested in.

Nevertheless, the rise of the money-makers is the most worrying aspect of social media. The 'collective allotment' of social media space – as I described it rather optimistically in chapter 1 – is not collectively *owned*. Instead – to repeat the observation made earlier in this chapter – you license your material to a giant media company such as Google, who presents it in a manner over which you have little control, and who can slap unpredictable adverts alongside or even on top of your carefully-made content. This is far from being a perfect solution.

In this case, funnily enough, we can again turn to Wikipedia for an alternative model – not in terms of how the content is produced, but in terms of how the service is funded. Wikipedia carries no advertising and exists as a 'public service' kind of offering run by the Wikimedia Foundation, which survives on donations and grants:

> The Wikimedia Foundation, Inc. is a nonprofit charitable organization dedicated to encouraging the growth, development and distribution of free, multilingual, educational content, and to providing the full content of these wiki-based projects to the public free of charge. The Wikimedia Foundation operates some of the largest collaboratively edited reference projects in the world, including Wikipedia, a top-ten internet property.
>
> Imagine a world in which every single human being can freely share in the sum of all knowledge. That's our commitment.[29]

Some of these attractive goals are also claimed by profit-making companies, of course – Google, for instance, presents its story as building on the vision of its founders 'to organize the world's information and make it universally accessible and useful'.[30] But the Wikimedia Foundation is able to make much more convincing claims regarding its mission to do these good works without charging for access and without including intrusive advertising – or any other kind of ads or sponsorship.

So could we have something like YouTube (not *actually* YouTube, but something offering the same kind of services) offered in the same 'public service' kind of way?

It's certainly possible – in the sense that anything is possible, and helped by the fact that Wikipedia itself would seem to be a pipe dream, if not for the fact that it actually happened and really exists. But I think there are two main reasons why a public service user-generated encyclopaedia is more likely to exist than a public service user-generated video site, unfortunately. (I mean unfortunate that the very good public service encyclopaedia is unlikely to be joined, any time soon, by a very good public service video platform.)

The first is cost. In 2016, it cost the Wikimedia Foundation US $66 million to run Wikipedia and a few other services – including the costs of all servers and bandwidth, software development, advocacy, fundraising and salaries.[31] So that's quite a lot. But in the same year, YouTube was basically 100 times more expensive to run, at a cost of US $6.4 billion.[32] The Wikimedia Foundation can afford to survive, at the moment, because enough users are willing to make donations to support its public service, education-supporting ethos, and because it is mostly serving up lots of text. Serving billions of high-definition videos daily is not something the Wikimedia Foundation could do without a vast increase in income.

The second reason why I would guess that a public service encyclopaedia is in a stronger position than a public service video site is 'worthiness'. The Wikimedia Foundation has benefited from hundreds of thousands of smallish donations from everyday users,[33] as well as from major grant-making foundations, because Wikipedia seems so rare, valuable and worthwhile. A video-sharing site which was basically YouTube without ads (and probably, for some time, with less recognition and popularity), might not seem such a distinctive and admirable proposition.

It is appealing to think that a set of governments, or the United Nations, or something, might see the civic advantage in establishing a publicly-funded video-sharing site, where creative audiovisual work could be developed and shared in an online space free of advertising and commercial concerns. Running a public service version of YouTube for, say, US $500 million (around £400 million UK) isn't even *that* much – it's only 11 per cent of the operating costs of the BBC, for instance.[34] But a publicly-funded version of something that already exists commercially is, to say the least, unlikely – especially in the present economic climate.

We do need to do better, though, with our *systems* for the online sharing of human creativity. The creativity itself is just fine, and flourishing, as we have seen. But the systems are skewing the ways in which this creativity circulates, and are absorbing huge amounts of money which previously went – at least in part – to reward creative people for their work. In a world where everybody else gets paid for their labour, there's no reason why we should have mostly stopped paying for the information, entertainment and culture that we enjoy and benefit from. In recent years we have seen a great rise in people choosing to pay for professional screen entertainment with services like Netflix, and almost half of Spotify's users choose to pay the monthly subscription to use the music service without ads – exceeding 50 million paying subscribers in March 2017.[35] That's a lot. These services are not about the sharing of everyday creativity, which we are mostly talking about in this book, and Spotify is often criticized for paying out less than it might (although when artists complain about the low amounts of money they get from music streaming, it is often because their own record company has kept a big slice). But the point is that people are learning to pay for creative material again, and in the light of the discussions above, that's a good start.

8

MAKING CONNECTIONS AND THE CREATIVE PROCESS: FROM MUSIC TO EVERYTHING

This chapter, and the next one, on music – or, more broadly, on ideas to do with music and what we do with music in the world – is new to this second edition of *Making is Connecting*. I wanted to add something about music because it seemed that a lot of the book's themes play out in the field of music – both music making and music getting-it-out-there – in ways which are intriguing and which we can learn from; and because I've been working more with makers of music in recent years – in particular with my friend Matt Gooderson, who is a great thinker on the creative process; and also, last but not least, because I have started trying to make music myself.

I say *trying*. Making music is hard. In an earlier phase of hobbyist creativity, several years ago, I did oil painting. With oil painting you could spend many hours pushing around the material in the hope of achieving a pleasing effect. I find the same thing with music. Many hours, pushing the material around, hoping to achieve a pleasing effect. And that pleasing bit might just be a nice 10-second bit. *Time* is so central to music. Unlike a painting, which is clearly a *thing*, there in front of you, and remains so, music simply doesn't exist unless it's happening, and then it happens across a section of time, and then is gone again. We take music for granted, but in many ways it is too weird to contemplate. We will come back to this.

I wondered if it might be spurious to have a chapter or two 'on' music, when the rest of the book is basically about creativity in all its forms. Why music in particular? One answer is, as mentioned, that issues around music making and music sharing in the world seem to serve as fascinating archetypes of the challenges and innovations around making and connecting today. Another answer is that it's good to focus in, a bit, on a particular area (although music and how music is made and shared in the world is the hugest 'area' imaginable).

But eventually I realized one particular answer: making music, which humans have been doing for many thousands of years, is a matter of crafting, using the hands and the mind, something that you can't really touch or see – although there are ways of calling it into being, or making it more visible, or tangible – and so making music has a lot in common with making *digital* things.[1] The pleasures and problems of making and exchanging music things are the same as the pleasures and problems of making and exchanging digital things. And this connects us right back to what I was talking about at the start of chapter 4, on crafting the digital (where I said 'producing something for the digital sphere might be thought of as the opposite of the physical, material process of craft work . . . but in my experience, making things to share online is very much a craft process' – and so on).

MAKING MUSIC WAS ALWAYS MAKING CONNECTIONS

We have already, in this book, established the centrality of the creative *process*. It is through the *doing* of making-things that we develop a sense of ourselves as purposeful and inventive, bringing something forth, and *participating* in the world. For instance, in chapter 3, you will recall, Rozsika Parker said that the creative act 'affirms the self as a being with agency, acceptability and potency' – based on a study of women doing embroidery. We similarly saw, from Turney and from Stalp, that knitting and quilt-making were activities which were not ultimately about the creation of new objects but were about the pleasures, challenges and meanings of the process itself. This applies to all kinds of making, and, essentially, explains why people do it – because if they just needed to have the 'thing', they could typically acquire something similar more easily by paying or exchanging. But *making* has a power and a reason of its own.

The furniture-maker Peter Korn, in his reflective memoir *Why We Make Things and Why it Matters*, writes:

> What I have come to see, bottom line, is that creative effort is a process of challenging embedded narratives of belief in order to think the world into being for oneself, and that the work involved in doing so provides a wellspring of spiritual fulfillment.[2]

He arrived at this conclusion from thinking carefully about his designing and making of wooden furniture – or actually, to be more precise, he arrived at this conclusion from the *process* of making a book about that practice – but it applies just as well to making clothes, or scientific ideas, or music.

The 'spiritual fulfillment' mentioned here is not religious, but is based in a sense of identity derived from the *doing* of creative work. He says, 'My intuition from the day I first picked up a hammer was that making things with a commitment to quality would lead to a good life.'[3] Over time, as Korn narrates his story, he comes to understand the relationship between what he makes and who he is. Just before his fortieth birthday, having been a 'working craftsman' for seventeen years, he has an epiphany:

> My own values became clear when I eventually realised that the words I used to describe my aesthetic goals as a furniture maker – integrity, simplicity, and grace – also described the person I sought to grow into through the practice of craftsmanship.[4]

This realization, that the values embodied in his work are also the values he aspires to as a person, nicely summed up in three key words, is striking, and a valuable model. (By which I mean: it might be a good exercise for each of us to write down the three words we aspire towards in our creative work, and to see if this aligns with our life, and sense of identity.)

Korn is happy to have made things which go out into the world – making is connecting for Korn when his furniture provides both beauty and usefulness within people's everyday lives – but the existence of the finished object is clearly much less important than the experience of making it. This also helps to explain, in part, how he can bear to sell the objects and not see them again. It is again clear that the beating heart of creativity lies in the *process* of making rather than in the *product* of that making.

MUSICKING

If we turn back to music, this centrality of the creative process is brought into especially striking relief in Christopher Small's book *Musicking*,[5] which argues that we should understand music as a thing that people *do*. Indeed, Small suggests that we should use the term 'musicking' for this activity – because music itself does not exist. What? That's right: music does not exist.

Of course music exists, you say: I love music. But no. Look – right there on page 2 of *Musicking*, Small says it quite clearly: 'There is no such thing as music'. He explains:

> Music is not a thing at all but an activity, something that people do. The apparent thing 'music' is a figment, an abstraction of the action, whose reality vanishes as soon as we examine it at all closely.[6]

Small quickly gets to work demolishing the idea of music as a thing. Of course, you may have music *recordings*, and there are particular *works* of music, which in the traditional Western approach are captured within *scores*, their written form, which were produced so that the works could be performed at certain *events*. But we don't think about music primarily as an event – unless there is some extraordinary story to tell about an audience's response to hearing some music for the first time – and we don't usually think about it as a *performance*, Small says, even though there's no music until some people perform the work.

This string of surprising assertions makes most sense, as Small would be quick to point out, in the Western classical tradition dominant in music schools in the twentieth century – which Small seems to be coming from – where popular music didn't really count, and the study of music from elsewhere is bundled away under the rubric of 'ethnomusicology'. But in that classical context, at least, he's fascinatingly right:

> The part played by the performers in that perception [of musical works] does not come into consideration; when performance is discussed at all, it is spoken of as if it were nothing more than a presentation, and generally an approximate and imperfect presentation at that, of the work that is being performed. It is rare indeed to find the act of musical performance thought of as possessing, much less creating, meanings in its own right.[7]

In its purest form, this is the view that creativity happens when an individual creative genius lays a golden egg of meaning within a piece of work, a meaning which can later on be unlocked by an enlightened audience. In the case of classical music 'works', which take the form of a score, the most direct way to access this meaning would be to stare at the score itself. But as Small notes:

> One wonders, in that case, why we should bother performing musical works at all, when we could just sit at home, like Brahms, and read them as if they were novels.[8]

These points are all part of showing that music doesn't exist, or at least, not in the way we think it does. Of course, most people do like to *listen* to music. And people like to perform music. Indeed, Small notes, smaller classical works often came into being because they were commissioned as something for the patron and their friends to *perform*, not just to listen to.[9] And, to complete the circle, Small mentions a number of cases where the patron was also a pretty good composer themselves.

So music is not a 'thing' but is an activity – a process rather than a product. That's why, to ensure that we are unable to miss this point, Small talks about musicking rather than music. In a world where we are so used to buying and reviewing and praising or denigrating creative *things*, Small manages an unusual feat in ruling out the things altogether. It is the *act* of making that is important, not the object, he insists. Of course, the objects have importance – we might enjoy or be inspired by other people's objects, and we might hope that they attend to ours – 'but it is the object that exists in order to bring about the action', Small says, 'not the other way around'.[10]

In thinking about creativity, it is hard not to think about creative outputs, and difficult to focus purely on the *doing* of their creation – not least of all because other people's admirable outputs can be a powerful prompt to strive for particular things in our own work. For myself, I know I've spent quite some time trying to reverse-engineer, in my mind, particular elements of other people's paintings and writings and music, so that I might achieve some similar effect. I'm thinking about techniques or methods, but based on looking at finished works. We think about other people's good outputs and we want to make our own good outputs. It's hard to be in the creative moment without having a concern for outcomes.

Part of the problem is the one which becomes crystal-clear in the epiphany moment, somewhere in the middle of *The LEGO Movie*, where Vitruvius tells Emmet: 'Don't worry about what the others are doing. You must embrace what is special about *you*.'[11] Focusing squarely on *just* doing *just* your own thing, is hard. And that's true even when we know that worrying about the outcomes can spoil the pleasure of the process.

There's a bit in *Comedian*, the film which follows Jerry

Seinfeld's return to stand-up comedy, where Seinfeld is chatting with an up-and-coming comedian, Orny Adams, who is worried about whether all the hours he has put into his craft are ever going to pay off. Adams worries that his friends are making lots more money in regular jobs, and have mortgages, and so on. Seinfeld is aghast: 'Are you out of your *mind*? Is there something else you would rather have been doing?!'[12] By which I think he means that Adams is in the perfect spot *already* because he is at least *trying* to fulfil his creative ambitions. For Seinfeld, the *doing* of it is everything, and there could be nothing better.[13]

If we return to musicking, the activity itself is all that matters, but this activity is far from being meaningless, or just passing the time, or an entertainment. Far from it. As Small argues:

> Musicking is an activity by means of which we bring into existence a set of relationships that model the relationships of our world, not as they are but as we would wish them to be. . . . [Therefore] musicking is in fact a way of knowing our world . . . and in knowing it, we learn to live well in it.[14]

So the process of making music is about exploring the greatest way to be in the world, and it is intriguing to find that the furniture-maker Peter Korn arrived at that same view:

> The critical point, as I began to see it, was that all people who engage in creative, self-expressive work – visual artists, craftspeople, writers, composers and others – participate in the same essential human activity as a woodworker does at the drawing board and the bench. None of us enter our studios because the world desperately requires another painting or symphony or chair. But none of us take the work lightly, either, because it requires too much commitment,

> discipline, and risk of failure. . . . We engage in the creative process to become more of whom we'd like to be and, just as important, to discover more of whom we might become. We may make things because we enjoy the process, but our underlying intent, inevitably, is self-transformation.[15]

This is really well put. Nobody really engages in their creative act because the world *requires* another of those *things*, but at the same time, the *activity* has weight and power because it is deeply meaningful to the individual. And it is this investment of meaning and energy which brings about pleasing outcomes – the greatest *things*, where you can see the love and personal effort that has gone into them.

So there is a complete circle here: *passion* for doing good things leads to *actual* good things: they are good because we can see the passion that has gone into them. Brian Eno has said, 'Everything good proceeds from enthusiasm', which sums it up.[16]

TRANSFERABLE LESSONS FROM MUSIC-MAKING PROCESSES

The processes of music-making can offer valuable lessons for makers in other fields. This is especially the case with the modern form of music-making where a piece can be carved out in a studio or on a computer. The previous situation in pop music, where you needed to get any number of musicians playing their speciality instrument into a room where they could be recorded, either one by one or all together, with the original idea for the material – generated by an individual or a collective – being developed by the performers and shaped by a producer and engineer, was complex and collaborative. It was not noticeably like other kinds of art or craft activity, although it was quite a lot like putting on a theatre performance or making a film. But today it is often the case that the creator, producer and performer are all the same person – or a duo or small team collaborating on all these roles – which brings the activity closer to other art, craft and design practices.

I remember being deeply struck by the creative process of pop producers Xenomania, when I read about it in 2009. I knew I liked their output – the oddly-structured fizzy hits of Girls Aloud, and the Pet Shop Boys' *Yes* album – but I didn't know anything about how it was made. Xenomania's drive for perfection, and appetite for redundancy – making lots of things and throwing away most of them – seemed both inspiring and terrifying. Founded by Brian Higgins and Miranda Cooper, and based in a big house in the Kent countryside, Xenomania was – at least in its early days – an 'all under one roof' powerhouse of pop music.

The surprising production process went like this. They would start with a basic riff or idea, and then create multiple melodies; selecting the best of these, they would create a track; and then – rather than being pleased that the track had been 'finished', as others might do – they would put this first version on the shelf and start all over again, making a second, different version, and then another version, and so on. Having produced multiple iterations of the same basic idea, they would compare these tracks and seek to combine the best parts, found within any of them, into a final, ultimate version.[17]

As someone who doesn't like to throw anything away, it was the commitment to quality – to the extent that you would re-do things multiple times and throw most of the work away – that I found most striking. When I had finished writing the first edition of this book, I was pleased that it was done. I read it through, made some tweaks, and added a few bits. But I certainly didn't put this *Making is Connecting* aside and then start writing a whole new second book, also called *Making is Connecting*, and then a third, so that I could select the best one later. So, I *didn't* do that, but I'm not saying that's right. These people are better than me.

It might be comforting to identify some rationale or explanation – an excuse, in other words – for why I wouldn't go about my own work with the same rigour as Xenomania. But I don't have anything very convincing. Is it because they are pop music producers and they need to be very rigorous to achieve a hit? Well yes – but I also would be much happier with a big audience for my book, a hit rather than a flop, so there's no excuse there. Is it because they have time to do it, whereas I don't? Not really – everybody is as pressed for time as everybody else, aren't they?

My only workable explanation is that writing a book takes longer than writing a song: doing the three different versions of a book might take three years, whereas you can do a few different versions of a song in a week. But I still don't do this multiple-versions thing for pages, or chapters, which might be more comparable units, so this excuse doesn't really work either. I like to think that I do something as well as I can, polish it a bit, then put it out there and move on. I'm not feeling sorry for myself – I think many of us are like that. But if you're like me, it's worth knowing that there is a model of much more rigorous creative sifting out there, and it comes from the producers of *Biology* by Girls Aloud, a song which runs through at least four types of verse section before it reaches anything resembling a chorus, and has been described as the best pop single of its decade.[18]

MORE LIKE SCULPTURE THAN PERFORMANCE

If we want to learn about creativity from music-making processes, though, it's never going to be long before we turn to Brian Eno. The musician, producer, artist and thinker Brian Eno rose to fame as the eye-catching synth scientist in Roxy Music, and went on to invent 'ambient music' in solo work while collaboratively producing many hit records and establishing a reputation as a highly articulate theorist of creative practice. In the early 1970s Eno had recognized that technology enabled music-making to be freed from its taken-for-granted association with musicians and musical instruments.[19] He was attracted to making music with synthesizers because they came with no history, no cultural baggage, and there was no established way to play them.[20] This was coupled with his fascination with the ways in which recording technologies had profoundly changed music, discussed in his 1979 lecture 'The Recording Studio as a Compositional Tool'. Eno showed that once music had become something that would be listened to again and again, its creators put different things into it; and once studios moved beyond 4-track recording – which was the norm up to 1968 – through the speedy blossoming from 16 and 24 to 48 and 64 tracks, there were suddenly many opportunities for surprising additions and unusual experiments. Having a surplus of empty tracks meant that in-studio creativity became possible, with tracks being made by adding different layers, thoughtfully, one by one, and extra effects and sounds, which could be included or removed later, so that the making of a recording became more like sculpture than performance. Eno noted that this wouldn't necessarily lead to 'better music', but presented a new way of working, a new way of making music which could be done by people with no traditional musical training – such as himself – and would at least be *different*.[21]

This process led to two new categories of thing. One set of things is all the amazing music made by Eno himself and by David Bowie, Talking Heads, The Gift and others with Eno as collaborator and producer; plus, of course, all the other music made by people who became aware of the same opportunity. Another set of things are all the ideas and insights about the creative process which have arisen from Eno's studio work. Most famously these include the Oblique Strategies cards, created with Peter Schmidt and first released in 1975, a deck of over 100 cards which can be selected at any time during the process of making something. They offer questions or prompts such as: 'Honor thy error as a hidden intention', 'Take away the elements in order of apparent non-importance', 'You don't have to be ashamed of using your own ideas', 'Just carry on', and 'Is it finished?' Obviously, to take a card at random, and to take its message seriously – whatever it is – is quite different to reading a list of them in this book. The card often disrupts the assumptions which have settled around a piece, changes the mood, or offers a new way of thinking about the activity.

Roy Ascott, the 'maverick educator' who had inspired Eno at Ipswich Civic College, had argued that contemporary art should form a 'feedback loop' between artist and spectator, engaging the audience in 'decision-making play' that would generate new meanings and experiences. The Oblique Strategies cards can be seen as a way to short-circuit that process by offering random feedback that the artist can use to shake up their thinking and perhaps take the work in new directions.[22]

Put perhaps more simply, the cards prompt the creator to take a step back from their work and consider it more broadly. Eno explains that it's easy to get drawn into a focus solely on *details*, especially when time is tight or expensive – or both, as in a recording studio – and the cards function to pull the artist out of details-focus and to think properly about what they are doing.[23]

Brian Eno explains that this interest in disrupting assumed processes is why he has enjoyed so many collaborations:

> When you work with somebody else, you expose yourself to an interesting risk: the risk of being sidetracked, of being taken where you hadn't intended to go. This is the central issue of collaboration for me. I work with people who I believe are likely to engender a set of conditions that will create this tangent effect, that will take me into new territory.[24]

Eno's enthusiasm for experimentation and trying out a wide range of things, drawing on as many cultural influences as possible, is infectious. (Any creative person will benefit, I think, from watching any of the many videos of Eno being interviewed that you can find on YouTube.) Eno found that playful and serious experimentation – not just done privately, but when shared more widely – could be a way to see what might later blossom within culture. He persuaded Island Records to let him curate a label of avant-garde and experimental artists called Obscure Records by suggesting it would be a fruitful strategy for innovation:

> In a nod to Anthony Stafford Beer's theories on business organisation and process, he [Eno] proposed that they [Island Records] launch a few things out of the mainstream and watch their progress very closely.[25]

Ultimately, Brian Eno is concerned with creating spaces where we can think and feel differently about things, in art and indeed in politics. And to achieve that, he uses processes or generates experiences where he and his collaborators are themselves knocked into a different state – a different but productive state – which is part of enabling that outcome. Eno has said:

> I think that when you make something, you offer people the choice of another way of feeling about the world . . . and as soon as people start practicing another way of feeling about the world, they actually *create* that world. As soon as you acknowledge the possibility of a certain type of being or a certain type of environment, you create that environment, because you tend to select and nourish those facets of that environment.[26]

Connecting across disciplines, again, we can see that this evokes the statements by Peter Korn (earlier in this chapter) and William Morris (in chapter 2) about creating the kind of world in which we would like to live. In all of these accounts, from different fields, we see that it is through *making* that our sought-after world can be both *revealed* to us, and brought *closer* to us, as we create pockets of an aspirational, visionary world within our own.

9

DOING IT YOURSELF: MORE LESSONS FROM MUSIC MAKING AND CONNECTING

There are issues shared between music-making and digital-making which are central to any discussion of 'making is connecting' today, as the previous chapter established. In this chapter we will see how these especially converge around 'do it yourself' (DIY) practices and opportunities – having the tools to make what you want to make, and getting it out to other people – and ways in which we might support our creative activities, both financially and practically, with the help of communities of supporters. This will lead us to revisit the value of the 'long tail', and to discuss whether new technologies can be especially enabling for women to do creative work on their own terms.

DIY AND MANY POSSIBILITIES

There is a strong 'DIY' ethic around both music and digital creativity. Of course, in either field you can have extensive training in tools and techniques, and some spheres of music favour the virtuoso who has had years of formal and informal learning. But exciting work is often done by people who have just picked up relevant equipment, played around, and had a go. As with most things, it takes *time* to become a skilled user, but starting and getting going are open and possible.

In any sphere there will be seasoned users of the most sophisticated tools, who perhaps inevitably start to think that their forbiddingly expensive and complex equipment is necessary for there to be an acceptable level of quality – but then there will be others, like electronic music artist Grimes, who made her first three albums using Apple's free Garageband software.[1] Her technology was not complex and expensive, but by using it skilfully, and with imagination and experimentation, she was able to make great work.

Like the best kinds of digital creativity, music-making is a 'low floor, high ceiling, wide walls' experience. (This notion, covered also in chapter 10 on platforms for creativity, comes from Mitch Resnick of MIT Media Lab.) The 'low floor' means it is easy to step into the experience and get going. That doesn't mean it is simple or easy – doing it really *well* can be a lot of hard work. The 'high ceiling' means you can take it to a very advanced level in terms of techniques, tools or complexity, like J. S. Bach's *Passacaglia and Fugue in C Minor* – said by Robert Schumann to feature variations 'intertwined so ingeniously that one can never cease to be amazed' – or the endless hours of studio reinvention and remixing by Trevor Horn and colleagues on Grace Jones's *Slave to the Rhythm*. But you don't need to get that complicated. The 'wide walls' mean you can do whatever sort of thing you want – anything at all – a beautiful simple thing with handbells, a symphony, a 12-hour piece to be played with spoons, ferocious heavy metal, or something we've never heard anything like before. Or, you know, *anything*.

So what music can sound like, or what other digital things

can be like, is basically limitless, but there are certain given forms and ways of doing it that you may want to work within. You might want to fit within a recognizable genre – the 8-minute trance anthem, for instance, or the 3-minute comedy sketch – or at least within certain typical limits for a certain form, like a 50-minute album or a 100-minute film. Or you may want to break those expectations too. All such possibilities are available, and you can do all this yourself.

We should note that 'endless possibilities' may not be the ultimate situation for creativity, in music or anywhere else. In an online conversation between music producers Matt Gooderson and David Sheppard, Gooderson explains that he was surprised to hear some of his own recordings from ten years ago, and find that they seemed creatively vibrant, even though made on very basic equipment. Whereas today he has equipment and software that can do virtually anything, reasonably easily, but this can have less striking outcomes. Sheppard responds that infinite possibilities are not helpful. He says, strikingly: 'Limiting the palette on new recordings, from the outset, is, I have found, the only way to navigate the technological and musical torrent that we sit amid today.'[2] So too many possibilities can be bewildering. But it's still good that we can actively choose our palette, and make creative choices.

THINGS, EXPERIENCES, AND MEANINGS

Having no necessary physical form offers a huge advantage: most obviously, with digital material – including digital music – that you can share these things around the world, instantly, at basically zero cost. But this brings other challenges, as humans often like to engage in embodied experiences, and to have physical objects to see and touch.

There is something rewarding about a thing you've made

having an obvious physical existence, and, for instance, it's hard to give an immaterial thing as a very satisfying gift. Hands-on learning, thinking and play can be more powerful than purely screen-based activity, and intangible music can become more powerful when integrated with movement, touch, visuals and experiences. An obvious thing about the relationship between physicality and digital experiences is that there must be many innovations yet to be devised. At the forefront of these developments, we often find game machine producers such as Nintendo, who invented the Wii and the Switch – systems that got people doing all kinds of things with their bodies.

Another clear downside to the intangible and readily shareable nature of digital recorded music is that it is now much harder to charge money for – the obvious and well-known headache for record companies over the past twenty years. (We discussed this as a purely bad thing in chapter 7.) For artists themselves, the internet meant that a record company was no longer necessary for distribution of their work, but they still faced the often unwelcome but interesting challenge regarding how to make money in a digital world. And they have been quite inventive. When the record company is bypassed altogether, artists can sell material directly to their fans; but today's music-lovers might be reluctant to pay much for some MP3s which they could probably access for free anyway. So then we get a new range of responses to this situation, where live gigs, merchandise and luxuriously packaged vinyl editions turn out to be where the money can be made, as long as you have some good material and are able to get noticed.

The diversity of ways in which music can be made physical can be seen in the range of products offered by creative people on Kickstarter. In Kickstarter terms, these are the 'rewards' offered to those who have 'invested' in enabling a thing to be made. Often the digital music file will be the lowest-priced item. Larger sums can bring attractively packaged vinyl and CD editions, posters, clothing, booklets, and so on – things that can bring greater engagement with the world of the artist through touch or reading – and at the most expensive end are live happenings – things you can *experience* – such as a small 'masterclass', or an intimate concert, or a meal and conversation with the creator.

In one case that I found especially memorable, singer/songwriter Sam Lee offered the most generous of his crowdfunding investors – those paying £250 or more – this opportunity in the English countryside:

> Take advantage of Sam's knowledge of edible and medicinal plants to join him for a songful and edible walking journey [... and then] accompany Sam on a dusk journey into the springtime woods to hear nightingales and experience the true magic of these nocturnal songsters. Dinner cooked by Sam is included. [This] will be a late night event which will end after midnight. Includes a signed CD.[3]

The cheapest thing on offer is a download of Sam's new album. At the opposite end of the spectrum, and costing more than twenty times as much, is this unique experience with the artist himself – something that you could never download: in a beautiful natural setting, with other people, singing together, listening intently to the sounds of the forest and the song of the nightingales.

That experience nicely illustrates this maxim from Kevin Kelly:

> The internet is this huge copying machine – that's what it does. How do you create things of value, if anything can be copied indiscriminately? I think the answer is that the

> things that become valuable are the things that *cannot* be copied.[4]

I love that quote because it sets up, simply and neatly, a common and fascinating challenge faced by artists, creators and companies today – how to create something that people will truly value, and will be willing to pay for, in an age where you can download so much good stuff for free. We seem to be implying here that these things will be *experiences* that cannot be conveyed over the internet – which is often the case – but as Kelly points out, you can have unique and tailor-made things online, or live and interactive online experiences, or bespoke individual coaching, which happen to be delivered online but which still 'cannot be copied'.

Cyrus Bozorgmehr has written that this is a paradox:

> 1. Physicality establishes that bond between us and the experience we seek. Holding something, paying for something, mounting it on a shelf – all these actions invest inanimate objects with meaning and bonds us into an understanding of its value. Hence 'things' are important.
> 2. Possessions have been superseded in value by experiences. Recent studies demonstrate people would rather purchase an experience than a new possession. Hence 'things' are no longer important.[5]

How can things be both important and unimportant? I think really, we like some things and we like some experiences, but what really counts is the *meaning*. Pondering how to save the music world from the trap where people just expect music to be free, Bozorgmehr suggests:

> It's about reinvesting the acquisition of music with drama and excitement – creating a wider narrative and a sense of

> mystique that then manifests through increased emotional value.[6]

The loss of 'drama and excitement' in finding and getting new music is certainly what is mourned by older music fans. But perhaps this is what services like Kickstarter bring back – a sense of being on a *journey* with an artist, with whom you have some *connection*, and that you are a part of their unfolding *story*.

MAKING A LIVING WITH '1,000 TRUE FANS'

Kevin Kelly, mentioned above, also proposed a memorable model of how musicians – and all other kinds of creator or artist – could make a living in the digital age, in a blog post called '1,000 true fans', first published in 2008, and revised in 2016.[7] The key point of this much-discussed piece is that an artist only needs a certain number of dedicated fans – the sort who will buy everything they do, including fancy special editions, and will travel some distances to see them speak or perform – in order to make a living. In the simplest formulation, if you can get $100 from 1,000 people then you have $100,000.

> Here's how the math works. You need to meet two criteria. First, you have to create enough each year that you can earn, on average, $100 profit from each true fan. That is easier to do in some arts and businesses than others, but it is a good creative challenge in every area because it is always easier and better to give your existing customers more, than it is to find new fans.
>
> Second, you must have a direct relationship with your fans. That is, they must pay you directly. You get to keep all of their support, unlike the small percent of their fees you

> might get from a music label, publisher, studio, retailer, or other intermediate. If you keep the full $100 of each true fan, then you need only 1,000 of them to earn $100,000 per year. That's a living for most folks.[8]

Kelly is quick to admit that all kinds of variations may be needed to this crude sum. Maybe you can only realistically expect to be getting $50 a year from your best fans, say, in which case you need 2,000 of them. That's still okay, though. Most strikingly, there is the question of what it costs you to deliver the artistic experience to the generously-paying fan. Having 1,000 true fans who collectively spend $100,000 on your work is magic, but if the cost of making, showing and/or delivering that work to them comes to $100,000 then you're still ending up with zero. This is the familiar tragedy of Kickstarter, where a creator is amazed and delighted to get $250,000 'investment' – 'I'm rich!' – but then realizes that the cost of simply making and getting all that stuff to thousands of investors is going to be at least $250,000. They will have gained reputation and experience which might be invaluable, and more profitable, when it comes to their *next* project, but the money, after this first project, has come in at nothing.

Getting a high level of *profit* – in other words, money to live on – if you are putting on an elaborate theatre production, or making large ceramic sculptures, is going to be really hard. To be keeping most of the money spent by fans, you need purely digital outputs, which you can make ideally without leaving the house, and which you can sell directly over the internet. Writing, music and software are the most obvious contenders, and perhaps animation or video. But we have already established that people are unwilling to spend much on downloadable experiences, and crave more physical stuff. As we have seen, the typical list of Kickstarter 'rewards' begins with some cheaper downloadable things, which might be sold to a few thousand 'standard' supporters, and a small number of distinctly personalized, intimate and expensive things, sold to a 'superfan' elite.

Since most fans are not the kind of superfans who would spend more than $100 a year on a particular artist, you probably need a lot more than 1,000 of them. The ease with which you can get good stuff for free online has, I guess, changed expectations, so that spending as much as $20–$40 a year on the work of a beloved artist now seems like quite a lot.

But let's try not to get too hung up on the numbers. The '1,000 true fans' argument is essentially intended as an encouraging one for today's creators who can make things and sell them directly to people via the internet, without all those publishers and distributors in the middle, taking huge percentages of the money. Kelly knows that we are aware that superstardom is almost always unattainable, and seeks to remind creators that it's no longer such a binary stardom-or-nothing game. With thousands, rather than millions, of fans 'you can make a living – if you are content to make a living but not a fortune'. In the social media age, having a few thousand followers is something we can picture:

> A thousand customers is a whole lot more feasible to aim for than a million fans. Millions of paying fans is not a realistic goal to shoot for, especially when you are starting out. But a thousand fans is doable. You might even be able to remember a thousand names. If you added one new true fan per day, it'd only take a few years to gain a thousand.[9]

Kelly seems to appreciate that the maths on just 1,000 fans might not quite work, but says:

> It's about an order of magnitude. [This approach says] you don't need a million fans to make a living, if you have direct contact with them. You don't need even a hundred thousand. You need in the thousands.[10]

He also notes that this approach is not for everybody – developing and maintaining engagement with a community of fans on social media takes a lot of work, and not all artists would want to put in that amount of time on that kind of activity.

It might seem that the promising argument that you only need 1,000 'true fans' to make a good living just unravels entirely. It was, perhaps, a simplified way of expressing something positive, which turned out to be a bit *too* simplified. And because it sounded so positive, we feel doubly disappointed. Getting $100 profit from each superfan, of whom there needed to be 1,000, turns out to be just too hard. It's actually easier to think of smaller amounts from a wider pool of people. If you can get just $5 from 10,000 people, plus $10 from 5,000 people, you've reached Kelly's $100,000 by a gentler path. And these $5 and $10 items could all be downloads. Getting those numbers is still not easy, but I think it's easier to picture, and offers a route for a moderately successful but perhaps still rather experimental artist to make a living, without needing conventional superstardom and without needing 1,000 superfans.

BUILDING SUPPORT BY GIVING AND ASKING

Amanda Palmer, rock star and enthusiastic early-ish adopter of online communities and crowdfunding, has set out some further ideas on how to get engagement from a particular, dedicated constituency. Before her music career took off, Palmer used to perform as a 'living statue' in Harvard Square, Cambridge, Massachusetts. Wearing a wedding dress and with her face painted white, standing on some crates, she was the 'eight-foot bride', who would come alive and hand a flower to anyone who stopped to give her money. People would sometimes shout at her, 'Get a job!', but Palmer knew, as she says, that she *had* a job. She was *doing* it.[11]

She discovered that the money was steady, and much better than her previous $9.50-an-hour work in an ice cream parlour.

> The consistency of the income really did amaze me. If the weather held, I could count on making about $40 to $50 an hour from random people walking by and making random decisions to give me a random amount of money. How was it possible that it was so predictable?[12]

She asked that question on Twitter, but the responses of economists were not especially clear or memorable. Palmer herself reduced it to a simple conclusion:

> *Given the opportunity, some small consistent portion of the population will happily pay for art.*[13]

And she finds that it doesn't matter if *most* people have no interest in her work, as long as *some* people are willing to pay attention, and a reasonable fraction of those might even like to pay.

Her approach is very much about collective and mutually supportive activity, and having the courage to ask for help. Palmer explains that although she has been called the 'Queen of DIY', she has no interest in actually doing everything herself. 'I'm much more interested in getting everybody to help me.'[14] She therefore distinguishes between two forms of DIY:

> 'Minimal DIY' is the kind of DIY where you literally try to Do It Yourself. The emphasis is on total self-reliance and individualism.

> Don't have a huge budget for food/can't afford takeout/have no kitchen? *Just buy a box of ramen in bulk and cook it in the coffeemaker you got for $5 at a yard sale.*
>
> Can't afford to hire a full choir of people? *Record your own voice fifty times, singing slightly differently at different spots in the room.*
>
> Car runs out of gas on a long stretch of road? *Grab the empty canister out of your trunk and start walking, sucker.*
>
> Then there's 'Maximal DIY', which is more about expansion and asking. The emphasis is on collectivism; you throw the problem out to your circles to see what solutions will arise.
>
> Don't have a huge budget for studio food? *Ask if anyone local feels like helping/cooking/bringing you leftover food from their job at the bakery.*
>
> Can't afford to hire a full choir of people? *Send out a blog and have your fans come in and sing with you. They may sound amateur, but it'll be fun, and people love being on a record.*
>
> Car runs out of gas on a long stretch of road? *Put your thumb out. Someone will eventually give you a lift.*
>
> As you can see, the underlying philosophy is actually the same: Limitations can expand, rather than shrink, the creative flow. Minimal DIY doesn't rely on trust; it relies on ingenuity. Maximal DIY relies on trust *and* ingenuity. You have to ask with enough grace and creativity to elicit a response, and you also have to trust the people you're asking not to ruin your recording session, not to poison your food, not to bludgeon you with a hammer as you sit in their passenger seat.[15]

Palmer's collective approach is about achieving her *own* objectives, which might appear potentially selfish – a manifesto for exploiting the goodwill of her adoring fans. But it is clear that Palmer, at other times, goes to some lengths to help others. So, as we saw at the end of chapter 2, creative individualists can thrive when supported by a network of supportive friends who are also, in other moments, creative individualists themselves.

This only works when time has been spent on *building* that supportive community – through engagement and conversation and generous giving – *before* anything is asked for. Palmer explains with a story told by her yoga teacher:

> Since ever, in China, bamboo farmers have planted baby bamboo shoots deep into the ground. And then, for three years, nothing happens. But the farmers will work, diligently watering the shoot, spreading hay and manure, waiting patiently, even though nothing is sprouting up. They simply have faith. And then, one day, the bamboo will shoot up and grow up to thirty feet in a month. It just blasts into the sky.
>
> Any small, sustainable artist-fan community works like this. Crowdfunding works like this.
>
> There's years and years of authentic work, tons of non-monetary exchanges, massive net-tightening, an endless collection of important moments. Good art is made, good art is shared, help is offered, ears are bent, emotions are exchanged, the compost of real, deep connection is sprayed all over the fields.
>
> Then, one day, the artist steps up and asks for something. And if the ground has been fertilized enough, the audience says, without hesitation: *Of course.*
>
> But it isn't magic. That first part can take years. Decades.[16]

Inevitably, building a base of followers who both love your work and feel that they know and trust you as a person is time-consuming and takes a lot of effort. Engaging with an online (and real-world) community of fans involves a two-way process – perhaps you can't deal with every comment and suggestion, all the time, but it should at least look like you are *trying*. This is not for everyone, as Kelly and Palmer agree. A sense of personal connection and even some intimacy has to be cultivated. As Palmer observes:

> Effective crowdfunding is not about relying on the kindness of strangers, it's about relying on the kindness of your crowd. There's a difference.[17]

There are various ways that this support can be leveraged, in different crowdfunding models. Amanda Palmer moved on from Kickstarter to Patreon, where instead of an all-or-nothing race to get a large amount of money for one project, artists ask their followers to promise small, consistent amounts of money every time they make a new song, comic, video, or whatever kind of thing they produce. Other such services may rise and fall. But all of them rely on trust – and their chances of success are closely aligned with the extent to which they seem to be delivering a 'real' and 'genuine' service.

Whilst all this is apparently about raising money, it is ultimately about how we can create and support a sustainable ecosystem for creative people to make a living in a predominantly digital world. Palmer suggests that we will need to 'create a world in which people don't think of art just as a product, but as a relationship'[18] – which is okay for some, but having to build and sustain all those 'relationships' can be an unwelcome development for some creative people. Then again, art was never really just 'product' – art and creativity have always been about ideas and relationships.

THE LONG TAIL REVISITED

Chris Anderson's 2006 book *The Long Tail*, which I mentioned in chapter 7, inspired lots of people with its clear articulation of the value of the huge 'long tail' of items that are – or can be made available – online. The phrase refers to the incredibly long tail end of a chart which shows the current sales or attention attracted by cultural products such as music, books, or films. On the left of this chart you have the highest point, with the current 'hit' items which are getting thousands of sales, views or listens today. There are only a small number of hits at any one time, and the curve quickly goes down through the moderate current successes and then bottoms out with literally millions of things which are mostly not being enjoyed by anyone much at the moment. That's the long tail. You've probably got things in there. Any of my YouTube videos, for instance, are deep in that long tail. My most popular video has been one called 'Participation culture, creativity, and social change', with 25,100 views as of November 2017. Sounds okay, but in its nine-year life that's only eight views per day. Maybe nobody will watch it today. But a few people might watch it tomorrow. The long tail is full of things like that, including items that were hugely successful in the past but which are mostly forgotten now. There may be some things that haven't had much attention *yet* but will have a surge later, probably when their creator gets noticed for something else. Typically, of course, the trend over time is down.

But the long tail doesn't have to be seen as old things and failures. The long tail is *exciting*. The edgy and experimental, naturally, live here. All the new things that are brilliant but which haven't become part of the mainstream live here – which is pretty much everything that can really claim to be cool.

Chris Anderson is mostly remembered for highlighting the *economic* value of this long tail: if you can sell a vast catalogue of digital stuff without having to worry about shelf space, you can make just as much money from the millions of mostly-unwanted things as you can from the bestseller chart of much-in-demand things. Anderson was also keen to highlight the cultural and creative richness amongst all the things that don't happen to currently be hits. A decade on, this point only seems even more pressing and vital to me. It's about the immediate availability of a much more diverse range of things made by all kinds of people. It's got to be much better than if we *didn't* have that. Down in the long tail, life is messy and imperfect, but full of good stuff.

Over time – particularly since *The Long Tail* book was quite a hit in itself – people have sought to show that the idea doesn't really work. They like to point out that we still have big hits in popular culture – in some fields, bigger hits than ever before. (This is the approach, for instance, in a 2017 article in *The Economist* subtitled 'Forget the long tail').[19] But the persistence of big hits doesn't show that Anderson was wrong: *The Long Tail* clearly acknowledged that there would always be bestsellers and blockbusters, but was about how the previous hits-or-nothing culture had changed into a hits-and-everything culture.

Others have pointed out that our choices of music, video and writing increasingly come to us via a small number of huge near-monopoly empires such as Google, Amazon and Apple, which represent the opposite of a long tail of distributors or sellers;[20] and they point out that the biggest hits of all are typically financed by a handful of mega-rich corporations such as Disney and Netflix, representing the opposite of a long tail of producers.[21] None of this makes the 'long tail' argument wrong in terms of artists and their work, however. Everybody agrees that there has been an explosion of creative content and that we can now access a vast array of things made by many and diverse people. The distributors of this work, such as Google, Amazon and Apple, have followed the 'long tail' logic – which, to be fair, they invented – by making money from both the small body of big hits *and also* the enormous long tail of everything else.

Recent studies of major tranches of data have found that the availability of a vast array of material online – both popular and not-popular things – benefits, in terms of sales or downloads, the niche items more than it benefits the hit items.[22] This is evidence that, although we still live in a world with big hits – which is perhaps inevitable, and is not really a problem – it is also true that the more unusual and homemade music, films, writing and software are finding more of an audience. The undeniable good thing about the long tail is that it's *always* going to be much better for us to be in a world where almost anyone can make and publish their own creative stuff.

The problem, arguably, comes with the question of whether anyone will ever *find* your amazing stuff. The troubling view on this appears in the same 2017 *Economist* article, and at first it looks like they've identified what's *really* wrong with the long tail:

> Despite all these available choices, technology increasingly shapes what humans select, steering them towards what is most popular and most distracting. . . . Until recently [the success of hit items] was seen as a natural consequence of the physical limits on production and distribution. It now turns out that – even in a potentially unlimited digital marketplace – social networks, rankings, recommendation algorithms and the like focus people's attentions on just a few items in the same way. The story of mass entertainment in the internet age is a paradox. Technology has given

> people too many choices, and then instantly relieved them of the need to make them.[23]

In some cases or on some platforms – looking at you, Netflix – this may be more or less true. But research has shown that the best recommendation algorithms are those which offer some unusual and surprising items in with the comforting and familiar.[24] And on the proper long tail platforms, such as YouTube or even Twitter (when used to link to good stuff hosted wherever), users can indicate approval and can recommend things to their networks, a social recommendation system that no sensible algorithm would want to get in the way of.

The powerful thing about the long tail is that there is always the *potential* to be moving up to bigger audiences or bigger conversations. Creators do have to work hard to get noticed, it's true, but there are ways of doing that, and there are many millions of people online eager to see something new and engaging. Or to be more specific, there are a certain number of people online who are interested in *your kind of thing* and would be pleased to see this new thing from *you*.

So although Disney may have worked out a pretty reliable way of getting incredibly big profits from incredibly expensive movies, that has nothing to do with, and makes no difference to, the kinds of homespun or small-scale creativity that we're talking about in this book. For us, it's great that we can get our stuff out there, and that there are ways of connecting with like-minded others and having a conversation about it.

For instance, digital music specialist Robert Strachan notes the huge number of amateur music-makers online, who use platforms such as Soundcloud, Reverbnation and YouTube to share and discuss their work. He cites a 2006 study of online music-making communities by Miikka Salavuo, which found that

> respondents framed their involvement within such networks in terms of affirmation, collaboration, sociality and the opportunity to get feedback on their work. Here, just 10 per cent named the 'economic benefits, such as obtaining a recording contract or becoming famous and making money through offering songs, as important factors for their participation'.[25]

For these people, the long tail is where they build supportive communities, and the question of whether a business somewhere else is having hits is irrelevant.

Ultimately, the great power of the long tail lies in its capacity for *inspiration*. This is partly because it's such a rich, diverse and enormous mix of stuff. So many ideas, which people have not only had, but also done something about. Some of that stuff is not of amazing quality, for sure. But that's also a reason why the long tail is inspiring: it contains things that are brilliant, which you can aspire to be as good as, and it contains things that are humdrum, which you can already do better than. And I think that's helpful. I explained in chapter 4 about how I decided to start making videos for YouTube because I had seen a video by a famous author which wasn't very good,[26] so my prompt was literally 'Oh, I can do better than *that*'. There are many accounts of creative people who felt emboldened to start making things – or to show what they could do publicly – because they had seen a public display of something which they thought was less than amazing. So that thing, itself, was not inspiring, but it played an inspiring role in someone's thinking.[27] On other occasions, of course, we might be inspired by something that is genuinely brilliant, which challenges us to see if we can reach similar heights.

It's this vibrant long tail which, for instance, enables independent creative women to become visible on their own terms, as discussed next.

CREATIVE WOMEN ON THEIR OWN TERMS

In a rich example of Michel Foucault's principle of power/resistance – where repression of something prompts an eruption of contrary brilliance – in the traditionally rather male-dominated spheres of digital-making and music-making, we find women doing brilliant and innovative things.[28]

Now I don't want to be a naïve and patronizing man, 'explaining' how things are all different nowadays for women. Most of the accounts from women that I've read or seen begin from rather the opposite point – that sexism in the music industry has not gone away (although things have, of course, changed over time). Indeed, this dismal situation has typically been a key motivation for women to strike out on their own and control all parts of the process themselves – not only music production, but also promotion and distribution. And at the same time, as discussed at the start of this book, we have seen a rise in appalling misogynist abuse online, especially directed at women who strive to be independent. So it's far from being a wholly positive environment. Nevertheless, the inspiring examples of women using new technologies to build their creative lives and share brilliant work are definitely worth highlighting. I guess I must refer again to the world as simultaneously piles of good things and piles of bad things, as on page 6 of this book. If the bad things stopped us talking about the inspiring things – the things with potential to change how things currently are – then we would be in a much worse place.

Developments in music-making technology mean that would-be music producers, especially at the electronic, dance and pop end of things, can now create and mix whole polished tracks at home. It's a hobby you can easily spend hundreds of pounds on, but is now far cheaper than when you had to hire a studio, a producer and an engineer, all handsomely paid by the hour. The DIY 'at home' approach also means you can specifically avoid the hassles associated with the potentially sexist studio environment. You can learn skills from the staggering number of often very good YouTube tutorials on recording, mixing, mastering, equipment, hardware and software.[29] And of course, music can be shared, distributed and sold online, straightforwardly, and the same online space is where you can promote and talk about your work, yourself, without expensive marketing costs or advisers.

These opportunities are open to all, basically (as long as you can work out how to access the internet and some basic music-making kit, which means, at minimum, an iPad or other tablet, or – at a bit of a push – a smartphone). Some smart women have seized this chance with particular vigour. I already mentioned Grimes, who started making music with free software, bending technology to her will. Grimes said in 2017:

> I think it's really great that there's so much new software and hardware out there for musicians. We're hearing from a much more diverse range of people. It's democratizing music. I think we're probably still ten years out from seeing the real change. I mean, the music industry is still controlled by white men and rich people.[30]

The wider context, as noted here, changes slowly. Little Boots, the artist name of Victoria Hesketh, has written powerfully about the pressures on female artists to conform to stereotypical looks and behaviours,[31] and about how the male-dominated industry, whilst changing in some good ways, can still be shamefully sexist.[32] For these reasons she walked away from a major label and founded her own, On Repeat Records, with her friend Lauren Verge, an artist manager, DJ and musician. I interviewed Victoria for this book. She reports that overall her move to independence has been a very positive experience:

> Setting up my own label and being able to maintain creative control of my output, both musical and of the project as a whole, has been a hugely empowering and liberating process. I now have complete creative control of everything I do. I can be much more reactive and direct with my fans, and I can choose what I want to focus on, when and where.[33]

She acknowledges that she learned a lot from being on a major label. The label was able to fund greater marketing efforts and could get her work seen by new audiences, and had access to lucrative 'sync' opportunities (getting an artist's music used in adverts or films). Being independent, by contrast, she says:

> I had to learn very quickly how to not just be an artist but run a business, in a way that allowed me to have creative freedom but also to function and fund my output, which meant motivating my fan base and particularly engaging my superfans in new and meaningful ways. The internet, and easier access to home production and release methods, means that there is an extremely saturated market of new music, and so it's harder than ever to break through and be noticed. But I don't believe this is always a bad thing, as it forces creators to think differently and challenges you to stand out from the crowd.

Despite the inevitable pressures and challenges of doing it all herself, Victoria says, 'I couldn't be happier with the way I create and run my business now. I feel in control and confident I can more or less create and release whatever and whenever I want.' Another brilliant and multi-talented artist, Emika, also felt compelled to establish her own label, Emika Records, in order to be fully in control:

> The sexism in music breaks my heart but I am coping with my sadness and producing anyway. Running my own label gives me a lot of security and freedom to produce music without making any sacrifices. I can cope with sadness because changing the world is more important than how I feel inside. I love what I do so much, that the passion and fire will always burn down all the negativity which I am faced with.[34]

So here overall we have a positive story, about how new digital technologies have enabled bold and brilliant women to leapfrog the constraints of a male-dominated industry, but at the same time we have the depressing story about that unreformed industry and the wider context of how female artists are treated. These things are changing, but slowly. The DIY route is not easy, but it does means that a lot of old-school power can be circumvented.

Beyond the music-making world, we find that women (and some men) are increasingly speaking out about sexism in the tech industry, and organizing to overcome it.[35] They are also starting and running their own outstanding creativity-building companies, such as LittleBits, founded by Ayah Bdeir, and Technology Will Save Us, founded by Bethany Koby. In the public and private makerspaces where we might expect innovation and new ideas to flourish, there can be a strong 'male-dominated' presence, and aesthetic, as documented by Sarah Davies in her book *Hackerspaces: Making the Maker Movement*.[36] But again, where there is an exercise of dominant power, there is also resistance, and feminist makerspaces – as well as more generally diverse and accessible creative environments – have begun to emerge.[37] As in music, the preponderance of the conventional and conservative set of things prompts us to imagine delightful and inspiring alternatives. That's not as good as if we were living in a properly egalitarian and respectful utopia already, of course, but it's exciting to be establishing new things, and finding colourful, inclusive and antisexist ways to support creativity – which, as it happens, is the subject of the next chapter.

10

PLATFORMS FOR CREATIVITY

For all of the reasons outlined in previous chapters, I believe that we need to develop more, better, and more inclusive opportunities for people to explore their creative abilities in everyday life – and to exchange ideas, have creative conversations, and inspire each other.[1] In the years since the first edition of this book was published, I have adopted the term 'platforms for creativity' to point to any and all kinds of events, spaces, environments, tools, or toys that might enable people to take some steps into the world of creativity. Often I am thinking of platforms that anyone can access – ideally – but you can also have platforms that are particular to certain groups or workplaces.

'Platforms for creativity' are not necessarily online, though they could be. The value of a platform might be enhanced through some hybrid of offline and online activity. They can be big or small. An imaginative programme of events and interactions across a network of museums might be a very large platform for creativity. Two people tinkering with a handful of LEGO would be an example of a very small platform. These platforms, whatever their size or type, are about offering people opportunities to creatively express themselves. Platforms for creativity can help people to connect with each other and build shared understandings. Over time, they can potentially contribute to social change, community resilience, and sustainability.

Platforms for creativity typically present an *invitation* to do something. This activity can be something very simple, but the fact that a platform has been created for it tends to make it more meaningful. A good example of this is the Global Cardboard Challenge. It's a very straightforward idea: the Global Cardboard Challenge invites you to make something out of cardboard, on a particular day. You might do it with others, and you are encouraged to share pictures of the activity online. But that's all. Clearly, this is very simple. It's barely an idea at all. Anybody who wants to make something out of cardboard, you might observe, can do that anyway, any time. The thing that makes it magic is that people have been *invited* to do it, as part of some larger shared project – a 'global challenge'! – and with an inspiring starting-point (in this case, the online video 'Caine's Arcade', the true story of a nine-year-old boy who made a whole world of arcade machines out of cardboard).

Other platforms offer similarly open, unspecific invitations. Online, YouTube invites people to fill it with videos about anything. Wikipedia invites articles about whatever you like. Minecraft invites you to build anything you can imagine within its world.[2] Offline, knitting groups invite people to come together and knit. Makerspaces invite you to tinker and make whatever you fancy with 3D printers, electronics, wood. Forward-looking libraries open their doors to people who like to create together.

All of these are broad and unspecific invitations – things

you could probably do anyway and elsewhere – but it's the particular *invitation* to share an experience with others, with a simple bit of framing to give it meaning, which makes it an actual *thing* that people like to do together.

So when we think about platforms for creativity, we should think about how they engage people – in terms of both minds and bodies – and the materials or environments that are offered, as well as how the invitation is framed, and the use of inspiring prompts, things, or people. Doing all of this thoughtfully means that we can develop opportunities for people to be expressive and creative, and consequently help to ensure that we live in thriving communities of people who are engaged with the world around them. We can help people to recognize that they can make and shape their own worlds, and do not merely have to consume stuff made by others. It is in this way that platforms for creativity can be fun and nourishing, and also vitally important for society and culture.

SUPPORTING CREATIVE IDENTITIES

There are a number of theoretical models of creativity, typically produced by social psychologists, which often position rather obvious elements in overcomplicated and/or clunky diagrams which can leave the reader with a strong feeling of 'so what?'[3] Here, though, if we are thinking about developing optimum platforms for creativity, it might be useful to have a meaningful model of the relationships between a person's sense of their own creative identity, and external factors such as other people, tools and environments. The most fruitful of these seems to be a model presented by Vlad Petre Glăveanu and Lene Tanggaard in a 2014 article called 'Creativity, identity, and representation: Towards a socio-cultural theory of creative identity'.[4]

Glăveanu and Tanggaard begin by observing that over the decades since the mid-twentieth century, when the field of psychology started taking creativity seriously, creativity has been studied either as a property of individuals, 'a system of personality traits and cognitive abilities' to be dissected, or else – in deliberate contrast – as something that emerges from social systems and environments, and not much to do with particular qualities of individuals at all (the latter being the approach of Mihaly Csikszentmihalyi, discussed in the early chapters of this book). The authors note that the role of creative *identity* has been largely neglected, but is absolutely central, linking up the individual and their social context:

> The creative person therefore, far from existing as an isolated unit, is a social actor able to co-construct his or her own sense of creative value in communication with others and in relation to societal discourses about what creativity is. In the end, there is creativity in identity construction just as there is identity construction in the most mundane forms of creative expression. Most importantly, identities conducive for creative performance are not just 'given' but built over time in interactions that are often marked by struggles and acts of resistance.[5]

This is of relevance here because platforms for creativity would need to help individuals to recognize and nurture their own creative identity. Glăveanu and Tanggaard argue that this creative identity is a 'representational project constructed within self–other relations'. In other words, we each create some kind of sense of ourselves as creative people, or perhaps not-creative people, with particular strengths and weaknesses and interests, and we work out this picture of ourselves – that's the 'representation', even if we never actually speak about it or make it explicit – in a kind of dialogue with other people and things we see in the world. And of course it changes over time.

So creative identity is forged through the interactions between three things: one, the individual; two, multiple others; and three, societal discourses around creativity (which might favour, say, the idea of the lone genius, or the notion that creativity is primarily collaborative, and may support or denigrate the amateur). These three elements can be seen as the three sides of a triangle, but then we have to add the dimension of time – as creative identity is an unfolding phenomenon – which drags out the triangle as a prism and gives the model its memorable shape, looking like a Toblerone, the popular Swiss chocolate bar. You've seen a Toblerone, right? The three sides of each triangle represent the individual, others, and social ideas about creativity; and it goes on and on lengthwise because of the passage of time. And it has chunky bits and flat bits because over time, sometimes there's more going on and sometimes there's less.[6]

Now, I know this model doesn't sound *amazing*. The fact that it feels rather blandly correct is to its credit, in a context where people hadn't managed to put these elements together very cleverly before. There's a long history in psychology, matched by an even longer one in everyday public discourse, which sees creativity as a set of individual characteristics that we might, potentially, measure, or nurture. So that's a focus on the individual, which is not *wrong* as such – it's certainly true that people are all different, and have had different experiences, and they have different kinds of creative capacities and inclinations that I do believe you can nurture. So a focus on the individual is not wrong but it disregards other things – the social and cultural dimensions of creativity. And similarly, you can take approaches which look at the social or collective ways in which creativity is brought into being, or you can focus on how creativity is considered within different cultures at different times, and these are very valid and important factors to look at, even though they disregard individual qualities and passions. On top of all this, it's relatively easy to forget that things change over time.

All of this explains why Glăveanu and Tanggaard, with their Toblerone, have done something noteworthy, because they have managed to bring together these components in one integrated model. It's fundamentally straightforward but it doesn't leave anything out.

And once we've got our heads around that, we can see the value when Glăveanu and Tanggaard suggest that individuals trace a line through the Toblerone, over time, developing their creative identity as 'an identity project fostered by the self and accomplished within social encounters'.[7] The 'project' of your own creative identity is owned by you but is both expressed in, and shaped by, social interaction with other people and with the culture at large. Glăveanu and Tanggaard show – based on interviews with makers and teachers in Denmark, and with folk-art egg decorators in Romania – that a creative identity, far from being a straightforward thing that each person proudly develops, is often denied, or problematic, or a source of anxiety. A particular creative identity shapes a creator's engagement with their own work, so the choices of what to do and how to do it are decisions at particular points in time influenced, of course, by the individual, social and cultural dimensions that pull on them from the three sides of the triangle. So we should keep all these things in mind as we consider effective platforms for creativity.

PRINCIPLES OF PLATFORMS

In 2011, I wrote an article which drew together what I had learned from collaborations that I had been involved in with the BBC, S4C and LEGO. Each of those projects had been about, in different ways, creating online platforms that should support and foster people's creativity. The article appeared online in 2012, and in a longer form in my book *Making Media Studies* in 2015. In this work I proposed eight principles for the design of platforms for creativity, based on what I had learned in these collaborations – sometimes prompted by things that *hadn't* been done, or *hadn't* worked, rather than all positive successes. Since then I have realized that although the eight principles were originally meant to be about the design of digital platforms, they are actually relevant to any kind of 'platform for creativity', large or small, online or offline, or both.

Here are the eight principles for the design of platforms for creativity:

1. Embrace 'because we want to'.
   – *A platform should go with the grain of what people already want to do; enable a sense of 'flow' by allowing them to do what they want to do in a way that feels natural, rather than compelling them to fit their ambitions into an imposed-from-elsewhere framework.*
2. Set no limits on participation.
   – *A platform should enable people to take their creativity as far as they like. There can, of course, be other kinds of limits (such as prohibition of harassment). Rather than requiring people to do certain types of thing, all different ways to participate should be supported. Platforms should undergird the self-efficacy beliefs of individuals: that is, their sense that they can make a difference in the world, and that this difference can be attributed to their own deliberate actions.*[8] *These beliefs are likely to be fostered by platforms which enable users to make their mark, and which are designed to encourage constructive interventions from others.*

3. Celebrate participants, not the platform.
   – A platform should be designed to showcase the inspiring things that people can do there, and help them to make connections, rather than promoting its own identity or brand, or that of its creators.
4. Support storytelling.
   – A platform should enable people to exchange and connect through stories, because storytelling is a fundamental way in which people come to comprehend the world, understand themselves, and connect with each other.[9] *Stories are not necessarily long things – they can be as short as a sentence – but a story connects experience, identity, and the wish to share something.*
5. Some gifts, some theatre, some recognition.
   – A platform should provide a space in which creative 'gifts' can be given and received; should offer a performative space, a stage on which people can show off their creative identity to others; and should enable individuals to explicitly recognize and give credit to the creative abilities of others. As we saw in chapter 4, creators typically value the sense of being part of a community, and they like unambiguous ways to be seen, and to be recognized and appreciated.
6. Online to offline is a continuum.
   – A platform should seek to connect the digital realm and the physical everyday world in imaginative ways. There can be exceptions – generally where a platform is purely offline, which can be refreshing in a world where so much is online – but usually it is valuable to create pathways for connection between people's online and offline existence.
7. Reinvent learning.
   – A platform should enable people to learn from each other. Writers on education and learning such as John Holt and Ivan Illich – as we saw in chapters 3 and 6 – argued that learning is a natural process which flourishes when learners can follow their own interests, and explore whatever engages their curiosity.[10]

Platforms for creativity can support this kind of informal, spontaneous learning, where people can learn through being inspired by other learners.

8. Foster genuine communities.
   – A platform should enable a meaningful community – or multiple sets of meaningful communities – to form around creative work. Although the term 'community' is used quite freely to describe online gatherings of users, a truly effective community is based around relationships of respect, trust and support. Platforms should be designed so that users are encouraged to give useful feedback to others, and to form connections with identifiable users over time.

This isn't meant to be the definitive list or final word on the subject. But it seems to have stood up well. I do like a numbered list, so I'm going to tell you about a further three-point thing, as well as a four-point thing, which complement the principles above.

TWO MORE KEY SETS OF PRINCIPLES

There are two more sets of principles which strike me as incredibly helpful and relevant, and both of them come from Mitch Resnick and colleagues at MIT Media Lab. I've worked with Mitch for a decade now, on and off, connected by LEGO and the LEGO Foundation, and we strongly share the same values – well, in fact, I probably learned them from him – that people should have tools which they can play with very openly and freely, rather than the tools coming with prescribed meanings and purposes. This applies to children and toys, as well as – I like to think – everything else. And we believe that people should be able to *make* things in a very open and unlimited environment, because we learn through putting things together, tinkering and making things – the idea of *constructionism*, pioneered by Seymour Papert, who was Mitch Resnick's mentor and supervised his PhD.[11]

Resnick has worked on various projects to enable this kind of play and learning to happen, most spectacularly by creating Scratch, the global phenomenon that enables children (and anyone) to click together code on screen to create computer programs. By summer 2017, as Scratch celebrated its ten-year anniversary, 20 million users had created 24 million projects in Scratch, and had made 120 million comments on each other's work.

In developing such tools, Resnick champions the idea of a 'low floor, high ceiling, wide walls' experience.[12] (I mentioned this in the previous chapter, in relation to music.) It was Papert who suggested that for a technology to effectively support learning and creativity, it should be easy for people to step into the experience and get started – that's the low floor – and it should also enable people to work on increasingly complex projects as their skills and ambitions develop – that's the high ceiling. Resnick added the notion of wide walls, which mean that the path from simple to complex is not one straight-upwards path but can take many different directions.[13]

So if we take the case of LEGO, for instance, the LEGO system offers a 'low floor' because it is easy and natural for anyone to pick up a few bricks and pieces and put them together to make something. But there's a high ceiling because you can make incredibly complex architecture, or spaceships. And there are wide walls because it doesn't have to be architecture or spaceships at all – you can use LEGO to make birds and flowers, marble runs, jewellery, machines, or whatever you want.

So ideally all platforms for creativity should offer 'low floor, high ceiling, wide walls' experiences. And in a different angle on the same topic, Mitch Resnick and his team have identified the '4 Ps' which are crucial to platforms like Scratch, and other creative learning activities: Projects, Peers, Passion and Play. Resnick summarizes the point of each as follows:

- *Projects:* People learn best when they are actively working on meaningful projects – generating new ideas, designing prototypes, refining iteratively.
- *Peers:* Learning flourishes as a social activity, with people sharing ideas, collaborating on projects, and building on one another's work.
- *Passion:* When people work on projects they care about, they work longer and harder, persist in the face of challenges, and learn more in the process.
- *Play:* Learning involves playful experimentation – trying new things, tinkering with materials, testing boundaries, taking risks, iterating again and again.[14]

This excellent list captures all of the elements most vital to fostering creative experiences that are going to be both enjoyable and valuable, and which will therefore be sustainable, because people will want to keep going and doing new things.

PLATFORMS FOR CREATIVITY IN PRACTICE

In the rest of this chapter I will give a few more examples of platforms for creativity. I think the online ones are straightforward and I don't need to explain much more about them. For instance, YouTube is a classic platform for creativity for the reasons set out in chapter 4, and for all the ways in which it matches up with what I've said about such platforms above, which I am sure you can recognize. Also my computer tells me that the word 'YouTube' has already appeared in this book 150 times, so we seem to be well covered there. (YouTube is also at the epicentre of some of the economic woes discussed in chapter 7, but that doesn't stop it from being an effective platform for creativity.) The digital game Minecraft became phenomenally successful – more than 130 million copies sold by 2017, the second best-selling video game of all time (after Tetris) – due to its open invitation to do anything within its environment, and to create stories yourself, rather than having them created for you by a professional developer elsewhere. Indeed, 'game' is not necessarily the right word for it – Minecraft is a toy, and a platform, and a sort of social network. It is also a stage upon which numerous performances are delivered and captured in phenomenally popular YouTube videos. (And we're back to YouTube again; it's not without reason that Kevin Kelly identifies YouTube as 'the center of our culture'.[15]) In the world of real-life construction, LEGO is a good example of a physical tool which is a great platform for creativity, for all the above reasons. LEGO is again boosted by a huge online community of YouTube video-makers, as well as multitudinous other enthusiasts who exchange images and ideas across numerous blogs, sites and networks, as well as physical events.

So let's consider other kinds of things that might be considered platforms for creativity. In 2014 I was contacted by the team at De Chocoladefabriek in Gouda, the Netherlands. De Chocoladefabriek was an old chocolate factory, as the name suggests, which had been converted into a new home for several different civic services and societies – the city library, the regional archive, a printing society, workspaces, a media workshop, a youth workshop and a restaurant all made their home there. Their vision was inspired, they said, by the first edition of *Making is Connecting*, which was one of the nicest things I had ever heard. Their idea was that all of these organizations and facilities would come together in one place, and think of themselves holistically as facilitating creativity in the community. They developed a 'cultural programme' together, and I found it memorable that the restaurant people had just as much of a say in the cultural programme as did the library people or the printing people. They used wooden pallets, which had previously been used for cooling chocolate, to show off creative work by the people of Gouda in prominent places around the building. I liked their sense of doing this all as part of one collective creative mission, and that they wanted to invert the idea of the library, so that it was not just a place where you went to find the written-down expertise of others, but where you could go to make and explore the knowledge and inspiration of your own community.[16]

So the idea of the city library was expanded from being like a bookshelf – a *repository* of knowledge – to being a platform – a place where the community *make* knowledge *together*. Rather like an online platform, it was a place that *invited* people to come in and do something, and to create the experience together, in terms of tone and feel and planning, as well as actual content. It's in this way that a physical place or environment can be a platform, just as a toy can be, or a digital social media enterprise can be.

SOCIAL ENTREPRENEURS BUILDING PLATFORMS FOR CREATIVITY

Through my work with the LEGO Foundation and Ashoka – the global network that aims to build and cultivate a community of change leaders – I have been able to meet and work with astounding social entrepreneurs who have established organizations that are changing how young people learn around the world. I will discuss three of them here.[17]

Imagination Foundation

The Imagination Foundation (more recently styling itself as Imagination.org) is the organization that runs the Global Cardboard Challenge, mentioned above. The Foundation grew out of the huge response to a short online film, 'Caine's Arcade', which went viral in 2012, the true story of a nine-year-old boy who made an arcade-game centre out of cardboard, in his father's Los Angeles car parts store, just for fun. The 11-minute video included a link for people to donate to Caine's college fund, which raised over $60,000 on the first day, and nearly $250,000 overall. This was matched with funding from the Goldhirsh Foundation, and quickly led to the launch of the Imagination Foundation. It was Nirvan Mullick who made the film and raised the money, but he hadn't been planning to run a foundation, so the Imagination Foundation quickly appointed Mike McGalliard as its passionate and hard-working Executive Director.

As well as the annual Global Cardboard Challenge, since 2014 McGalliard has been supporting people to launch Imagination Chapters, which are 'pop-up learning spaces that foster creativity, entrepreneurship and 21st century skills through creative play'. There are already more than 120 Chapters around the world, in libraries, community centres, and other spaces, as well as in schools, using a range of tools and materials, from cardboard to advanced electronics. Chapters usually meet weekly, and Chapter Leaders, who come from all walks of life, have formed a highly active online social network for idea-sharing and support. Like the Cardboard Challenge, it's a very simple idea – a weekly meetup to make stuff, essentially – but becomes a platform for creativity because of the *invitation* and the *shared experience*, both within each Chapter and shared around the world online.

It still takes some organizing. McGalliard recalls that the first Imagination Chapters were weekly two-hour sessions where participants could build whatever they wanted. 'People said, "This is great, we love the freedom, but actually we need more direction".' Therefore the Foundation has been developing tools for support – to provide a rich seam of inspiration, as well as personal support for leaders. McGalliard says, 'We communicate with people a lot online, but they are still very personal interactions. Our Chapter Leaders are from all walks of life; half are teachers but half have no teaching experience at all. They support and inspire each other all the time.' Imagination Chapters were conceived as an out-of-school activity, but it has turned out that in some cases they are being used by teachers who want to change their systems. McGalliard calls them tools of 'modest disruption'. They slip in under the radar: 'The Chapters are such a positive thing – nobody's actually going to stop you.' But the Chapters open up a playful space which is unlike most other kinds of school learning, and they are beginning to have a knock-on impact on how learning is conceived in other parts of those schools. So platforms can begin simply, but then their reach grows, and can change how people think about schools, libraries, and other taken-for-granted places.

Design for Change

It was another unexpected moment that led to the global platform Design for Change. In Ahmedabad, India, in 2001, Kiran Bir Sethi was so dismayed by the regimented and impersonal style of her son's education that she removed him from school one day, and started her own, in her home. Trained as a designer, she couldn't help noticing that education had been designed to satisfy the demands of parents, not children. Sethi insisted on listening to children, co-creating learning with them, and designing learning experiences that would enable them to flourish. 'In India', she explains, 'design was always thought of as happening only in design studios – an ideal. Nothing to do with children and education. I think that's what I really understood. Design thinking, and how design thinking should shape education.' This meant listening carefully to the needs of children and collaboratively designing a system which would enable them to learn in the best possible way.

Her school quickly grew to become the Riverside School, in Ahmedabad, with 390 students and an outstanding reputation as one of the best schools in India. Creating this school led Sethi to articulate design processes in ways that made sense to young learners, and she developed her idea that schools should build the 'I Can' mindset – where children instinctively know that they can do things and make a difference in the world. By 2009, Sethi realized she could have an impact beyond her own school, and launched these principles as an inspiring national and then international movement, Design for Change. The core elements of design thinking were reduced to a memorable four-step process: 'Feel – Imagine – Do – Share'. 'Feel' means to empathize with the people facing a problem; 'Imagine' is about brainstorming possible solutions; 'Do' means selecting and executing a plan; and 'Share' is about communicating the story to inspire others.

Since then, Design for Change has empowered children in more than 200,000 schools in over forty-four countries to create 18,000 stories of change, uploaded to the Design for Change website. Riverside School is the base, and offers training to other educators, but the Design for Change ideas and resources are spread for free. 'We really simplified it', Sethi explains, 'and we said it was open source, so you could download, you could customize, you could change. We would support you in any way we could. That's what made it global.'

The platform of Design for Change *invites* young people to tackle any kind of problem in a creative, playful way, using the four-step design thinking process. Sethi considers: 'I think one of the things that design thinking has removed is that there's no such thing as a problem – it's an opportunity. There is no failure, it's responsibility. Just as in play, there is no failure, just an opportunity to do something different, do something better.'

Skateistan

Perhaps the most unusual and thrilling of all these examples is Skateistan, founded in 2007 by Oliver Percovich. Skateistan runs skate schools, first in Afghanistan, and then also in Cambodia and South Africa, which offer a combination of skateboarding and arts-based learning to deprived children.

At first Ollie Percovich can seem diffident – you get the impression, at any time, that he would rather be outside skateboarding. But his gentle determination to create opportunities for girls in Afghanistan has been incredible. Of course, we should give full credit to his team, and the communities which enabled the schools to open, and the young women themselves who seized this chance. But the story starts with Ollie, who went to Afghanistan because his then-girlfriend was working for an NGO there.

He was immediately struck by the sheer unfairness of the situation for young women in Afghanistan. He explains, 'I didn't see any women driving a car, or serving me in a shop, or anywhere – they're just invisible in society.' But when he was skateboarding on the streets of Kabul, it turned out that both girls and boys were eager to have a go. Because there were no cultural rules forbidding girls from skateboarding, they found an opportunity to flourish. Percovich took this as an opportunity to show girls that they could succeed.

'I *wanted* the girls to beat the boys', he admits. 'In every sphere the boys were saying they were better than the girls, simply because they've had the opportunities to do those things. They practised things so they had got better. The girls had opportunities cut off. They were told they couldn't do anything, but they didn't have any opportunities to do anything in the first place. I thought that was grossly unfair. I could get away with enabling skateboarding because skateboarding hadn't been seen before. Nobody had made up rules saying that girls shouldn't do it.'

Skateistan was established with a particular emphasis on recruiting and supporting girls – 'We put 80 per cent of our effort into getting 50 per cent girls.' This involved gaining support from the community and religious leaders, and working within cultural norms, such as having separate days for boys and girls, and having only female teachers with female students. Step by step, they were able to get girls skateboarding and then get girls into the classroom. And step by step, following the interests of students, they became interested in subjects such as photography, social media, art and the environment. Because they felt comfortable and safe, the girls and boys became eager learners. Older and more confident children became teachers to others.

This led, amongst other things, to a delegation of the Skateistan girls going to speak in the Afghan parliament, and at UN conferences in other countries. Percovich reflects, 'It was amazing, first just getting them to school, and then getting to represent Afghan youth around the world through the bridge that the skateboard created.' In Afghanistan where female literacy is less than 25 per cent, Skateistan ensures participation of at least 40 per cent girls on all its programmes. Afghanistan now has the highest proportion of female skateboarders in the world.

This may not sound like the most straightforward example of a platform for creativity – and it isn't – because it is many things, including being a school, a school with a significant emphasis on one activity, skateboarding. But you may not have realized – I didn't, initially – that skateboarding *itself* is a platform for creativity. It invites you to do whatever you like with that one bit of equipment, the skateboard. Ollie Percovich asserts that skateboarding is intrinsically playful because, unlike other sports, there is no 'correct' way to do it. Skateboarding tends to create a community of people who, whatever their own ability, are highly supportive of others and welcome innovation rather than competition. 'It's important that there is no right and wrong way. The more playful you are, the more inventive and creative you are with the skateboard, that is what is celebrated in skateboarding culture. You're not actually doing it right, unless you're somehow breaking the rules.' Skateistan is an incredible and inspiring platform that has unlocked the creativity of individuals and contributed to real social change.

PLATFORMS FOR CREATIVITY: KINDNESS AND THE FUTURE

As we have seen, platforms for creativity are not necessarily technological, and can take many forms. Social media services are often referred to as platforms, but may not be platforms for *creativity* unless they actually invite creative participation. For instance, Facebook is usually more a place for communication and social organization, and sharing things found elsewhere, and not so much a platform for creativity *per se*, although it can be used in that way. (Also, Facebook is creepy for reasons discussed in chapters 6 and 7.) But it's not clear-cut that certain things 'are' or 'are not' platforms for creativity – it depends what you do with them. I think that Twitter is *more* of a platform for creativity, because of its invitation to craft little gems out of 140 (or 280) characters, and the ways in which it enables users to show and connect their creativity with others, including others that they don't know. But that's not how it is used by everybody. YouTube is more of a platform for creativity than either of these because it comes with a clear invitation to participate by producing quite substantial creative works. Of course, the people who create videos are heavily outnumbered by the people who only view videos, and not all of the content is non-professional material, but the invitation – the sense of 'you can do this too' – is part of YouTube's identity. (And this remains true even if we recognize that the reasons why YouTube wants users to feed it free videos are commercial.) Of course there are also non-commercial online platforms for creativity, such as Scratch, mentioned above, and open source systems such as Elgg and Buddycloud, which power social networks that are not commercial and not vehicles for advertising.

With online platforms there is a particular need to develop environments which facilitate kindness. It would be nice to think that human kindness just emerges *anyway*, but we have seen that that is not always the case. Tim Wu, professor of law at Columbia Law School and author of *The Attention Merchants*,[18] observes that 'to maintain spaces that bring out the best in us' there need to be very carefully designed structures.

> Looking back at the 2000s, the great mistake of the web's idealists was a near-total failure to create institutions designed to preserve that which was good about the web – its openness, its room for a diversity of voices and its

> earnest amateurism – and to ward off that which was bad: the trolling, the clickbait, the demands of excessive and intrusive advertising, the security breaches. There was too much faith that everything would take care of itself – that 'netizens' were different, that the culture of the web was intrinsically better. Unfortunately, that excessive faith in web culture left a void, one that became filled by the lowest forms of human conduct and the basest norms of commerce. It really was just like the classic story of the party that went sour.[19]

Wu suggests that this is not exactly a new depressing discovery, because we have known for a long time that key public institutions such as parks, universities and museums need to be carefully framed and protected. We don't just let people or businesses do whatever they like with them – we look after them, for everyone, for the greater good, and for the future. So we need to start thinking more about how online platforms can be set up and run in ways that foster kindness and supportive behaviour, and which also do not have to adopt a corporate business model with continuous pressure for revenue growth.

And as we have seen in this chapter, platforms for creativity can take many forms. They do not need to be online at all, although the connecting properties of the internet can often add value. They can be single happenings, or orchestrated multiple events – like the Cardboard Challenge, or Hey Clay, a day of free pottery sessions across the UK run by the Crafts Council[20] – or can be toys, toolkits, schools, or other kinds of things and environments. Not all kinds of platforms suit all kinds of people, so there is a wide-open opportunity for us to develop new platforms to engage different groups and give them opportunities to unlock previously unrecognized creative potential.

11

CONCLUSION

In this concluding chapter I will begin by summarizing and pulling together key arguments from the book. This starts with a section about our philosophical heroes, John Ruskin and William Morris, as I want to reiterate their core points and connect them with today's issues. Then everything else is boiled down into a set of seven key principles, namely:

1. A new understanding of creativity as process, emotion and presence
2. The drive to make and share
3. Happiness through creativity and community
4. A middle layer of creativity as social glue
5. Making your mark, and making the world your own
6. All media are social media
7. Do it yourself and self-transformation

I will outline each of these, and then discuss some of the political connotations of the 'making is connecting' thesis.

Finally, I will offer some positive thoughts about building and connecting creativity.[1]

THE LESSONS OF RUSKIN AND MORRIS

We started the book with a discussion of the ideas about everyday creativity suggested by the Victorian social critics John Ruskin and William Morris. These arguments, after 150 years, remain extremely powerful and relevant. We saw that making things is part of the process of thinking about things. Making leads to pleasures and understandings, gained *within* the process of making itself, which otherwise would not be achieved.

We also saw how amateur craft, and what I call everyday creativity, has been consistently derided over two centuries. The manufacture of everyday objects, and the media of entertainment and information, has become professionalized, and it is in the interests of those companies and professionals to run down the work of amateurs (although they do not *always* do so)[2]. Meanwhile, 'art' itself has also become a professional field of experts and elites, who carefully police the borders of their practice. A significant part of the joy of craft, and online creativity, is of course that it does *not* rely on hierarchies of experts and elites to be validated, and does not depend on editors and gatekeepers for its circulation.

Ruskin made the excellent point that roughly-made and non-professional things embody a kind of celebration of humanity's imperfections – the very fact that we are *not* machines. The collaborative mish-mash that characterizes many social media services is a heightened version of this. Ruskin argued that human creativity must be unleashed, and should risk failure and shame, so that the richness of humanity could be properly expressed. You may remember that he was thrilled by the sometimes silly and ugly sculptures to be found ornamenting Gothic cathedrals, as they were signs of the uninhibited life and freedom of quirky individual artisans. This is rather like the point made by internet commentator Clay Shirky, in his book *Cognitive Surplus*, that even daft websites – such as those collecting silly photos of cats with comic captions – reflect a zesty, everyday, creative liveliness which we should embrace and value, especially because they suggest to other everyday amateurs that 'You can play this game too'.[3]

Ruskin also helped us to make the connection from *individual* creativity to the 'big picture' of social stability and vitality. He showed that societies may establish apparently rational systems, which are intended to 'cure' inefficiencies, but which as a side-effect silence individual voice and strangle independent creativity, and so ultimately create a much greater sickness. This Ruskin point also has a modern-day counterpart, in the recent work of Nick Couldry, which we will discuss in a few pages.

Ruskin's enthusiastic supporter, William Morris, was a creative *producer* throughout his life, as well as critic of industry and politics. He drew our attention to the fact that we need *models* of good practice. Criticizing present realities is important but insufficient. It can be hard to picture what the future would look like, and so to be making things, as examples of future creative diversity, in the here and now, offers a powerful and tangible form of inspiration to others – and challenges the apparent inevitability of the present. This idea is shared by the makers of punk zines, and the knitters, stitchers and guerrilla gardeners, as well as the makers of YouTube videos and Soundcloud recordings, who show by vivid example that you do not have to accept all of mainstream culture, and can start to create your own alternatives instead.

Morris contended that people need to be able to make

their mark on the world, give shape to their environments, and share knowledge, ideas and self-expression. Ivan Illich made the same points, in a different way, 100 years later. Both thinkers observed that these opportunities provide a feeling of joy – or, when they are lacking, a dull misery. These arguments are today more vital than ever, and since we live in a world with so many media – and, now, so much *potential* for everyday personally made and distributed media – they offer a kind of prescription for how we should proceed.

Since – as critics of this book may like to point out – the majority of people remain, most of the time, viewers and consumers of mainstream professional stuff rather than makers and sharers of amateur material, this is a prescription that may seem ambitious and radical. But there are clearly many signs of this potential – not least of all in the staggering growth of people using social networks where personal creative material is shared.

SEVEN KEY PRINCIPLES

This book has highlighted a number of key principles, which I offer as tools for thinking about everyday life, creativity and media. Here, I have tried to draw together the main points, and numbered them from one to seven.

1. A new understanding of creativity as process, emotion and presence

The standard definition says that creativity should be judged on its outcomes, which are required to be original and paradigm-shifting. I argued that this way of understanding creativity is unsatisfactory because it rejects everyday activity that we would normally describe, in a 'common-sense' way, as creative; and especially because it is about the final product, rather than the process. There also seemed to be a philosophical flaw in a definition of creativity which would not enable anyone to identify 'creativity' unless they happened to be in possession of a God-like overview of the history of previous innovations in that sphere. A new definition was therefore proposed, in longer and shorter forms (see the discussion on pages 84–90). The shorter one was this:

> *Everyday creativity refers to a process which brings together at least one active human mind, and the material or digital world, in the activity of making something which is novel in that context, and is a process which evokes a feeling of joy.*

This approach to creativity is valuable, I would say, because it correctly recognizes the imaginative process of, say, knitters and bakers, amateur engineers, gardeners, LEGO enthusiasts, bloggers and YouTube video-makers, as the creative activity that it is – engaged in because the makers *want* to, and because it gives them *pleasure*. In the longer version of the revised definition of creativity, we also recognized that others may be able to sense the *presence* of the maker, in the thing they have made – the unavoidably distinctive fingerprint that the thinking-and-making individual leaves on their work, which can foster a sense of shared feeling and common cause, even when maker and audience never meet.

2. *The drive to make and share*

It is clearly the case, as we have seen from a range of offline and online cases mentioned in this book, that people like to make and share things. This may not be *all* people, partly because modern life has sought to render personal creativity unnecessary, but it is *some* people, with the potential to be many. They enjoy making and sharing things without the need for external rewards such as money or celebrity; although low-level recognition and reputation – being able to impress the people around you – may be a motivating force. But people do just do it anyway.

In the discussion of motivations in chapters 3 and 4, we saw that people often spend time creating things because they want to feel alive in the world, as *participants* rather than viewers, and to be active and recognized within a community of interesting people. It is common that they wish to make their existence, their interests and their personality more visible in the contexts that are significant to them, and they want this to be *noticed*. The process of making is enjoyed for its own sake, of course: there is pleasure in seeing a project from start to finish, and the process provides space for thought and reflection, and helps to cultivate a sense of the self as an active, creative agent. But there is also a desire to connect and communicate with others, and – especially online – to be an active participant in dialogues and communities. These are impulses which should be supported and developed by the websites and technologies of the future – as well as the toys and games, education and government programmes, and everything else of the future, as we will discuss in the 'implications' section below.

3. Happiness through creativity and community

We have seen that humans are very bad at predicting what will make us more happy. Indeed, it is a matter of historical and current fact that we typically allocate time to activities which are the wrong ones, working harder in an attempt to increase wealth, at the expense of the social engagement which can actually improve our enjoyment of life.

Happiness research shows that happiness is strongly

associated with the quality of our relationships and our connections with others. Nothing else comes close. Richard Layard, a leading economist and happiness researcher, even ends up saying: 'Increasingly, research confirms the dominating importance of love.'[4] In chapter 5 we saw that happiness is also heavily associated with self-esteem, and having projects to work on; and that work needs to be *meaningful* if we are to be satisfied and healthy. Crucially, we saw that although the happiness research identifies a number of variables and circumstances which should be able to assure humans of greater happiness, we cannot simply line up the 'correct' lifestyle elements and expect happiness to flood in. Happiness has to be worked towards, and it flows from action, not passivity.

All of this suggests that creative projects, especially when either online, or offline but linked via online platforms, are invaluable for human happiness. We should also remember Layard's stark warning that shared purpose is essential for human stability, otherwise we can find ourselves unexpectedly crushed by loneliness and stress. 'The current pursuit of self-realisation *will not work*', he says, least of all from the consumption of readymade products.[5] Communication, exchange, and collaboration in the production of everyday life, ideas and community, are much more rewarding.

4. A middle layer of creativity as social glue

Social scientists have traditionally analysed social life at the level of individuals, groups and families – the down to earth 'micro' level – or in terms of organizations, institutions and governments – the more abstract 'macro' level. More imaginative analysts, such as sociologist Anthony Giddens, have sought to connect the two levels by showing how the perception of macro-level expectations influences individual micro behaviour, and how everyday practices can in turn reinforce, or change, the macro established order.[6]

The discussion in this book, however, has often concerned activity in what we might call a middle layer. Social capital theory, as we saw in chapter 5, suggested that 'meso-level social structures' could act as 'integrating elements' between individuals and society.[7] Making and sharing activities, online and offline, can be seen as a disorganized (or, rather, lightly self-organized) cloud of creative links which can bind people together. These ties may not necessarily forge links between individuals and formal institutions, but they certainly connect people with others in unexpected, unplanned and perhaps rather anarchic ways. This creative cloud carries no single coherent message, but its existence, representing people doing what they want to do, *because they want to do it*, raises a challenge to the lifestyles of individual consumers, and to the ambitions of organized businesses and governments. These are people who want to make their own stuff, rather than only having stuff that is made commercially or on an industrial scale; and who are interested in that kind of thing made by others.

5. Making your mark, and making the world your own

Human beings need to be able to make their mark on the world, and to give shape and character to the environments that they live in. They need tools to do this, as Ivan Illich showed (see chapter 6). Ideally, these are tools which can be used in any way that a person likes, to do whatever they want. Tools which only offer a predetermined set of opportunities, or which are scaled up to provide uniform 'solutions', Illich warned, deny creativity and impose the fixed meanings of others. But mastery of a creative tool means that an individual can invest the world with meaning, and thereby 'enrich the environment' with the fruits of their vision.[8] This is not a specific roadmap towards a better society: the vision is only that there must be the ever-present possibility and potential of unpredictable and unplanned creativity – and that the *tools* for this must be readily available and easy to use.

This mention of such tools may lead modern readers to immediately think of online services, and it comes with implications for how such digital tools should be designed. It means that social media tools should be as open and as inviting of creativity as possible; and offer platforms where people can truly make their mark, express themselves, and shape the environment. As Jaron Lanier has argued (see chapter 7), it cannot involve simplistic templates where identities are reduced to a tick-box level. Expressive messiness, rather than Facebook-style neatness, is therefore to be encouraged – even by those of us who, for whatever psychological reason, prefer things to be tidy. Furthermore, distinctive creative contributions, and individual expressive voices, should be distinguishable – not mushed-together – so that we can respect and recognize each other as individuals.

Ideally, we need *sustainable* online platforms, offering a service to citizens without advertising or unnecessary surveillance, underpinned by the common good rather than profit-seeking motives. This may sound expensive and unlikely in modern societies, but for example, in the UK the BBC collects £3.7 billion in licence fee income each year to support its public service media operation.[9] The greatest public service that such an organization could offer today would be a fully non-commercial online video and social network service, guaranteed for the long term, a platform for the creativity of everybody.

Furthermore, as we saw in chapter 10, society would benefit from 'platforms for creativity' of all kinds – not just online platforms but also events, environments, tools and toys that support people to initiate creative projects and share their work with others. These platforms typically come with an *invitation* to do something, and should be open, easy to engage with, and foster helpful communities. Sometimes these communities come to take on a particular character, or attract certain kinds of person, which is fine, but it means also that we need to ensure that there is a broad *diversity* of making platforms and opportunities, so that people of different backgrounds and experiences and preferences feel that there are creative communities that they can become a part of.

6. All media are social media

When people were first starting to talk about 'social media' – meaning digital platforms where people could connect and interact – some old-schoolers liked to say 'of course, all kinds of media have always been social media'. What they meant was that we shouldn't forget about old media like radio and television because there was a long tradition of people writing letters to broadcasters and newspapers – which were essentially ignored – although in a tiny proportion of cases they were published or broadcast before being ignored. I'm not making that point. I don't really care about those emphatically one-way vehicles – they barely ever counted as mediums (media) of communication at all, if you think that communication is a two-way process, which it is. (And when I say 'two-way' here I mean 'two-or-more way', of course.)

But I do want to embrace the wide meaning of social media, so that we do count in all of the genuinely two-way or participatory means of exchanging information, emotion and ideas – so it's a happy yes to pianos, paint and sticks, and a hearty thumbs-up to pens, wool, LEGO, clay, stickers and charcoal. And a whole load of other nouns.

The point of considering media this broadly is to connect and integrate how we think about all the different ways in which humans can exchange, engage and relate. It's easy to think of digital media as a unique new part of human experience, and to focus on specific gadgets and services, and the things that people do with them. But I think the greater understandings come from thinking about this hardware, software and activity as part of arts, crafts and culture more generally; and to think of the feelings and needs that they engage with as essentially *timeless* human emotions and yearnings.

7. *Do it yourself and self-transformation*

The 'do it yourself' (DIY) ethos runs throughout this book, unsurprisingly, since making and connecting are things that you have to do yourself.[10] And you do them for yourself because they're good for you – and, perhaps, for others. In terms of which media we would be talking about, the *opposite* of DIY would be those twentieth-century types of one-way media, such as broadcast radio and television, and things that don't want you to participate or play with them. DIY is not powerful because of the stuff that is made, but because of the feelings and meanings of the process.

Making something yourself can be both a pleasure and a challenge – most probably a mix of both, and of course the challenges can heighten the pleasures. Making things can be about building external relationships, but is also about self-worth. I think the essence of this was captured by Peter Korn when he explained, rather beautifully, in chapter 8: 'None of us enter our studios because the world desperately requires another painting or symphony or chair. . . . We engage in the creative process to become more of whom we'd like to be and, just as important, to discover more of whom we might become.'[11]

In making and reflecting – in seeing what we can do, and how we can prompt feelings of fascination, curiosity, pride and joy in ourselves and others – and connecting with others through the social practices surrounding creative endeavour – we encounter great opportunities to learn, grow and change.

THE POLITICAL CONNOTATIONS OF 'MAKING IS CONNECTING'

This book is built on a broad general understanding that people are happier, more engaged with the world, and more likely to develop or learn, when they are doing and making things for themselves, rather than having things done and made for them. This obviously lines up with liberal and countercultural notions of self-reliance and independence, but at the same time could appear to steer close to core right-wing or reactionary ideas: that the poor and disadvantaged do not deserve our support, as they are simply people who have failed to do the necessary things to ensure their own well-being; who expect to have 'things done for them' rather than solving their own problems. Of course, this is not my intention. 'Making is connecting' suggests that society is stronger, and kinder, when we take time to listen to the voices around us, when we pay attention to the diverse stories presented through the everyday creativity of our fellow human beings, and when we engage helpfully in the world. To suggest that it is rewarding and inspiring to make and fix things for oneself, rather than relying on external forces, is not at all to say that there should not be external services which provide security and support for individuals, families and communities.

In particular, when we are talking about media, art and culture, a kind of do-it-yourself individualism, or do-it-with-others collaboration – with wide participation across the population – is highly defensible, since otherwise we only have a choice of large-scale *monolithic* solutions (such as broadcast television stations) or more distinctive but *elite* ones (such as the artworld system of 'star' artists and international galleries, where having the right kind of education, sponsors, and jargon, are necessary markers of worthiness). Compared with mass-market populism on the one hand, and pretentious elitism on the other, the multitudinous and diverse fruits of the 'make it yourself' ethic, or the 'make it with others' ethic – as seen across YouTube and the rest of the Web, and in craft fairs, guerrilla gardening interventions, and elsewhere – are easily the winners.

The DIY ethic in everyday culture is wholly different from, say, the Thatcherite do-it-yourself notion which is encapsulated in Norman Tebbit's famous 1981 statement that his unemployed father had 'got on his bike and looked for work', a phrase often slightly misremembered as a direct command to the unemployed to 'get on your bike' (which, although a misquote, represents the implied meaning). This right-wing version of self-reliance, which implies that poverty or unemployment are a consequence of personal laziness, stems from the view that all of life is fundamentally a marketplace, within which some products (or people) will succeed, whilst others fail. This is the mindset which today is known as neoliberalism – the idea that markets and market forces are the primary way to understand and organize not only economics, but also politics and society.

I would say that the ideals associated with 'making is connecting' – individual and collective creativity, self-expression and sharing – offer a *challenge* to the neoliberal vision of society, consumerism and education. I am helped in this by the recent work of Nick Couldry, the LSE, University of London professor who has emerged as one of the sharpest analysts of the intersection between politics, culture and communications on multiple levels. In his book *Why Voice Matters: Culture and Politics after Neoliberalism*, Couldry charts the ways in which neoliberalism has become naturalized in social and political life over the past couple of decades, and argues that human 'voice' may be the most powerful tool to erode its power. As he explains:

> Voice as a process – giving an account of oneself and what affects one's life – is an irreducible part of what it means to be human; effective voice (the effective opportunity to have one's voice heard and taken into account) is a human good. 'Voice' might therefore appear unquestionable as a value. But across various domains – economic, political, cultural – we are governed in ways that deny the value of voice and insist instead on the primacy of market functioning.[12]

Being opposed to neoliberalism does not mean that one is opposed to markets *per se*. Markets may be a good way to organize a number of things, such as trade and employment – with some regulation to ensure decent practices, such as minimum wage laws. Neoliberalism, however, is the belief that markets are the *only* lens through which to run anything, or to assess the value of anything. It is manifested in many ways, and becomes apparent when individuals are seen as simply customers and consumers, and workers become faceless 'service providers'. It means that the 'voice' of people is denied, because they can only express themselves through choices within the existing market, which is not genuine self-expression at all.

The perspective of neoliberalism, Couldry argues, seeps into all aspects of society and culture, shaping our assumptions and expectations, and ultimately making some approaches common-sense and other views alien. For example, in education, the influence of neoliberalism means that students become 'customers' who assume that their purpose is to purchase and extract a qualification as simply as possible, rather than engage in a process of discovery, learning and growth. For their teachers, the work becomes a matter of handing over the relevant packages of 'knowledge' in a uniform manner – the practice which can be most simply unified and audited, at the cost of individuality and creativity. In businesses and organizations, the influence of neoliberalism means that individuals become 'brand representatives', whose work takes over more and more of their lives and demands a particular performance of passion and enthusiasm, the better to sell the brand, but not as an invitation to genuine self-expression. In media and communications, this trend led, for instance, to the rise of 'reality TV', which appears to give a voice to individuals but only as part of an edited package produced by professionals, not as an actual vehicle for self-expression.

CREATIVITY AND BEING HEARD

My own argument here would be that, although mass-market broadcasting, consumerism and 'neoliberal rationality' are currently well embedded in our society and culture, we have seen in this book the seeds of a possible new direction. Part of the way people may now be finding a voice is by using the internet in particular ways. Couldry's *Why Voice Matters* acknowledges online communication at various points but is not primarily concerned with it; and his brief discussion of online political practices generally involves a conventional understanding of political activity (such as online circulation of photographic evidence by activists; antiwar and environmental campaigning websites and networks; and other online means to communicate and organize protest and opinion to governments). However, he does also point towards a rethinking of what politics means – a 'politics of politics' which would aim to reimagine and re-enable collective participation in public affairs[13] – which, in the 'everyday' contexts we are concerned with here, could, I think, involve finding new meaning within our own participation in society through creative making and sharing.

If we are willing to consider an optimistic possibility, I would argue that the 'making is connecting' power of the internet, which in turn may be seeding and inspiring other offline (or both on- and offline) activities, offers us a potential way to disrupt the inevitability and dominance of the one-size-fits-all broadcasting and consumerism model, and to enhance the power of voice. For voice to be meaningful, people need opportunities and tools for self-expression, but – as Couldry asserts – they also need to be effectively *heard*. As we saw in chapter 7, the existence of social media technologies, or companies, does not guarantee this in any way, and indeed the commercial nature of the tools can be the basis of significant concern. Furthermore, the resources of skills, techniques, networks and contacts which can help some people to get heard are not equally distributed – some people can speak with much louder voices than others. This can be seen on Twitter, where there seems to be a class of 'ordinary' users, who typically have fewer than 500 followers, and a class of high-status Tweeters, who are likely to have well over 5,000, and are much more active. And of course, a majority of people are not on Twitter at all. Similarly, the very point of the 'long tail' of videos on YouTube is that most videos, whilst available, are very rarely watched by anybody.[14]

However, what we do know about online communication is that, although the capacity to be 'heard' is not evenly distributed, it does not only follow traditional or straightforward patterns either. In terms of being able to make attractive online content, an individual needs to acquire and develop certain skills. Anyone with the basic equipment can do this, although some amount of literacy and computer literacy is necessary, and a certain flair for design, and self-promotion, can also be helpful. In terms of becoming *heard* – a distinct further step, once the content has been created – the sensible individual makes use of existing online networks in a bid to push their material in front of others who may then pass on the links to yet more others. The same kind of 'anyone' can do this too. Previously-existing fame or status can definitely help – that's a fact – but it is not at all necessary. Many people have become popular bloggers and YouTube video-makers even though they had no previous platform, celebrity, or relevant contacts. In the online discussion of social and political matters, it is true that college-educated professionals, and in particular already-established journalists, commentators, politicians, organizations and think-tanks get a huge boost in visibility (which is largely the point of Matthew Hindman's book *The Myth of Digital Democracy*)[15]. But it is still true that unconventional, minority and non-professional voices also can get heard.

It is worth noting that in order to feel supported and encouraged in their creative efforts, people do not necessarily need a huge audience or network. The pleasure in connecting with other people through creativity, and therefore feeling more connected with the world – becoming heard and recognized, and starting to feel that there may be some point in trying to make a difference – can develop through interactions with small numbers of like-minded people. We should also remember that for those who wish to have a voice, and be heard, all of this is much, much different to the previous situation, just twenty-five years ago, where you had to be one of the absolute elite, employed by a media organization, and selected to produce content, to even get to speak. Today, a lot of non-elite, non-professional people are creating and sharing media, making their mark on the world and sharing what they have to say about an incredibly diverse range of spheres and subjects, from parenting to painting, ecology to economics, diabetes to discrimination, lifestyles, poetry, science, and everything else. They also make things which are simply meant to be beautiful, inspiring, or entertaining.

It is partly for these reasons that this book has not primarily concerned itself with explicitly 'political' activity online, or with the work of 'craftivists' who combine craft activity with political activism.[16] I have not focused on these more obvious centres of political activity because this book is about the idea that making and sharing is *already* a political act. Taken bit by bit, it's small stuff. Each little pebble of creative activity is easily lost in the general landscape, which is dominated by various big beasts such as social institutions, popular broadcasters and giant supermarkets.[17] But those pebbles all add up, and *cumulatively* could reach as high as any of the big beasts. We have already seen that the huge numbers of people engaging with a vast array of homemade things on YouTube present a severe challenge to the professional mass-market TV stations, which until recently had assumed that they were the natural providers of what people wanted. If we are willing to be optimistic, this could just be the start of a substantial shift from the one-size-fits-all industrial fast food culture of the twentieth century, towards a homemade, slow-cooked, highly diverse feast of meaningful engagement, sharing and playfulness in the twenty-first. This would be based on an ethics of understanding, self-expression, recognition and respect, rather than a general assumption that people shouldn't mind parking their own personalities under a readymade platter of mass-market identities.

If you're *not* optimistic, you can note that the ways in

which the internet has connected up the narrow-minded and supported them to mutually reinforce their views have led to darker days. The internet reflects the world, and sometimes the world is much less kind than you would wish. But awful political surprises such as Trump and Brexit emerge because people feel disenfranchised, so talking about activities and technologies that will give people more of a voice *ought* to be part of the solution. If it is the perceived divide between the elites and the masses that causes the masses to vote for disruptive change, even when the change in question seems rationally dreadful, then a more level playing field of creative and cultural communication and exchange should be helpful. In any case, more people having a voice – rather than a small elite having a voice – has got to be better. And if we can develop widely-used tools for meaningful creative conversations then maybe we can start to build our way out of this mess.

Now for a change of gear as we head towards the end of the book. Here's the penultimate section, which is both more cheerful and hopefully more useful.

DEVELOPING AND CONNECTING CREATIVITY

Since the first edition of *Making is Connecting* was published, it has become apparent that lots of the people who read it are makers themselves. They like to make things, and they are interested in the meaning of this activity, and how they can do more of it, and maybe have more recognition and exchange as well. In other words, they want to do more making and they want to do more connecting.

So in this section, I will mention a few things I've worked out, or picked up, about how we can develop and share our creativity.

Feel the fear and do it anyway

Am I *really* offering you advice ripped straight from the cover of a thirty-year-old self-help book? Definitely. The thing is, I had always liked the well-known title, *Feel the Fear and Do It Anyway*, but hadn't read the actual book, by Susan Jeffers. Then I was invited to do a talk about creativity to some music students. I'd not met these music students before and had decided to purely say inspiring things to them. I had to reply to an email where they wanted me to give a title, and I was in a rush, so I suggested 'Creativity – Feel the fear and do it anyway'. It wasn't an *accident*, and I was going to give due credit. But then later I thought, if I'm doing a lecture which has *Feel the Fear and Do It Anyway* in the title, then I'd better read Susan Jeffers' book. And, good news: it's a great book.[18] Clearly, a lot of it is in the memorable title. I had already found that useful, without ever having seen the book. It's self-explanatory, and inspiring.

From the book, I took away a slightly more complex understanding of Jeffers' approach – though it's still simple enough to be memorable. The first point is, 'the fear' – such as the fear of doing a new creative thing that you've not done before – is not really a bad thing. It's an indicator that you are pushing yourself, for sure – but it's good to be challenging yourself. Therefore, if you continue to push yourself creatively, then some amount of fear is not, in fact, going to go away. And the way to get on top of the fear – to reduce it, or understand it, or live with it – is by *doing* the challenging thing. The 'doing it' has to come before the fear can be diminished.

Jeffers knows also that the fear can be associated with self-esteem. We might think, 'When I feel better about myself – then I'll do it.' But, crucially, she points out that we will only feel better about ourselves *through* doing the thing, and, as she says in an especially neat sentence, 'The "doing it" comes *before* the feeling better about yourself.'[19] We only get better at things by *doing* them – therefore there can be no good reason for holding back. That is perhaps the greatest lesson of the book: it's all about the power of just *doing* things, making things, getting on with it, learning through the process, and growing as a person through the process. But none of the learning and growing can happen without the *doing*.

Jeffers has two more strong points. First, she points out that while you will experience fear when on unfamiliar territory, *so does everyone else*. This is one of those statements which seems predictable and obvious on the one hand – and we don't really believe it on the other. Clearly, people *do* experience different levels of anxiety when faced with the prospect of doing a creative or performative thing – but the less anxious people are those who had that fear more strongly before, and have learned to deal with it by *doing* the thing – not because they were already superhuman, or better than you. I note, for example, that in the more than 200 interviews with stand-up comedians in the *Comedian's Comedian* podcast series by Stuart Goldsmith,[20] almost all of them talk about considerable fear, anxiety and self-doubt, at least at some point in their performing lives. And in all cases, the only way to get beyond this fear of performance was by *doing* more performances.

Second, Jeffers says: 'Pushing through fear is less frightening than living with the underlying fear that comes from a feeling of helplessness.'[21] She suggests that if we 'protect' ourselves by not taking creative risks, we actually feel a lot worse, and for longer – potentially, forever. Doing things, and so eventually coming to feel competent at those things, feels much better than not daring to even try to do them.

If you don't like it, it wasn't meant for you anyway

When we make things and put them out there, that is already a brave thing to do. We are allowing ourselves – directly or through our work – to be seen, and judged. That's not easy. As Brené Brown has said, if you step into the creative arena – the place where we make things and show them to others – 'you *will* get your ass kicked'.[22] It is wise to accept from the outset that a creative life will bring some negative feedback, as well as – hopefully – more positive responses. But Brown adds this: 'If you aren't in the arena *also* getting your ass kicked, I am *not* interested in your feedback.' Hearing from other creators, and people who want to engage meaningfully, is worth doing. But some people are only there to criticize, and they are welcome to come and look at what you do, but you really have to ignore what they say.

This connects with two other points. First of all, if they don't like it, it wasn't for them anyway. It's so easy to feel bruised by the one person who didn't happen to like your thing, and to forget about the 100 people who did. But a fact that we already know is that not everybody likes everything. That's obvious. Not everybody likes everything, so of *course* there will be people who don't like *your* thing. That's a totally inevitable statement. We can tell you, right now, before you make a thing, whoever you are, and without us needing to know what it is, that there will be people who don't like it. If we can remember this, then any unhelpful criticism of your creative work can be met with an absolute blank: 'OK. So, it wasn't for you.' And then you can get on with doing the things you like to do.

The second point about 'wasn't meant for you anyway' is the positive flipside, and connects with what we learned during the '1,000 true fans' discussion in chapter 9. If 98 per cent of all people have absolutely no interest in what you are doing, it sounds like you're doing really badly. But out of every million people, there are 20,000 who might like it. That's a lot. Focusing on the potential positive reception from a certain sphere is likely to be more rewarding than worrying about a zero or negative response from other larger groups that are probably just not your kind of people anyway.

Make the time

Finally, and very pragmatically, it's easy to feel disappointed or annoyed that we have not made more things, and the explanation is often that we just didn't manage to carve out the *time* to make the things. Although we may like to imagine that delightful creative moments 'just happen', in fact they are distinctly more likely to occur if we write them down on the calendar in advance.

The musician and producer Ill Gates has a striking methodology for getting things done, presented in his online 'Ill. methodology' workshop – some of which can be seen on YouTube.[23] He knows that electronic music-makers can have an endless capacity to tinker with equipment, tweak sounds and play with software, even where they have strong positive intentions to seek music gold. Promoting his method, Gates says, 'I went from finishing a tune every six months, to finishing one or more a day.' Basically it is about marking out creative time in your schedule, so there's a clear block of time set out within which you aim to get something *completed*.

During creative sessions we might tend to 'take a moment' to send some messages, do admin or promotion, look online for information and tutorials, or email friends to ask for feedback. Gates says you have to remove *all* of these distractions from your allocated creative session, and do them at other times. The creative session needs to have a clear ticking clock. Depending on your craft, lifestyle and commitments, this length of time might vary. For Gates it is twenty hours – 'I like to imagine what I call the 20 hour guillotine: there's this guillotine hanging above my studio desk, and if I don't finish that song in 20 hours, you just gut it for parts, put them in the library, and move on with your life.'[24] You get things done by setting out limited blocks of time within which the thing has to be done. And again, to go back to Susan Jeffers' message, it might feel scary to say 'I must complete this whole task in the next six hours', but it is only by setting that fixed amount of time aside, and then *doing* it, that you get things done and start to build a sense of confidence and achievement.

IN CONCLUSION

This book has been about the shift from the 'sit back and be told' culture which became entrenched in the twentieth century, towards the 'making and doing' culture which could flourish in the twenty-first. Although I think there is an appetite for such a change, we could hardly say that this will be an easy shift. Many people have become comfortable with the undemanding role that contemporary culture expects us to enjoy – it appears pleasant enough, allows us to consume wall-to-wall entertainment, and nothing very bad seems to happen. But at the same time, we are not left feeling very whole, or fulfilled, or creative. And bad things *are* happening – see all the evidence of social isolation, fragmented communities, environmental pollution and climate change in particular – which we choose to not really notice.

It doesn't seem right to suggest that people just don't know what's good for them: but the empirical research on happiness and well-being does show a clear mismatch between the things which we say help us to feel positive, alive and connected, and the things which we actually spend most time on. It sounds illogical, but we all do it. And because modern life is often tiring and complicated, we are often likely to welcome the blessed relief of the 'sit back and be told' elements which don't require us to *do* very much. The 'making and doing' culture does require a bit more effort – but it comes with rich rewards.

Making things shows us that we are powerful, creative agents – people who can really *do* things, things that other people can see, learn from, and enjoy. Making things is about transforming materials into something new, but it is also about transforming one's own sense of self. Creativity is a gift, not in the sense of it being a talent, but in the sense that it is a way of sharing meaningful things, ideas, or wisdom, which form bridges between people and communities. Through creative activity – where making really is connecting – we can increase our pleasure in everyday life, unlock innovative capacity, and build resilience in our communities. The potency that comes from doing and making things yourself is irresistible, and means that we can face future challenges with originality, daring and joy.

NOTES

PREAMBLE TO THE SECOND EDITION

1. Jonathan Taplin, *Move Fast and Break Things* (London: Macmillan, 2017).
2. GSMA, 'The mobile economy 2017', 27 February 2017, https://www.gsma.com/newsroom/press-release/number-of-global-mobile-subscribers-to-surpass-five-billion-this-year/
3. On 24 September 2014: https://twitter.com/davidgauntlett/status/514729040364986368
4. Detailed at length in the Wikipedia article 'Gamergate controversy', https://en.wikipedia.org/wiki/Gamergate_controversy
5. Wikipedia again has a summary: https://en.wikipedia.org/wiki/Ghostbusters_(2016_film)#Controversy
6. Such statistics are compiled, for instance, by Internet Live Stats, which in July 2016 stated that there are 3.4 billion internet users in the world, where a user is 'an

individual who can access the Internet, via computer or mobile device, within the home where the individual lives'. See http://www.internetlivestats.com/internet-users/

7. This is from near the end of the *Doctor Who* episode, 'Vincent and the Doctor', spoken by Matt Smith as the Doctor, written by Richard Curtis, first broadcast on BBC One in the UK on 5 June 2010. I realize it sounds like something corny – like 'life is like a box of chocolates' – but life *isn't* like a box of chocolates. It *is* like a pile of good things and a pile of bad things, which don't actually cancel each other out.

1 INTRODUCTION

1. David Gauntlett, *Creative Explorations: New Approaches to Identities and Audiences* (London: Routledge, 2007).
2. Charles Leadbeater, *We Think: Mass Innovation not Mass Production* (London: Profile Books, 2008). Clay Shirky, *Here Comes Everybody: The Power of Organising Without Organisations* (London: Allen Lane, 2008). Clay Shirky, *Cognitive Surplus: Creativity and Generosity in a Connected Age* (London: Allen Lane, 2010).
3. I expect Charles Leadbeater is doing some of this, implicitly if not explicitly, in some of his other work, such as his ideas on education reform; see www.charlesleadbeater.net
4. A powerful critique of this situation is: Guy Claxton, *What's the Point of School?* (Oxford: Oneworld, 2008); and see Guy Claxton and Bill Lucas, *Educating Ruby: What Our Children Really Need to Learn* (Bancyfelin: Crown House, 2015).
5. For the latest data, see www.nielsen.com. Summaries of television viewing appear in the 'Insights' section.

6. For the latest, see www.barb.co.uk. Summaries of television viewing appear under 'Viewing data'.
7. David Gauntlett, *Moving Experiences, 2nd edition: Media Effects and Beyond* (London: John Libbey, 2005).
8. Max Horkheimer and Theodor W. Adorno, *Dialectic of Enlightenment* (London: Verso, 1979).
9. Sigmund Freud, *'A Case of Hysteria', 'Three Essays on Sexuality' and Other Works* (London: Vintage, 2001).
10. Karl Marx, *Capital: A Critique of Political Economy, Volume 1* (London: Penguin, 2004).
11. Claxton, *What's the Point of School?*
12. YouTube statistics: https://www.youtube.com/yt/about/press/
13. Instagram statistics: https://instagram-press.com/our-story/
14. Josh Constine, 'Facebook now has 2 billion monthly users – and responsibility', *Techcrunch*, 27 June 2017, https://techcrunch.com/2017/06/27/facebook-2-billion-users/
15. For instance, the resurgence of interest in craft activities is one of the key findings of the 'Living Britain' report, an independent study by The Future Laboratory, commissioned by Zurich, published 2007. Although commercially funded, the study draws on a wide range of data and expertise, and Zurich has no apparent vested interests in this kind of finding. http://www.zurich.co.uk/home/Welcome/livingbritain/. Similarly, Joanne Turney cites a number of statistics which suggest that significantly increased numbers of people are taking up knitting, in *The Culture of Knitting* (Oxford: Berg, 2009), p. 1.
16. The various manifestations of these shifts were, in part, documented in the EU-funded project that I was a part of, 'Digital DIY', 2015–17, http://www.didiy.eu

17. *Make* is a physical magazine, but also has a comprehensive website at http://www.makezine.com
18. Ellen Dissanayake, 'The pleasure and meaning of making', *American Craft*, April–May 1995, quoted at the American Craft Council website, http://www.craftcouncil.org/html/about/craft_is.shtml
19. Mihaly Csikszentmihalyi, *Creativity: Flow and the Psychology of Discovery and Invention* (New York: Harper Perennial, 1997), p. 8.
20. Ibid., p. 6.
21. Ibid.
22. Gauntlett, *Creative Explorations*, p. 19.
23. Charles J. Lumsden, 'Evolving Creative Minds: Stories and Mechanisms', in Robert J. Sternberg, ed., *Handbook of Creativity* (Cambridge: Cambridge University Press, 1999), p. 153.
24. Matthew Crawford, *The Case for Working with Your Hands: or Why Office Work is Bad for Us and Fixing Things Feels Good* (London: Viking, 2010). Mark Frauenfelder, *Made by Hand: Searching for Meaning in a Throwaway World* (New York: Portfolio, 2010). Peter Korn, *Why We Make Things and Why it Matters: The Education of a Craftsman* (Vintage: London, 2017).
25. Richard Sennett, *The Craftsman* (London: Allen Lane, 2008). And for a particular focus on doing things by hand, see Frank R. Wilson, *The Hand: How its Use Shapes the Brain, Language, and Human Culture* (New York: Vintage, 1999).
26. Rob Hopkins, *The Transition Handbook: From Oil Dependency to Local Resilience* (Totnes: Green Books, 2008). Rob Hopkins, *The Power of Just Doing Stuff: How Local Action Can Change the World* (Totnes: Green Books, 2013). Shaun Chamberlin, *The Transition Timeline: For a Local, Resilient Future* (Totnes: Green Books, 2010).

For an introduction, see Rob Hopkins' TED talk: http://www.ted.com/talks/rob_hopkins_transition_to_a_world_without_oil.html

2 THE MEANING OF MAKING I

1. Peter Dormer, 'The Status of Craft', in Peter Dormer, ed., *The Culture of Craft* (Manchester: Manchester University Press, 1997), p. 18.
2. Richard Sennett, *The Craftsman* (London: Allen Lane, 2008), p. 7.
3. Ibid., p. 11.
4. Ellen Dissanayake, 'The pleasure and meaning of making', *American Craft*, April–May 1995, quoted at the American Craft Council website, http://www.craftcouncil.org/html/about/craft_is.shtml
5. Dormer, 'The Status of Craft', p. 18.
6. Peter Dormer, 'Craft and the Turing Test for Practical Thinking', in Peter Dormer, ed., *The Culture of Craft* (Manchester: Manchester University Press, 1997), p. 154.
7. John Ruskin, *Selected Writings*, edited by Dinah Birch (Oxford: Oxford University Press, 2009), p. 279.
8. Clive Wilmer, 'Introduction', in John Ruskin, *Unto This Last and Other Writings* (London: Penguin, 1997), p. 24.
9. Ruskin, *Selected Writings*, p. 100.
10. A good short introduction to this context appears in Clive Wilmer's 'Introduction'.
11. By 'moral' I refer to strong ethical beliefs, but not the narrow code of 'Victorian morality'.
12. John Ruskin, 'Unto This Last: Essay IV: Ad Valorem', in *Unto This Last and Other Writings*, edited by Clive Wilmer (London: Penguin, 1997), p. 222.
13. Ibid.

14. See Wilmer, 'Introduction', p. 22.
15. William Morris, 'Preface to The Nature of Gothic', in *News from Nowhere and Other Writings*, edited by Clive Wilmer (London: Penguin, 2004), p. 367.
16. John Ruskin, 'The Nature of Gothic', in *Unto This Last and Other Writings*, edited by Clive Wilmer (London: Penguin, 1997), p. 83.
17. Ibid.
18. Ibid.
19. Lars Spuybroek, *The Sympathy of Things: Ruskin and the Ecology of Design – Second edition* (London: Bloomsbury Academic, 2016), p. 49.
20. Ibid.
21. Ibid., p. 50.
22. Ibid., p. 24.
23. Ibid.
24. Ruskin, 'The Nature of Gothic', p. 84.
25. Ibid.
26. Ibid., p. 85.
27. Ibid., pp. 85–6.
28. Adam Smith, *An Inquiry into the Nature and Causes of the Wealth of Nations*, available at Project Gutenberg, http://www.gutenberg.org/etext/3300. The quote is from the start of chapter 1.
29. Ibid. This quote is in Book Five, chapter 1, part 3.
30. Karl Marx, *Economic and Philosophic Manuscripts of 1844*, in the chapter 'Wages of Labour', http://www.marxists.org/archive/marx/works/1844/manuscripts/wages.htm. These writings were not published until 1932.
31. P. D. Anthony, *John Ruskin's Labour: A Study of Ruskin's Social Theory* (Cambridge: Cambridge University Press, 1983), pp. 171–2.
32. Ruskin, 'The Nature of Gothic', p. 87.
33. Ibid., p. 90.

34. Ibid.
35. Anthony, *John Ruskin's Labour*, pp. 171–2.
36. Viscount Snowden, in his untitled contribution to *William Morris 1834 – 1896: Some Appreciations* (London: Walthamstow Historical Society, 2003, first published 1934).
37. E. P. Thompson, *William Morris: Romantic to Revolutionary* (London: Merlin, 1977), p. 4.
38. Ibid., p. 28.
39. 'Interview with William Morris', *Clarion*, 19 November 1892, reprinted in Tony Pinkney, ed., *We Met Morris: Interviews with William Morris, 1885–96* (Reading: Spire Books, 2005), pp. 63–4.
40. 'The Kelmscott Press: An Illustrated Interview with Mr William Morris', *Bookselling*, Christmas 1895, reprinted in Pinkney, ed., *We Met Morris*, pp.114–15.
41. 'The Poet as Printer: An Interview with Mr William Morris', *Pall Mall Gazette*, 12 November 1891, reprinted in Pinkney, ed., *We Met Morris*, p. 56.
42. As the company history on Penguin's website explains, 'Penguin paperbacks were the brainchild of Allen Lane [who] found himself on a platform at Exeter station searching its bookstall for something to read on his journey back to London, but discovered only popular magazines and reprints of Victorian novels. Appalled by the selection on offer, Lane decided that good quality contemporary fiction should be made available at an attractive price. . . . The first Penguin paperbacks appeared in the summer of 1935 and included works by Ernest Hemingway, André Maurois and Agatha Christie. They were colour coded (orange for fiction, blue for biography, green for crime) and cost just sixpence, the same price as a packet of cigarettes' (http://www.penguin.co.uk/static/cs/uk/0/aboutus/aboutpenguin_companyhistory.html)

43. Tony Pinkney, 'Introduction', in *We Met Morris*, pp. 18–19.
44. Clive Wilmer, 'Introduction', in *William Morris, News from Nowhere and Other Writings* (London: Penguin, 2004), p. xxii, emphasis added.
45. Ibid., p. xxiii.
46. Thompson, *William Morris*, p. 126.
47. William Morris, 'The Lesser Arts', in *William Morris, News from Nowhere and Other Writings*, p. 252.
48. Ibid., p. 253.
49. Ibid., p. 235.
50. Ibid.
51. William Morris, 'Useful Work versus Useless Toil', in *William Morris, News from Nowhere and Other Writings*, p. 288.
52. Ibid., pp. 288–9.
53. Ibid., pp. 291–2.
54. Morris, 'Preface to The Nature of Gothic', p. 369.
55. Morris, 'Art Under Plutocracy', quoted in Thompson, *William Morris*, p. 642.
56. Ibid.
57. Clay Shirky, *Here Comes Everybody: The Power of Organising Without Organisations* (London: Allen Lane, 2008), pp. 81–108.
58. William Morris, 'The Art of the People', in *Hopes and Fears for Art*, available at http://www.marxists.org/archive/morris/works/1882/hopes/
59. Thompson, *William Morris*, p. 686.

3 THE MEANING OF MAKING II

1. Paul Greenhalgh, 'The History of Craft', in Peter Dormer, ed., *The Culture of Craft* (Manchester: Manchester University Press, 1997), p. 22.

2. The 1785 edition is online at: http://www.archive.org/details/dictionaryofengl01johnuoft
3. Greenhalgh, 'The History of Craft', p. 22.
4. Ibid., p. 23.
5. Ibid., p. 25.
6. Elizabeth Cumming and Wendy Kaplan, *The Arts and Crafts Movement* (London: Thames & Hudson, 1991).
7. Greenhalgh, 'The History of Craft', p. 35.
8. Ibid., p. 35.
9. Cumming and Kaplan, *The Arts and Crafts Movement*, p. 178.
10. I found this quote via the helpful Wikipedia article on 'Do it yourself'. A full transcript of the event is available at http://www.vallejo.to/articles/summit_pt1.htm
11. John Holt, *How Children Fail* (London: Penguin, 1990, first published 1964). John Holt, *How Children Learn* (London: Penguin, 1991, first published 1967).
12. See also the very good John Holt, *Instead of Education: Ways to Help People Do Things Better* (Boulder: Sentient, 2004, first published 1976).
13. Fred Turner, *From Counterculture to Cyberculture: Stewart Brand, the Whole Earth Network, and the Rise of Digital Utopianism* (Chicago: University of Chicago Press, 2006), pp. 69–70. See also Stewart Brand, 'Photography changes our relationship to our planet', http://click.si.edu/Story.aspx?story=31
14. A facsimile of the 1968 catalogue is available online at http://www.wholeearth.com. The word 'defects' is missing from the online reproduction but this seems to be a typographical error which may or may not have been in the original. It is included in Brand's discussion of this statement of purpose at http://wholeearth.com/issue/1010/article/195/we.are.as.gods

15. Amy Spencer, *DIY: The Rise of Lo-Fi Culture* (London: Marion Boyars, 2008), p. 11.
16. Ibid., p. 13.
17. David Gauntlett, 'Web Studies: A User's Guide', in David Gauntlett, ed., *Web.Studies: Rewiring Media Studies for the Digital Age* (London: Arnold, 2000), p. 13.
18. Spencer, *DIY*, pp. 19–20.
19. Ibid., p. 50.
20. Betsy Greer is quoted in Spencer, *DIY*, p. 61. See also her website, http://www.craftivism.com, and her book, *Knitting for Good! A Guide to Creating Personal, Social, and Political Change, Stitch by Stitch* (Boston: Trumpeter, 2008).
21. John Naish, *Enough: Breaking Free from the World of Excess* (London: Hodder and Stoughton, 2009), p. 4.
22. For information and links, see the Wikipedia article, 'Great Pacific Garbage Patch', and the Greenpeace report at http://www.greenpeace.org/international/cam paigns/oceans/pollution/trash-vortex/
23. Anthony McCann, 'Crafting gentleness', http://www. hummingbirdworkshop.com/helpful-resources/
24. Ibid.
25. Carl Honoré, *In Praise of Slow: How a Worldwide Movement is Challenging the Cult of Speed* (London: Orion, 2004).
26. This relationship was explored in the exhibition *Taking Time: Craft and the Slow Revolution*, developed by Helen Carnac and Andy Horn, which toured the UK from 2009 to 2011. For information see http://makingaslowrevolu tion.wordpress.com and for a related Twitter application see http://www.tweave.co.uk
27. Marybeth C. Stalp, *Quilting: The Fabric of Everyday Life* (Oxford: Berg, 2007), p. 9.
28. Ibid.
29. Faythe Levine, 'Preface', in Faythe Levine and Cortney

Heimerl, eds, *Handmade Nation: The Rise of DIY, Art, Craft and Design* (New York: Princeton Architectural Press, 2008), pp. ix–x.

30. The internet, of course, also gives a home to more surprising interests. IKEA Hacker (http://www.ikeahackers.net/), for instance, is a community sharing ideas and instructions on ways to customize and redeploy IKEA furniture in novel ways. There we can see that Martina from Austria has posted instructions on how to turn the IKEA Expedit bookcase into an elaborate hamster home; a user called Steffen shows how to build a model railway inside the IKEA Vinninga coffee table; and David Mingay from Cornwall demonstrates how to make a pinhole camera out of the IKEA Bjuron plant pot holder.
31. Garth Johnson, 'Down the Tubes: In Search of Internet Craft', in Levine and Heimerl, eds, *Handmade Nation*, pp. 30–5.
32. Illustrated in Levine and Heimerl, eds, *Handmade Nation*, p. xx.
33. Interviewed in Levine and Heimerl, eds, *Handmade Nation*, p. 26.
34. Ibid.
35. Matthew Crawford, *The Case for Working with Your Hands: or Why Office Work is Bad for Us and Fixing Things Feels Good* (London: Viking, 2010).
36. Interviewed in Levine and Heimerl, eds, *Handmade Nation*, p. 10.
37. Interviewed in Levine and Heimerl, eds, *Handmade Nation*, p. 46.
38. Interviewed in Levine and Heimerl, eds, *Handmade Nation*, p. 50.
39. Ibid., p. 94.
40. Amanda Blake Soule, *The Creative Family: How to*

Encourage Imagination and Nurture Family Connections (Boston: Trumpeter, 2008), p. 7.

41. Ibid., p. 5.
42. http://www.afghansforafghans.org and http://www.fireprojects.org/dulaan
43. Rozsika Parker, *The Subversive Stitch: Embroidery and the Making of the Feminine*, new edition (London: I. B. Tauris, 2010), p. ix.
44. Ibid., p. xx.
45. Joanne Turney, *The Culture of Knitting* (Oxford: Berg, 2009), p. 217.
46. Ibid., p. 220.
47. Stalp, *Quilting*, pp. 129–40.
48. Ibid., p. 132.
49. Richard Reynolds, *On Guerrilla Gardening: A Handbook for Gardening Without Boundaries* (London: Bloomsbury, 2008), p. 16.
50. See also Barbara Pallenberg, *Guerrilla Gardening: How to Create Gorgeous Gardens for Free* (Los Angeles: Renaissance Books, 2001), and David Tracey, *Guerrilla Gardening: A Manualfesto* (Gabriola Island: New Society, 2007).
51. Mihaly Csikszentmihalyi, *Flow: The Classic Work on How to Achieve Happiness*, revised edition (London: Rider, 2002, first published 1990).

4 THE MEANING OF MAKING III

1. To be fair, software did exist to support webpage and website creation in 1997, but I didn't have it. As it turned out, the early tools which created HTML on your behalf were not very good or precise anyway, so it was much better to be able to write the code yourself.
2. Miguel Helft, 'YouTube: We're bigger than you

thought', *The New York Times*, 9 October 2009, http://bits.blogs.nytimes.com/2009/10/09/youtube-were-bigger-than-you-thought/

3. YouTube statistics: https://www.youtube.com/yt/about/press/
4. I saw this video a few years ago, and now it is difficult to track down which one it was; but it would be one of the ones on Chris Anderson's YouTube channel for this particular hobby, at http://www.youtube.com/user/zlite or at http://diydrones.com/profile/zlitezlite
5. John Ruskin, *The Seven Lamps of Architecture* (London: Waverley, 1920), p. 155. Available at http://www.archive.org/details/1920sevenlampsof00ruskuoft
6. Ibid., p. 154.
7. John Ruskin, 'The Nature of Gothic', in *Selected Writings* (Oxford: Oxford University Press, 2004), p. 45.
8. Ibid., p. 46.
9. Some parts of this discussion of YouTube were originally written by me as part of my contribution to Edith Ackermann, David Gauntlett and Cecilia Weckström, *Systematic Creativity in the Digital Realm* (Billund: LEGO Learning Institute, 2010).
10. See Jean Burgess and Joshua Green, *YouTube: Online Video and Participatory Culture* (Cambridge: Polity, 2009), and Pelle Snickars and Patrick Vonderau, eds, *The YouTube Reader* (Stockholm: National Library of Sweden, 2009).
11. Mark Andrejevic, 'Exploiting YouTube: Contradictions of User-Generated Labor', in Snickars and Vonderau, eds, *The YouTube Reader*; or see any of the many Christian Fuchs publications, such as *Social Media: A Critical Introduction*, second edition (London: Sage, 2017).
12. Virginia Nightingale, 'The cameraphone and online image sharing', *Continuum: Journal of Media and Cultural Studies*, 2007, 21 (2): 289–301.

13. Patricia G. Lange, 'Videos of Affinity on YouTube', in Snickars and Vonderau, eds, *The YouTube Reader*.
14. Clay Shirky, *Here Comes Everybody: The Power of Organising without Organisations* (London: Penguin, 2008), p. 85.
15. Martin Creed, interviewed in Illuminations, eds, *Art Now: Interviews with Modern Artists* (London: Continuum, 2002), p. 101.
16. This is as true in 2017 as it was ten years earlier. Jean Burgess and Joshua Green, 'The Entrepreneurial Vlogger: Participatory Culture Beyond the Professional–Amateur Divide', in Snickars and Vonderau, eds, *The YouTube Reader*.
17. Ibid., p. 105.
18. Henry Jenkins, 'What Happened Before YouTube', in Burgess and Green, *YouTube*, p. 116.
19. Ibid.
20. See Jenkins, 'What Happened Before YouTube', p. 120, and Lewis Hyde, *The Gift: How the Creative Spirit Transforms the World* (London: Canongate, 2007).
21. Leisa Reichelt, 'Ambient intimacy', 1 March 2007, http://www.disambiguity.com/ambient-intimacy
22. Ibid.
23. Interview with David Jennings, London, 2 July 2010.
24. Amanda Blake Soule, 'Snapshots', posted on *SouleMama* blog, 31 March 2009, http://www.soulemama.com/soulemama/2009/03/oldest-youngest.html
25. Studies discussed included: Rosanna E. Guadagno, Bradley M. Okdie and Cassie A. Eno, 'Who blogs? Personality predictors of blogging', *Computers in Human Behavior*, 2008, 24 (5): 1993–2004; Asako Miura and Kiyomi Yamashita, 'Psychological and social influences on blog writing: An online survey of blog authors in Japan', *Journal of Computer-Mediated Communication*, 2007, 12 (4): 1452–71; David R. Brake, *'As if Nobody's*

Reading'? The Imagined Audience and Socio-Technical Biases in Personal Blogging Practice in the UK (PhD thesis, London School of Economics, 2009), available at http://eprints.lse.ac.uk/25535/; and Nancy K. Baym and Robert Burnett, 'Amateur experts: International fan labour in Swedish independent music', *International Journal of Cultural Studies*, 2009, 12 (5): 433–49.

26. Modified from Rozsika Parker, *The Subversive Stitch: Embroidery and the Making of the Feminine*, new edition (London: I. B. Tauris, 2010), p. xx.

5 THE VALUE OF CONNECTING

1. Richard Layard, *Happiness: Lessons from a New Science* (London: Penguin, 2006), p. 42.
2. Daniel Gilbert, *Stumbling on Happiness* (London: Harper Perennial, 2007). Drake Bennett, 'Perfectly happy', *Boston Globe*, 10 May 2009, http://www.boston.com/bostonglobe/ideas/articles/2009/05/10/perfectly_happy/
3. Layard, *Happiness*, pp. 48–9. Paul Taylor, Cary Funk and Peyton Craighill, *Are We Happy Yet?* (Washington, DC: Pew Research Center, 2006), http://pewresearch.org/pubs/301/are-we-happy-yet
4. Taylor et al., *Are We Happy Yet?*
5. Layard, *Happiness*. Taylor et al., *Are We Happy Yet?*
6. Interviewed in Joseph T. Hallinan, *Errornomics: Why We Make Mistakes and What We Can Do to Avoid Them* (London: Ebury Press, 2009), pp. 201–8.
7. Ibid., p. 201.
8. David A. Schkade and Daniel Kahneman, 'Does living in California make people happy? A focusing illusion in judgments of life satisfaction', *Psychological Science*, 1998, 9 (5): 340–6.
9. Deborah D. Danner, David A. Snowdon and Wallace V.

Friesen, 'Positive emotions in early life and longevity: Findings from the Nun Study', *Journal of Personality and Social Psychology*, 2001, 80 (5): 804–13.

10. Layard, *Happiness*, p. 63.
11. Ibid.
12. Ibid., pp. 64–5.
13. For up-to-date information on the legal status of officially-recognised same-sex partnerships, Wikipedia has a detailed article entitled 'Same-sex marriage'.
14. Layard, *Happiness*, p. 66.
15. Ibid., p. 68.
16. Taylor et al., *Are We Happy Yet?*, p. 32.
17. Bruno S. Frey and Alois Stutzer, 'Happiness, Economy and Institutions', Working Paper No. 15 (Zurich: Institute for Empirical Research in Economics, University of Zurich, 1999). Available at http://www.iew.uzh.ch/wp/iewwp015.pdf. See also Bruno S. Frey and Alois Stutzer, *Happiness and Economics: How the Economy and Institutions Affect Human Well-Being* (Princeton: Princeton University Press, 2001).
18. Frey and Stutzer, 'Happiness, Economy and Institutions', pp. 11–12.
19. Layard, *Happiness*, p. 72.
20. Taylor et al., *Are We Happy Yet?*, p. 6.
21. Ibid.
22. Layard, *Happiness*, p. 73.
23. Tibor Scitovsky, *The Joyless Economy: The Psychology of Human Satisfaction* (New York: Oxford University Press, 1992, first published 1976).
24. Sonja Lyubomirsky, Kennon M. Sheldon and David Schkade, 'Pursuing happiness: The architecture of sustainable change', *Review of General Psychology*, 2005, 9 (2): 111–31. Available at http://www.faculty.ucr.edu/~sonja/papers.html

25. Kennon M. Sheldon and Sonja Lyubomirsky, 'Change Your Actions, Not Your Circumstances: An Experimental Test of the Sustainable Happiness Model', in A. K. Dutt and B. Radcliff, eds, *Happiness, Economics, and Politics: Toward a Multi-Disciplinary Approach* (New York: Edward Elgar, 2009). Available at http://www.faculty.ucr.edu/~sonja/papers.html
26. Lyubomirsky et al., 'Pursuing happiness', pp. 118–20. Julia K. Boehm and Sonja Lyubomirsky, 'The Promise of Sustainable Happiness', in S. J. Lopez, ed., *Handbook of Positive Psychology*, second edition (Oxford: Oxford University Press, 2009), pp. 671–3. Available at http://www.faculty.ucr.edu/~sonja/papers.html
27. Paul Anand, *Happiness Explained: What Human Flourishing Is and What We Can Do to Promote It* (Oxford: Oxford University Press, 2016), pp. 115–17.
28. Richard Wilkinson and Kate Pickett, *The Spirit Level: Why Equality is Better for Everyone* (London: Penguin, 2010).
29. Kate Raworth, *Doughnut Economics: Seven Ways to Think Like a 21st-Century Economist* (London: Random House, 2017), p. 11.
30. Layard, *Happiness*, p. 234.
31. Governments can also, of course, offer tax breaks and financial help for married couples, although this can be perceived as lifestyle discrimination and unwarranted meddling in personal lives.
32. L. J. Hanifan, 1916, quoted in Robert D. Putnam, *Bowling Alone: The Collapse and Revival of American Community* (New York: Simon & Schuster, 2001), p. 19.
33. Pierre Bourdieu, *Distinction: A Social Critique of the Judgement of Taste* (London: Routledge & Kegan Paul, 1984). Pierre Bourdieu, 'The Forms of Capital', in John G. Richardson, ed., *Handbook of Theory and Research for the Sociology of Education* (New York: Greenwood, 1986).

34. Pierre Bourdieu, in Pierre Bourdieu and Loïc J. D. Wacquant, *An Invitation to Reflexive Sociology* (Chicago: University of Chicago Press, 1992), p. 119.
35. See for instance the report, 'Unleashing aspiration: The Final Report of the Panel on Fair Access to the Professions' (http://www.cabinetoffice.gov.uk/media/227102/fair-access.pdf) commissioned by the UK Prime Minister and published in July 2009. Its findings are succinctly summarized in *The Guardian*'s headline: 'Britain's closed shop: Damning report on social mobility failings – Wealth and private school remain key to professions', 21 July 2009.
36. James S. Coleman, 'Social capital in the creation of human capital', *American Journal of Sociology*, 1988, 94 (Supplement: Organizations and Institutions: Sociological and Economic Approaches to the Analysis of Social Structure): S95–S120.
37. Ibid., pp. 104–5.
38. Ibid., p. 109.
39. Alexis de Tocqueville, *Democracy in America, Volume II* (1840, translated by Henry Reeve, 1899), section 2, chapter 5. The text is available online, e.g. http://xroads.virginia.edu/~HYPER/DETOC/
40. Ibid.
41. Ibid.
42. De Tocqueville, *Democracy in America, Volume II*, section 2, chapter 7.
43. John Field, *Social Capital*, second edition (London: Routledge, 2008), p. 35.
44. Putnam, *Bowling Alone*, p. 19.
45. Ibid.
46. Ibid., p. 53.
47. Ibid., p. 283.
48. Ibid., p. 221.

49. Ibid., p. 231.
50. Ibid., p. 241.
51. Some of whom seemed to be behind the badly-conducted 'media effects' studies that I discussed in the book *Moving Experiences* (London: John Libbey, 1995, second edition 2005).
52. Putnam, *Bowling Alone*, p. 287, emphasis added.
53. Ibid., p. 311.
54. Ibid., p. 312.
55. Ibid., pp. 288–9.
56. David Gauntlett, ed., *Web.Studies: Rewiring Media Studies for the Digital Age* (London: Arnold, 2000).
57. Howard Rheingold, *The Virtual Community* (1993). The book is available free online at http://www.rheingold.com/vc/book/
58. Putnam, *Bowling Alone*, p. 171.
59. For readable introductions to the broader field, see for instance John Field, *Social Capital*; Michael Edwards, *Civil Society* (Cambridge: Polity, 2004); and David Halpern, *Social Capital* (Cambridge: Polity, 2005).
60. Field, *Social Capital*, second edition, p. 160. This quote is slightly edited here: Field attributes the notion of 'meso-level social structures' to a 1997 article by Bob Edwards and Michael W. Foley, and the three dimensions of social capital to a 2007 article by Sara Ferlander.
61. Ibid., p. 161.

6 TOOLS FOR CHANGE

1. Some parts of this discussion of Ivan Illich appeared previously in David Gauntlett, 'Media studies 2.0: A response', in *Interactions: Studies in Communication and Culture*, 2009, 1 (1): 147–57.

2. Ivan Illich, *Deschooling Society* (London: Marion Boyars, 2002, first published 1970), pp. 2–3.
3. Ibid., p. 3.
4. Ibid., p. 72.
5. Ibid., p. 75.
6. Ibid., p. 110.
7. Ivan Illich, *Tools for Conviviality* (London: Calder & Boyars, 1973), pp. 20–1.
8. David Cayley, *Ivan Illich in Conversation* (Toronto: House of Anansi Press, 2007), p. 108.
9. Illich, *Tools for Conviviality*, p. 11.
10. Ibid.
11. Ibid.
12. Ibid., p. xi.
13. In a later work, Illich suggests that immersion in the world of a book is a powerful experience that is lost when we live in a world of short electronic fragments of information, even if the latter are more accessible. See Ivan Illich, *In the Vineyard of the Text: A Commentary to Hugh's Didascalicon* (Chicago: University of Chicago Press, 1993). On the other hand, we learn from a memoir that Illich, in the early 1990s, 'did exchange his portable typewriter for a laptop and soon became the first person I knew in Germany who had somehow gained access to an on-line library catalogue, that of Pennsylvania State University, well before the pervasive onslaught of modems and Internet sources'. See Gesine Bottomley, 'Ivan Illich at the Wissenschaftskolleg', in Lee Hoinacki and Carl Mitcham, eds, *The Challenges of Ivan Illich: A Collective Reflection* (New York: State University of New York Press, 2002), p. 56.
14. Illich, *Deschooling Society*, p. 77.
15. Ibid., p. 77.
16. See the Wikipedia article on 'Community memory'.

17. Quoted in Charles Leadbeater, *We Think: Mass Innovation not Mass Production* (London: Profile Books, 2008), pp. 42–3. See also Patrice Flichy, *The Internet Imaginaire* (Cambridge, MA: MIT Press, 2007).
18. Illich, *Tools for Conviviality*, p. 20.
19. Ibid., p. 22.
20. Ibid., p. 21.
21. Ibid., p. 75.
22. Jonathan Zittrain, *The Future of the Internet and How to Stop It* (New Haven, CT: Yale University Press, 2008).
23. Ibid., p. 2.
24. For instance, an Apple press release from 5 January 2017 mentions that the App Store offered 2.2 million apps at that point, and that in 2016 alone, developers collectively earned over $20 billion. See http://www.apple.com/newsroom/2017/01/app-store-shatters-records-on-new-years-day.html
25. You may be wondering how often Apple rejects apps. The short answer is, not very often, but the detail is interesting. See the Wikipedia article on 'IOS app approvals', https://en.wikipedia.org/wiki/IOS_app_approvals
26. See https://developer.apple.com
27. https://twitter.com/notch/status/448586381565390848
28. Tim Berners-Lee, Testimony before the United States House of Representatives Committee on Energy and Commerce, Subcommittee on Telecommunications and the Internet, at the hearing, 'Digital Future of the United States: Part I – The Future of the World Wide Web', March 2007, http://dig.csail.mit.edu/2007/03/01-ushouse-future-of-the-web
29. Ibid.
30. Ibid.

7 ONLINE CREATIVITY NEEDS BETTER PLATFORMS

1. This kind of argument is made by commentators such as Mark Andrejevic, Toby Miller and Natalie Fenton.
2. Isabelle Risner and David Gauntlett, 'EU Digital DIY project output 5.3', *The Relationships Between Digital DIY and Social Change* (2017), http://www.didiy.eu/project/results
3. Chris Anderson, *Free: The Future of a Radical Price* (London: Random House Business Books, 2009).
4. Nicholas Carr, 'Web 2.0lier than thou', *Rough Type*, blog post dated 23 October 2006, http://www.roughtype.com/archives/2006/10/web_20ier_than.php. I am grateful to Stefan Sonvilla-Weiss, who drew my attention to this quote when he interviewed me for his book *Mashup Cultures*.
5. For detail on this, see David Gauntlett, 'Creativity, Participation and Connectedness: An Interview with David Gauntlett', in Stefan Sonvilla-Weiss, ed., *Mashup Cultures* (New York: Springer, 2010).
6. Toby Miller, 'Cybertarians of the World Unite: You Have Nothing to Lose but Your Tubes!', in Pelle Snickars and Patrick Vonderau, eds, *The YouTube Reader* (Stockholm: National Library of Sweden, 2009), p. 432.
7. These figures come from https://www.emarketer.com/Article/Googles-Gains-Slow-Big-Mobile-Growth-Continues/1013531 and http://tubularinsights.com/youtube-changes-33-percent-a-year/
8. The relevant figures for YouTube are typically buried within Google's overall accounts, but industry experts seem to agree on typical numbers. So in 2016, the operating cost of YouTube was said to be US $6.4 billion against advertising income of US $4.2 billion. Which

would be a loss of US $2 billion. Other reports suggest YouTube was just about breaking even by 2015. But the cost of running the beast certainly means they don't make billions in profit. See reports such as http://www.statisticbrain.com/youtube-statistics/ and https://fortunelords.com/youtube-statistics/ as well as YouTube's own https://www.youtube.com/yt/press/statistics.html

9. Miller, 'Cybertarians of the World Unite', p. 425.
10. Jonathan Taplin, *Move Fast and Break Things* (London: Macmillan, 2017).
11. Ibid., pp. 6–7.
12. Ibid., p. 121.
13. Ibid., p. 159.
14. Ibid., p. 85.
15. Ibid., p. 43.
16. Ibid., p. 280.
17. Jaron Lanier, *You Are Not a Gadget: A Manifesto* (London: Allen Lane, 2010).
18. Ibid., pp. 68–9.
19. Ibid., p. 48.
20. Ibid., p. 5.
21. Ibid., p. 50.
22. Charles Leadbeater, *We Think: Mass Innovation not Mass Production* (London: Profile Books, 2008). Clay Shirky, *Here Comes Everybody: The Power of Organising Without Organisations* (London: Allen Lane, 2008). Clay Shirky, *Cognitive Surplus: Creativity and Generosity in a Connected Age* (London: Allen Lane, 2010).
23. For example, the 95-minute film *Life in a Day* (Kevin Macdonald, 2011), assembled from 80,000 clips submitted to YouTube for this purpose, showing scenes from around the world on a single day, 24 July 2010. There have been other such projects – and, of course, *Star Wars Uncut*, discussed in chapter 3.

24. Chris Anderson, *The Long Tail: How Endless Choice is Creating Unlimited Demand* (London: Random House Business Books, 2006).
25. Chris Anderson, *Free: The Future of a Radical Price* (London: Random House Business Books, 2009), p. 81.
26. Ibid., p. 19.
27. This phenomenon is covered by Anderson, Ibid., pp. 153–8. It has also been the subject of numerous news and discussion articles – search for 'how do musicians make money' for some recent examples. The excellent book by David Byrne, *How Music Works* (New York: Three Rivers, 2012, second edition 2017) discusses this extensively, including illustrations drawn from the finances of his own projects.
28. See Lanier, *You Are Not a Gadget*, pp. 90–1.
29. From the Wikimedia Foundation website, http://wikimediafoundation.org (accessed on 27 February 2017).
30. Google, 'Our story', https://www.google.com/about/our-story/ (accessed on 27 February 2017).
31. Wikimedia Foundation financial report, https://annual.wikimedia.org/2016/financials.html (accessed on 27 February 2017).
32. See note 8 in this chapter.
33. In the second half of 2009, the Wikimedia Foundation received donations from 226,382 'community donors' at an average donation of $33.18. (See http://wikimediafoundation.org/wiki/Financial_reports/)
34. The BBC Full Financial Statements 2015/16 record that the BBC's total operating costs for the year ended 31 March 2016 were £3,493 million.
35. Jon Russell, 'Spotify reaches 50 million paying users', *Techcrunch*, 2 March 2017, https://techcrunch.com/2017/03/02/spotify-50-million/

8 MAKING CONNECTIONS AND THE CREATIVE PROCESS

1. On how many centuries human beings have been making music for – a bone flute found in Slovenia is believed to be 43,000 years old. See the Wikipedia article on 'Divje Babe flute'.
2. Peter Korn, *Why We Make Things and Why it Matters: The Education of a Craftsman* (London: Vintage, 2017), p. 8.
3. Ibid., p. 13.
4. Ibid., p. 102.
5. Christopher Small, *Musicking: The Meanings of Performing and Listening* (Middletown, CT: Wesleyan University Press, 1998).
6. Ibid., p. 2.
7. Ibid., p. 4.
8. Ibid., p. 5. This seems to me to be a good and funny line even without the context. But the context is higher on the same page, where Small tells us that some believe 'that music's inner meanings can never be properly yielded up in performance. They can be discovered only by those who can read and study the score, like Johannes Brahms, who once refused an invitation to attend a performance of Mozart's Don Giovanni, saying he would sooner stay home and read it.'
9. Ibid., p. 40.
10. Ibid., p. 108.
11. *The LEGO Movie* (2014), written and directed by Phil Lord and Christopher Miller. A clip which contains this bit can be seen at: http://youtu.be/9VeUoVKiyhE
12. *Comedian*, directed by Christian Charles (2002). I was helpfully reminded of this by Rob Bell, *How to be Here* (New York: HarperCollins, 2014), pp. 45–6. This quote is an edited selection of Seinfeld's responses.

13. Of course, Seinfeld is able to say this from the comfortable position he achieved from the vast success of his TV show. On the other hand, that success only began when its creator was thirty-four, and Adams is twenty-nine in this conversation. In any case, it seems clear that Seinfeld believes he would have been happy in his craft regardless.
14. Small, *Musicking*, p. 50.
15. Korn, *Why We Make Things*, pp. 103–4.
16. Brian Eno, in the interesting interview 'Brian Eno by Alfred Dunhill', https://youtu.be/5mqtc2Z3K8o, published 14 January 2013.
17. Based on rich description of the process in *Literally* – the magazine of the Pet Shop Boys Club – No. 34, 2009.
18. Peter Cashmore, 'New releases', *The Guardian*, 21 October 2006, https://www.theguardian.com/culture/2006/oct/21/previews.theguide10
19. We highlight here Eno's eloquence in thinking and writing about the studio as a compositional tool. He wasn't really the first to be *doing* it. Even, to pick a mainstream but pioneering example, the theme music for the BBC television series *Doctor Who*, created by Delia Derbyshire in 1963, was notable for the fact that it was made with no musical instruments, just electronically treated sound. This in turn built on the work of pioneers such as Pierre Schaeffer, who developed *musique concrète* in the 1940s.
20. Paul Morley, 'On gospel, Abba and the death of the record: An audience with Brian Eno', *The Guardian*, 17 January 2010, https://www.theguardian.com/music/2010/jan/17/brian-eno-interview-paul-morley
21. Brian Eno, 'The Recording Studio as a Compositional Tool', lecture at New Music New York, 1979; transcript at http://music.hyperreal.org/artists/brian_eno/interviews/downbeat79.htm
22. Kingsley Marshall and Rupert Loydell, 'Control and

Surrender: Eno Remixed – Collaboration and Oblique Strategies', in Sean Albiez and David Pattie, eds, *Brian Eno: Oblique Music* (London: Bloomsbury Academic, 2016), pp. 176–7.

23. Brian Eno interviewed by Jarvis Cocker on BBC Radio 6 Music, 8 November 2010, https://youtu.be/pRc7MUybCsE
24. Quoted in Marshall and Loydell, 'Control and Surrender', p. 178.
25. Michael Bracewell, *Re-Make/Re-Model: Art, Pop, Fashion and the Making of Roxy Music, 1953–1972* (London: Faber and Faber, 2007), p. 208, cited by Marshall and Loydell, 'Control and Surrender'. A similar point is made in a book about the success of the LEGO Group: 'More often than not, game-changing innovation doesn't come from one all-encompassing, ambitious strategy. It comes from persistent experimentation, which increases the odds that at least one effort will get you to the future first.' David Robertson with Bill Breen, *Brick by Brick: How LEGO Rewrote the Rules of Innovation and Conquered the Global Toy Industry* (New York: Crown Business, 2013), p. 18.
26. Gene Kalbacher, 'Profile: Brian Eno', *Modern Recording & Music*, October 1982. Thanks to Mark Edward Achtermann for picking out this quote. http://music.hyperreal.org/artists/brian_eno/interviews/mram82a.html

9 DOING IT YOURSELF

1. The albums were *Geidi Primes* (2010), *Halfaxa* (2010) and *Visions* (2012).
2. Matthew Gooderson, 'Creative limitations: A conversation between David Sheppard and myself (over SMS)', 11 May 2016, http://matthewclymagooderson.com/

creative-limitations-a-conversation-between-david-shep pard-and-myself/

3. This was offered by Sam Lee on the Pledge Music crowdfunding site in 2015, at http://www.pledgemusic.com/projects/samlee. Singing with Nightingales, on various dates with Sam Lee or other artists, became an in-demand venture in itself: https://www.singingwith nightingales.com
4. From the video of 'Kevin Kelly's 6 words for the modern internet', 22 June 2011, https://www.wired.com/2011/06/kevin-kellys-internet-words/
5. Cyrus Bozorgmehr, 'An advisor behind Wu-Tang Clan's single-copy album says this is where the music industry's headed next', 16 July 2017, https://www.linkedin.com/pulse/advisor-behind-wu-tang-clans-single-copy-album-where-music-cyrus
6. Ibid.
7. At Kelly's website you can read both the shorter 2016 version and the longer 2008 one, on the same page, at http://kk.org/thetechnium/1000-true-fans/
8. Ibid.
9. Ibid.
10. https://youtu.be/Wlg3808gDic
11. See Amanda Palmer, *The Art of Asking, or How I Learned to Stop Worrying and Let People Help* (London: Piatkus, 2014), p. 55, for more on her feelings about 'Get a job!'
12. Ibid., p. 44.
13. Ibid.
14. Ibid., p. 100.
15. Ibid., pp. 100–1. This quote has been shortened.
16. Ibid., p. 235.
17. Ibid., p. 244.
18. Ibid., p. 303.
19. *The Economist*, 'The battle for consumers' attention:

Forget the long tail', 9 February 2017, http://www.economist.com/news/special-report/21716460-forget-long-tail-battle-consumers-attention

20. For example, this conflation of two different things happens in David Hesmondhalgh and Leslie M. Meier, 'Popular Music, Independence and the Concept of the Alternative in Contemporary Capitalism', in James Bennett and Nikki Strange, eds, *Media Independence: Working with Freedom or Working for Free?* (Abingdon: Routledge, 2015).
21. As in Gady Epstein, 'Mass entertainment in the digital age is still about blockbusters, not endless choice', *The Economist*, 11 February 2017, http://www.economist.com/news/special-report/21716467-technology-has-given-billions-people-access-vast-range-entertainment-gady; and Anita Elberse, *Blockbusters: Why Big Hits – and Big Risks – Are the Future of the Entertainment Business* (New York: Henry Holt, 2013).
22. See Wenqi Zhou and Wenjing Duan, 'Online user reviews, product variety, and the long tail: An empirical investigation on online software downloads', *Electronic Commerce Research and Applications*, 2012, 11 (3): 275–89, https://ssrn.com/abstract=1742519; Laurina Zhang, 'Intellectual property strategy and the long tail: Evidence from the recorded music industry', *Management Science*, 2016, published online under Articles in Advance section, 11 November 2016, http://dx.doi.org/10.1287/mnsc.2016.2562
23. *The Economist*, 'The battle for consumers' attention'.
24. *The Economist*, 'How to devise the perfect recommendation algorithm', 9 February 2017, http://www.economist.com/news/special-report/21716464-recommendations-must-be-neither-too-familiar-nor-too-novel-how-devise-per fect

25. Robert Strachan, *Sonic Technologies: Popular Music, Digital Culture and the Creative Process* (London: Bloomsbury, 2017), p. 32. The article mentioned is Miikka Salavuo, 'Open and informal online communities as forums of collaborative musical activities and learning', *British Journal of Music Education*, 2006, 23 (3): 253–71.
26. Attentive readers will know that this famous author was Chris Anderson, author of *The Long Tail.* So it's an odd coincidence that he appears in this section both as the author of a relevant book and as the creator of a shoddy video. I could say 'it's a small world', but you might counter that I must be a Chris Anderson obsessive . . . or that I must have only ever read one book.
27. To pick one example, in *The Comedian's Comedian* podcast series by Stuart Goldsmith (http://www.comedianscomedian.com), featuring over 200 long interviews with stand-up comedians, there are many cases where someone had essentially decided to have a go at stand-up comedy because they believed that they could *at least* do better than some lacklustre performer that they had seen.
28. On the Foucault point, see Michel Foucault, *The History of Sexuality, Volume I: The Will To Knowledge* (London: Penguin, 1998), p. 95. A great celebration of these ideas appears in David M. Halperin, *Saint Foucault: Towards a Gay Hagiography* (New York: Oxford University Press, 1994), and is discussed in either edition of David Gauntlett, *Media, Gender and Identity: An Introduction* (London: Routledge, 2002 / 2008).
29. Strachan, *Sonic Technologies.*
30. Grimes interview at 'Grimes' exclusive soundpack sends an electromagnetic pulse', 30 June 2017, https://roli.com/stories/grimes-electromagnetic-pulse
31. Victoria Hesketh, 'Little Boots on how the music industry treats female artists', *The Independent*, 24 May 2016, http://

www.independent.co.uk/arts-entertainment/music/curvaceous-celebrating-pop-star-meghan-trainor-is-the-latest-to-suffer-from-photoshop-slimming-down-a7029436.html

32. Victoria Hesketh, 'Little Boots: "Why I'm still talking about sexism and the music industry"', 21 August 2015, http://www.thedebrief.co.uk/things-to-do/music/little-boots-why-im-still-talking-about-sexism-and-the-music-industry-20150850592
33. Email interview with Victoria Hesketh (artist name Little Boots), 24 July 2017.
34. Emika interviewed in Istanbul, 24 February 2016, http://bonemagazine.com/en/entry/emika-istanbulda
35. Katie Benner, 'Women in tech speak frankly on culture of harassment', *New York Times*, 30 June 2017, https://www.nytimes.com/2017/06/30/technology/women-entrepreneurs-speak-out-sexual-harassment.html
36. Sarah R. Davies, *Hackerspaces: Making the Maker Movement* (Cambridge: Polity, 2017).
37. Ibid., pp. 101–5.

10 PLATFORMS FOR CREATIVITY

1. This chapter draws on previous blog posts by me, 'Platforms for creativity: Introduction', 3 July 2015, http://davidgauntlett.com/creativity/platforms-for-creativity-introduction/ and 'Platforms for creativity: Eight principles revisited', 3 July 2015, http://davidgauntlett.com/creativity/platforms-for-creativity-eight-principles-revisited/
2. A fascinating account of Minecraft and its development is: Daniel Goldberg and Linus Larsson, *Minecraft: The Unlikely Tale of Markus 'Notch' Persson and the Game that Changed Everything* (London: Virgin, 2015).

3. An excellent overview of these theories and models, with a particular focus on those that relate to creative identity, appears in Mary Kay Culpepper, *I Make, Therefore I Am: The Birth of Creative Identity* (PhD thesis, Westminster School of Media, Arts and Design, University of Westminster, 2017). I suggest you search for publications that Culpepper has subsequently produced.
4. Vlad Petre Glăveanu and Lene Tanggaard, 'Creativity, identity, and representation: Towards a socio-cultural theory of creative identity', *New Ideas in Psychology*, 2014, 34: 12–21.
5. Ibid., p. 13.
6. I don't want to complicate matters further, but Glăveanu and Tanggaard rightly add that creative identity is not a singular thing, and a person may have a number of different creative identities – or at least *versions* of this sense of identity – which appear in different scenarios or with different groups. So you might have white, milk and dark chocolate Toblerones for different occasions.
7. Glăveanu and Tanggaard, 'Creativity, identity, and representation', p. 15.
8. Frank Pajares and Tim Urdan, eds, *Self-Efficacy Beliefs of Adolescents* (Greenwich, CT: Information Age Publishing, 2006). Dale H. Schunk and Frank Pajares, 'Self-Efficacy Beliefs', in Sanna Järvelä, ed., *Social and Emotional Aspects of Learning* (Oxford: Elsevier, 2011).
9. This idea was brilliantly explored in Paul Ricoeur's three-volume *Time and Narrative* (1984, 1985, 1988) and *Oneself as Another* (1992). A short outline appears in my book *Creative Explorations* (London: Routledge, 2007), pp. 166–72.
10. Discussed in chapters 3 and 6. John Holt, *How Children Fail* (London: Penguin, 1990, first published 1964). John Holt, *How Children Learn* (London: Penguin, 1991, first

published 1967). Ivan Illich, *Deschooling Society* (London: Marion Boyars, 2002, first published 1970), Ivan Illich, *Tools for Conviviality* (London: Calder & Boyars, 1973).

11. A brief introduction to Papert and constructionism appears in my book *Creative Explorations* (2007), pp. 130–1.
12. Mitchel Resnick and Brian Silverman, 'Some reflections on designing construction kits for kids', *IDC '05: Proceedings of the 2005 Conference on Interaction Design and Children* (New York: Association for Computing Machinery, 2005).
13. Mitchel Resnick, 'Designing for wide walls', 25 August 2016, https://design.blog/2016/08/25/mitchel-resnick-designing-for-wide-walls/
14. Mitchel Resnick, 'Give P's a chance: Projects, Peers, Passion, Play', *Constructionism and Creativity Conference*, Vienna, August 2014, http://web.media.mit.edu/~mres/papers.html
15. 'YouTube videos are viewed more than 12 billion times in a single month. The most viewed videos have been watched several billion times each, more than any blockbuster movie. More than 100 million short video clips with very small audiences are shared to the net every day. Judged merely by volume and the amount of attention the videos collectively garner, these clips are now the center of our culture' – Kevin Kelly, *The Inevitable: Understanding the 12 Technological Forces That Will Shape Our Future* (London: Viking, 2016), Kindle location 2867.
16. I made a YouTube video where you can see it. 'David Gauntlett at De Chocoladefabriek Gouda – Making is Connecting in action', 29 October 2014, https://youtu.be/4L0fBRV1MMw
17. The following text draws upon case studies that I wrote

for the LEGO Foundation, based on interviews with the individuals involved conducted in 2016.

18. Tim Wu, *The Attention Merchants: How Our Time and Attention Are Gathered and Sold* (London: Atlantic, 2017).
19. Tim Wu interviewed by John Naughton, 'Tim Wu: "The internet is like the classic story of the party that went sour"', *The Observer*, 8 January 2017, https://www.theguardian.com/technology/2017/jan/08/tim-wu-interview-internet-classic-party-went-sour-attention-merchants
20. http://www.craftscouncil.org.uk/what-we-do/hey-clay/

11 CONCLUSIONS

1. In the first edition of this book, there was a section in this Conclusion where I took the opportunity to describe some 'imagined futures', proposing implications of the book's arguments in the areas of media, education, work, and politics and the environment. I think these suggestions can have a tendency to seem either banal or fantastical, or both, and you can imagine the implications of this book perfectly well for yourself. So I've put that section online (at www.makingisconnecting.org), which means it's still perfectly accessible, but not taking up space here.
2. For instance, upmarket newspapers in the UK, especially *The Guardian*, have tended to be relatively curious and positive about online culture, although the bigger-selling tabloids, in particular the *Daily Mail* and *Daily Express*, have generally gone for ridiculous scare stories. The fear of the online amateur amongst media professionals is most lucidly expressed in Andrew Keen's book *The Cult of the Amateur: How Today's Internet is Killing Our Culture and Assaulting Our Economy* (London: Nicholas Brealey, 2007).

3. Clay Shirky, *Cognitive Surplus: Creativity and Generosity in a Connected Age* (London: Allen Lane, 2010), pp. 17–20. The 'lolcat' site he picks out is http://icanhascheezburger.com
4. Richard Layard, *Happiness: Lessons from a New Science* (London: Penguin, 2006), p. 66.
5. Ibid., p. 234, emphasis added.
6. A summary of this approach appears in the chapter on Giddens in either edition of David Gauntlett, *Media, Gender and Identity: An Introduction* (London: Routledge, 2002 / 2008).
7. John Field, *Social Capital*, second edition (London: Routledge, 2008), p. 160.
8. Ivan Illich, *Tools for Conviviality* (London: Calder & Boyars, 1973), p. 21.
9. The BBC Full Financial Statements 2015/16, http://www.bbc.co.uk/aboutthebbc/insidethebbc/howwework/reports/ara
10. You might say that if I was properly DIY I would publish a book myself, not have it done by a publisher like Polity. Well, I have done that. See David Gauntlett, 'A tale of two books', 29 April 2013, http://davidgauntlett.com/digital-media/a-tale-of-two-books/
11. Peter Korn, *Why We Make Things and Why it Matters: The Education of a Craftsman* (London: Vintage, 2017), pp. 103–4.
12. Nick Couldry, *Why Voice Matters: Culture and Politics after Neoliberalism* (London: Sage, 2010), p. vi.
13. Ibid., pp. 16–17.
14. This is the more gloomy way to express the argument made by Chris Anderson in *The Long Tail: How Endless Choice is Creating Unlimited Demand* (London: Random House Business Books, 2006). Anderson's point is that there is a very *high* demand for all these items in

aggregate, even though at an individual level each one may be requested rarely.

15. Matthew Hindman, *The Myth of Digital Democracy* (Princeton: Princeton University Press, 2009).
16. See for example the excellent books, Sarah Corbett, *How to be a Craftivist: The Art of Gentle Protest* (London: Unbound, 2017) and Betsy Greer, ed., *Craftivism: The Art of Craft and Activism* (Vancouver: Arsenal Pulp Press, 2014).
17. I apologize that this is a mangled remix of the pebbles – boulders – beach metaphor used by Charles Leadbeater to describe the rise of amateur/online producers in the media landscape.
18. Susan Jeffers, *Feel the Fear and Do It Anyway* (London: Vermilion, 2012, first published 1987).
19. Ibid., p. 25, her emphasis.
20. See note 27 in chapter 9.
21. Jeffers, *Feel the Fear*, p. 28.
22. Brené Brown, 'Why your critics aren't the ones who count', 99U talk, 4 December 2013, https://youtu.be/8-JXOnFOXQk
23. Ill Gates, 'ill.methodology workshop – chapter 1', 7 February 2012, https://youtu.be/XVQ8c19unnM, and see http://theillmethodology.com
24. Ibid. (YouTube video) at 9 minutes, 30 seconds.

INDEX